Toward a
Theology of
Holy Black Rage

Toward a
Theology of
Holy Black Rage

Editor: The Rev.Dr. Melinda Contreras-Byrd

AFRICA WORLD PRESS

Trenton | London | Cape Town | Nairobi | Addis Ababa | Asmara | Ibadan | New Delhi

AFRICA WORLD PRESS
541 West Ingham Avenue | Suite B
Trenton, New Jersey 08638

Book design: Dawid Kahts
Cover design: Ashraful Haque
Cover photo: Dr. Regina Langley

Cataloging-in-Publication Data may be obtained from the Library of Congress.

ISBNs: 9781569027196 (HB)
      9781569027202 (PB)

HOLY BLACK RAGE

The statue in the next page is the work of Rev. Dr. Melinda Contreras-Byrd, created as her artistic impression of how Holy Black Rage might look if it were embodied visually.

The overall piece was birthed from memories of traditional statues from African artists who attempted to create forms that would serve to represent an expressive anger that would be both dangerous and protective.

The horror of the rage from the experiences of living with racism is depicted in the battered and splintering brown skin of the figure.

The violence against Black bodies and psyches is represented by the nails that pierce the head of the statue.

On the brain and mind is the blood red cross, upon which the word Black is written, to name our community and its continued centering in the unique and destructive particularities of Black life in the Diaspora.

The eyes are glaring, reflective and engaging.   From them drip tear of blood from our collective and on-going suffering.

The mouth is open in a scream, and from this opened mouth comes the voices of fire that will end this horror.

There is a cry in the belly. On its chest we see that life and love have been turned upside down... and yet there remains a pure red heart in its chest.

Behind its back—but out of sight here—it is covered with the names of the never-ending multitudes of Black and brown men and women who have been murdered by armed U.S. peace keepers. It is this situation—this growing list of names—that creates and propels this Holy Black Rage that often remains unseen and unrecognized by the power structures of the Empire.

The ropes of the cross have formed a noose around the neck. And despite all the pain and horror, all the rage and suffering, this figure has the wings of holiness attached.

This is Rage.

This is Black Rage.

And this is why it must be Holy.

Melinda Contreras-Byrd
2020

Contents

Toward a Theology of Holy Black Rage

Melinda Contreras-Byrd, M.Div., Psy.D.

The world was facing one of the most terrifying times that the present generations had ever faced.

Those to whom we normally looked for answers admitted that they were baffled and likewise terrified about the possible implications of the world of deadly, unpredictable disease that we had now entered. People were dying in astonishing and growing numbers. Medical workers were overwhelmed, pushed to the precipice of human endurance in their attempts to save lives while protecting themselves from the invisible foe that was waging a world war. People became glued to their smart phones, iPads, and computers, hoping for some word that would help them to know how to protect their lives and the lives of those they loved. But panic set in as the world's health leaders fumbled in confusion to stave off this enemy, often giving out contradictory and inconclusive information. People died — quickly, unexpectantly, unexplainably — without the comfort of the presence of loved ones, solid prognoses, or even a chance to say goodbye.

1

Families were separated because of illness or fear of contamination. Smiles were covered by masks. Hopelessness set in. Just when it appeared that things could get no worse, evil reared its head and roared across the world in known tongues. Tempers flared. Trust evaporated. Perhaps it was the disillusionment. Maybe it was the hopeless and nihilism generated in response to the realities of living under CoVid-19. Or maybe it was the mounting fear, frustration, and suicidal ideation. No one can say unequivocally.

The Corona Virus pandemic morphed into an equal if not increased evil as racism drew a reviving breath.

Masks of civility and decorum crumbled and the specter that had been so long dismissed as merely the overactive imagination of a people already characterized as troubled, became a legion of flesh and blood.   No longer able to be contained, individuals and groups of bigots of every kind became emboldened to freely express and act out their hatred. "Karens" of diverse denominations crawled out of the bushes to harass, accuse, and threaten any Black people who they happened to come across.

Proud, weapon-carrying groups of White racists marched against interracial groups of Black Lives Matter advocates and other justice seekers and protesters. According to a July 13, 2020 article by The Brookings Institution, following the onset of the pandemic and the George Floyd killing, three million more guns were sold in the U.S. They note that the United States possess more guns than people, and that those having the most weapons are White.

The now customary cry of "I can't breathe" rang out once more, and the dying plea of yet another unarmed Black man—prone, tortured and murdered in what I can only characterized as an act of pure, unadulterated evil—was ignored by police. Like the sound of Rachel, "weeping for her children and *refusing to be comforted,* because they were no more," the dying voice of George Floyd, crying " mama," served as "the straw that broke the camel's back."

Those whose hearts had not been frozen by the evil of hatred and racism symbolically cried out in prophetic voices, like the prophet Amos, "Let justice roll down like water and righteousness like a mighty stream!"

In a recent article, titled, "Responding to the Murder of George Floyd," Robert Weissman, President of Public Citizen. Org (on which website the article appeared), noted that, in response to this murder, some 400 organizations " signed a letter led by the Leadership Conference of Civil and Human Rights that outlined key federal steps to scale back police violence and abuse. "

Protests and uprisings spread, from the hundreds of protesters surrounding the White House, to multiple cities and states across the U.S. In an article in the July 10, 2020 edition of Brookings.edu, speaking of the reaction to the death of George Floyd, Mary Blankenship and Richard V. Reeves wrote, "Floyd's murder ignited a wave that is leading to changes in symbols of racism—from flags to statues… in hopes of real police reform, and of overdue reparations to Black Americans…. By June 2nd the protest movement had spread across the nation and around the world." The title of Jen Kirby's June 12, 2020 article, " 'Black Lives Matter' Has Become a Global Rallying Cry Against Racism and Police Brutality," on Vox.com, sums up the story of this turbulent time of social unrest, protest, uprisings, and Covid-19 pandemic.

What we are seeing at the time of these writings is an almost universal expression of a longstanding level of anger over injustice: Belgian protest … Brazilian protest … unrest in the U.K. … protests erupting in Seoul, Korea, Sydney Australia, and Syria … signs lifted in outrage by groups in Spain, Germany, France, and Pretoria, South Africa. Words of condemnation have come from the head of the African Union, an organization representing 55 African nations. Some 200 people march in Kenya and in Lagos, Nigeria over the police shooting of a teen named Tina Ezekwe. In Accra, Ghana, a Black Lives Matter protest is staged, but then is halted by police and its leader arrested. Protests in support of the idea that Black lives matter take place in Liberia and Senegal.

As I try to grasp the world spinning around me, I am also invited to engage in new forms of mental health therapeutics, the ministry into which I have been called. Certainly, the situation of living under the health and safety restrictions of the Corona virus has set the perfect stage for the development of mental health challenges. People who have never struggled with mental health challenges are beginning to experience new and frightening symptoms. People who believed themselves to be strong in their faith have now come to a time of questioning—struggling with issues of theodicy, a theology of death and dying, increased stress reactions, depressed behavior, PTSD-like reactions, grief and loss, etc. And as I have worked with my clinical clients around these issues, Black churches and organizations have invited me to conduct Zoom presentations and discussions that would offer information and suggestions for coping with these issues.

After having offered several mental health presentations, I realized that there is one mental health issue of paramount importance that no one had asked me to speak about. It is an issue that had been with me throughout my life. It is an issue that causes me to talk aloud to the television news, to have early morning awakenings, and knots to form in my stomach.

And when I raised this issue unbidden in groups, the reaction was swift and visceral. There was excitement and self-disclosure and full attention...and, yes, even a little cussin'.

The topic that no one in the church was talking about was *anger*, and it was the elephant in the room.

This book seeks to begin a discussion as a first step in formulating what I have come to call "A Theology of Holy Black Rage."

My discussion of this topic began with a desire to unpack the issue of anger among Black Christians. It soon became apparent that "anger" didn't even come close to describing the true feelings that we were experiencing. My investigation of the difference between anger and rage disclosed definitions that characterized anger and rage as emotional expressions on a spectrum. While anger is described in ways that leave room for it to be seen in a positive light, rage is often described in only pejorative ways. Rage is characterized as excessive and often includes violent acting out. Rage is described as anger that is hostile and uncontrolled. Further descriptions of rage include ideas concerning its origins, based upon unacknowledged ideas about what is appropriate and acceptable. In my search of definitions distinguishing rage from anger, it occured to me that to make any accurate distinction requires more than linguistics or semantics. At least a consideration of cultural and hermeneutical factors is required. Assessed from a psychological standpoint, rage is considered to be a form of uncontrolled anger. It is defined relative to issues of self-control, which in turn is related to one's level of maturity. Terms such as "anger management" suggest that rage is an unacceptable and negative emotion, to be avoided and controlled. Mental health articles offer ways to manage and tame your anger. Other articles couple rage with "domestic violence," "road rage," and "temper tantrums." Expressions of rage are mixed with psychological diagnoses (narcissistic rage, borderline rage, etc.). The definitions seem to beg the question of whether there is any situation within which rage, defined as wrath or unrestrained anger, is a normal and expected reaction, on account of which the enraged can escape negative judgment and a mental health diagnosis.

A recent op-ed in the *New York Times* stated:

It is exhausting and infuriating and maddening to be forced to fight, always, for what for others is free. It enrages, when you realize that you're still fighting the same fight that your parents fought, and that their parents fought. It is an everyday struggle to neither fall into despair nor explode in anger. So, these people are in the streets, having their moment and having their say. And America would do well to listen and not try to silence them or soothe them. In fact, America listening and responding to these protests, respecting them, is one of the healthiest things the country can do, because as protester Kimberly Latrice Jones said at the end of her viral video, "They are lucky that what black people are looking for is equality and not revenge.[1]

I would contend that our religious beliefs have informed our ideas about what are acceptable versus unacceptable emotional expressions. But, assessed from a different angle and in a different context, is it possible for the expression of rage to signify that something positive has taken place? Is rage ever an acceptable response? Outlining the connection between racism and sexism, in her recent book, *Killing Rage*, writer bell hooks proposes that the Black rage resulting from the ongoing experiences of racism can serve to be "a healing source of love and strength and a catalyst for positive change."

Even the title of a book by Soraya Chemaly—*Rage Becomes Her: The Power of Women's Anger*—implies some agreement that the answer is *yes*, that there *are* positive psychological ramifications of expressions of rage. Chemaly argues that rage can signal a positive move *towards* self-determination, empowerment, and gender justice and *against* lives ruled by trying to adjust to living within a sexist patriarchy. Contrary to some clinical characterizations of rage as the action of an individual, occurring without thought, often with displaced or unconscious origins; within Chemaly's framework rage can be a gender group response to a history of identifiable inequality.

Is it possible then that rage can be analyzed as a reaction related to more than just an individual, a family, or a region? Could it be possible that ongoing egregious historical states of affairs could affect a mass diversity of persons whose only connection is their being members of the African Diaspora? Black psychiatrists Grier and Cobb thought so, as a result of their research on anger in the Black community. Their ground-breaking work culminated in the nuanced belief that because of all that we have suffered, all Black people are angry!

I contend that it is this repressed Black anger that has turned into rage and ignited a demand for justice that is spreading across the world.

I believe that the unusual times that we are living in has raised the need for Black theologians to begin to question and rethink the meaning of rage and anger. I think that this is the time to join together and question what constitutes acceptable responses to ongoing racism, violence against unarmed and innocent Black people, and a history of attempted genocide.

This collection of essays is about Black rage, because the writers are Black women and men sharing this experience from a personal and community standpoint. We seek to find and describe God's hand in the midst of a time of great unrest, rage, and destruction. We have come together to tell the truth—to bless the people, and to proclaim liberty to the captives...and the day of vengeance of our God.

The title of this book suggests not only the idea that Black people are angry, but, that we are enraged; and that, furthermore, this rage is not only acceptable, but *holy*:

> **Holy:** consecrated, sacred, having a holiness that is connected to and derived from God, set apart for the purposes of God.

We have collected our writings together in order to talk about and *encourage* rage—but not just *any* rage.

We want to talk about a rage that is centered in the *encountered* Black experience.[2]

We come together to define and distinguish distinctively *Black* rage.

We want to talk about an increased anger resulting in a rage that emerges from the mire of racism. We want to talk about a rage that is strategic and unrelated to psychiatric diagnoses—a rage that is not merely *justified*, but *commissioned and anointed as the work of the Kingdom of God.*

We offer up this collection in order to speak truths that will educate, redirect, and bless those who engage in uprisings with the goal of establishing a worldwide justice that is finally able to state unequivocally that "Black Lives Matter."

In the midst of unprecedented racial uprisings, I raised this challenge, and Black clergy from a variety of different backgrounds, denominations, and theological spaces have joined me in a terrifying and self-exposing quest—to speak out of their own experience of Black rage, and to find and outline its sacredness and its connection to "the things of God."

This book is the beginning of a discussion. It contains diverse, uncensored words given as a gift from the heart of each writer.

This collection constitutes an act of courage. It discloses personal stories of self-discovery, pain, and relentless theological inquiry.

It is our hope that this effort will engage our community and inspire them to discuss and add on to what we have shared in this collection.

"Sometimes we have to disturb the order of things. Sometimes we have to get in the way—or get in good trouble—necessary trouble—to bring truth to light."
–The Honorable John Robert Lewis (1940-2020)

Endnotes

1   Charles M. Blow, "An Insatiable Rage: It is an everyday struggle to neither fall into despair nor explode in anger" [Opinion], *The New York Times*, June 14, 2020.

2   By this I mean to say that "the Black experience" has an African history and cultures that are unrelated to those that developed as a result of the encounter with enslavers and oppressors.

CHAPTER ONE

Black Christians and the Problem of Black Anger:
Toward a Theology of Holy Black Rage

Melinda Contreras-Byrd, M.Div., Psy.D.

Abstract

B eginning with personal memories of growing up in the urban environment of Newark, N.J., this essay begins to unravel the unseen faces of a community's anger and rage, culminating in. the 1967 riots in Newark and elsewhere across the United States.

The essay argues that, within the context of the Black experience, rage is an appropriate and psychologically empowering reaction to the evil and unconscionable lives under which Black people have been forced to live. The writer further argues that not only are we entitled to be enraged, but actually are by Holy mandate directed by a holy mandate to act in accord with those measures that will achieve God's will for all people.

Based on basic psycho-social theory and a reinterpretation of relevant scripture, a call for the development of a theology

of holy Black rage is supported by the absence of voices advocating appropriate and culturally syntonic definitions of love
and forgiveness during the initial development of theological
points of view. Additional support for the development of
a theology of holy Black rage is given through examples of
how the life application of historical theological definitions
has served to hinder the ability of Black Christians to develop healthy boundaries against oppression and injustice. Black
Christians therefore should feel justified to protect themselves
by acting out the righteous and holy rage that is necessary to
bring about justice and meet the Biblical challenge to people
of faith.

>>>

I grew up in the inner city, where I didn't feel like I was
encountering much anger. At least I didn't recognize it as
such. There were skirmishes between neighborhood men on
Friday or Saturday nights. Much of the time, the participants
had been drinking. It wasn't until I was older that I learned
that angry people often act out their anger at those who are in
closest proximity to them. Low wage, unstable dead-end jobs,
where you are disrespected as a matter of course on a daily
basis, give rise to a kind of anger that, because of its potential
for devastating consequences, must be repressed at work.
This kind of anger results when men of color are denied the
ability to fulfill cultural norms that define worthwhile and real
manhood as successfully assuming certain responsibilities.
This anger builds as Black single mothers are chastised and
castigated at their jobs, in their children's schools, and within
the overall culture of the United States, as they often struggle
to meet the needs for shelter, food, and clothing and the
academic, moral, and spiritual education of children who are
being treated in the same fashion. I can now see that, quiet
as it was kept, we were all fighting that anger. The feelings of
helplessness that are generated by racism become a catalyst
for latent and manifest demonstrations of anger, as you watch

the daily effects of racism threaten your self-esteem and that of those whom you love.

In my neighborhood, there were many who were familiar with the effects of drugs and alcohol, because someone in their family lived in semi-controlled addiction. People exhibiting a variety of mental health struggles were also an accepted part of our neighborhood. Everyone knew their families and the stories that were told about how they came to behave in peculiar and tormented ways. I was growing up, but not yet able to see any connection between the issues in my neighborhood and the effects of living for generations under the siege conditions of genocidal racism.

The year was 1967. The city was Newark, New Jersey. I was a teenager, and something terrifying was happening that no one in my city had ever seen before. One morning, we awakened to find that there were tanks and White soldiers stationed in the middle of our block. We could hear gunfire going off in the distance. Armed members of a nearby Muslim Mosque and Amiri Baraka's Black Nationalist "Committee for a United Newark" were rumored to be exchanging fire. Black and Puerto Rican journalists[1] would later argue that, despite what the local newspapers reported, there had in fact been *two* "riots" going on in Newark, N.J. One was started when police snipers and sanctioned National Guard ratcheted up the conflict with military tactics and arms against a mostly inactive and unarmed city.

One night during the melee, my older sister and I snuck out of our apartment in the middle of the night and walked to the main street. Chaos was everywhere. People were running in and out of broken store windows and doors with arms full of stolen merchandise. By the next morning, our entire city was completely razed. Busses stopped running. Grocery stores were empty and in shambles. Hospitals had to turn off their lights to guard themselves and their patients from being hit by sniper bullets. Black-owned stores put up signs that read, "Soul Brother" and Latinx store owners displayed "Soul

Sister" signs as a way to signal to looters not to damage these stores because they were part of the neighborhood.

Martin Luther King's frequently repeated phrase offered an interpretation of the rioting that was breaking out all over the country, "Riots are the language of the unheard."[2] We now understand these actions to be more correctly labeled, "uprisings" and *not* riots.

Uprisings had first broken out in Birmingham, then Harlem, Watts, Chicago, Tampa, Cincinnati, and Atlanta; and once the Newark uprising ended, Detroit went up in smoke.

This season of turmoil was interpreted and presented in a variety of ways. The why's and what's of these circumstances were viewed in diametrically opposed ways in the memories and interpretations of those who were Black and brown as opposed to those who were White.

But not even the injustices of Newark's and Detroit's particular political racist and corrupt city governments could fully or honestly account for the great domino-effect firestorms that erupted in city after city.

Then, two Black psychiatrists joined the conversation with a theory that would prove both accurate and pivotal. They posited the existence of a particular socio-cultural and psychological condition that they named "black rage." A book by the same title[3] became a seminal piece in the psychological understanding of the psyche of Black Americans.

The truth that is often left unspoken, even in the 21st century, is that people of color in the U.S. have lived and are living under completely deranged circumstances that have become an acceptable norm in "American life."

I contend that we persons of color have to some extent come to tacitly accept this derangement as our burden to struggle against and bear.[4] As I say this, I want to make it *very clear* that I am *not* saying that we have *ever* summarily acquiesced to injustice. Anyone's assessment of the lives of people of color under oppressive regimes, from any vantage point, must bear witness to our ongoing history of struggle—from leaping overboard slave ships to marches, boycotts, uprisings, armed resistance, and the songs of protest that have been created by all people of color and of the African diaspora.[5] *We have not, and will not now, just take what has been dished out to us!*

But the point that I want to make is that too many of us are not as outraged as the situation calls for. It is important here to note that, clinically speaking, we *could not* maintain the level of on-going rage that is warranted by the egregious situation that we not only live under, but birth our children into. Such an enormous amount of rage would prove destructive to our minds, bodies, and spirits.

What I want to stress is that we Black people have the sanctified right to not only be angry, but to be *enraged!* To be enraged is part of our Holy calling to issue rightful expressions of works of justice for the kingdom of God. And I believe that we have been given a flawed theology, one that labels justifiable human reactions to gross injustice as ungodly and our only acceptable responses a strange form of inactive prayer and "godly" patience. This scenario assumes a Father-God as the only featured actor in its eschatology. Cuban theologian Miquel De La Torre writes:

> White Christianity in the United States damns Jesus. An underlying problem with white Christianity is its relegation of Christian beliefs to the personal, to the private…. With his eye on the eschatological promise, [Billy] Graham railed against any social program designed to alleviate human suffering. Graham remarked that the dream must be deferred: "only when Christ comes again will the little children of Alabama walk hand in hand with little black children. For Evangelical Christians like the Grahams, one can continue engaging in everything Jesus preached against as long as one decides to give oneself over to Jesus in some theoretical or partial sense that does not necessarily entail following or even intending to follow his own teaches and example."[6]

I believe that this present era—the Trump Era—has increased our unspoken anger, by taking us back to the time of free, acceptable, open, and government-sanctioned pronouncements of White supremacy, lynching, and unmitigated violence against Black people. Perhaps this is the time of American "greatness" that is connected to "making America great again"? The CoVId-19 pandemic has also served as a trigger causing us to realize anew the dangerous and deadly circumstance of racism and injustice under which we live.

Because of CoVid, we have been trapped in our houses, unable to earn funds to meet our responsibilities or seek comfort from the human touch or presence of our only support systems we have in the Black lives we lead. And because of the concurrence of the CoVid pandemic and the ongoing racism pandemic, our days and nights are filled with news of increasingly blatant aggressive behavior toward Black people and our allies, and the tweets and proclamations of a President who supports genocidal policy and those who proclaim White supremacy and privilege. As a consequence of this state of affairs, our anxiety and anger levels have increased and our political and spiritual understanding have been honed. Yes, the injustices of CoVid-19 have ratcheted up the unconscious rage of even the most moderate, peace-loving, and forgiving Black Christian.

What we need to see is that "America's on-going race problem" is correlated with Black anger and rage. And the problem of addressing this anger has been confounded for Black Christians by a dangerously flawed theology.[7,8] If I am correct, then it is time for Black Christians to create a viable theology of Holy Black Rage.

Our suffering entitles us to be enraged.

It is time for a Theology of Holy Black Rage because we have repeatedly been physically, mentally, and spiritually assaulted, demeaned, oppressed, as well as negatively stereotyped, ignored, passed over, maligned, massacred, misinformed, segregated; ostracized, held back, dangerously stressed, sold as chattel, used for medical experimentation, underestimated, placed under surveillance, mistrusted, falsely accused, tricked, traumatized—in a word, treated unjustly. We have been devalued, harassed, falsely imprisoned; given the harshest punishments, the most restrictive psychological diagnoses, the poorest medical care, the worst housing. The lighting in the food stores in our neighborhoods is oddly dim. There is a slight odor of something rotting. The vegetables are not fresh and the fruit is bruised. Our collective psyches hold the stories of our parents, grandparents, and great grandparents, whose sacred lands were confiscated, desecrated, reallocated, stolen, and taken by "Eminent Domain." Our children have been miseducated, failed, arrested, taunted, wrongfully placed in special education, and assessed by tools using White standards that found in the end that *they are not White* and thus are "Culturally Deprived" and lower in intellect, abstract reasoning, and overall ability to learn. Our children have been bullied, ostracized on playgrounds, even picked on and taunted by angry groups of White adults. Our children have been taught by those who despised them, set lower standards for them, and held lower expectations of them. They have entered schools where they were surrounded by peers who resented their presence, teased them, called them "nigger," laughed at them, defaced their lockers and books, threatened and bullied them—all with the full knowledge *of* and consent *from* their Church-going parents.

The windows of our homes and our stores and our churches have been broken, our cars vandalized and spray-painted with words of hate. The things that we have struggled together to build have been destroyed, burned, and forgotten— Black Wall Street, New York; Rosewood, Florida; Slocum, Texas; Seneca Village, New York; North Brentwood, Maryland; Weeksville/ Bedford Stuyvesant, New York; Mound Bayou, Mississippi; Glenarden, Maryland; and Blackdom, New Mexico.[9]

And yet we stand, still speaking of forgiveness, moving past these daily ongoing assaults to our very humanity. And we reach out with the little that we have been allowed to amass and give to those who are less fortunate—ever thankful to

God for whatever we have to share. *And still we stand,* known throughout the world for our spirituality and the gift of music that we share so freely and willingly. *Still we stand,* believing in a God who would fight our battles if we just kept still. Yes Margaret, "We have been believers, believing in the black gods of an old land, believing in the secrets of the seeress and the magic of the charmers and the power of the devil's evil ones, and in the white gods of a new land...."[10]

We need a theology of holy rage, because of all that I have pointed out from our life experience. We are an ENRAGED people, who are struggling to finally begin the road to recovery and justice.

We need a holy rage, because the faulty ethics of those theologies we have been taught have silenced our human-selves.

The absence of a balanced theology that allowed us to be human has served to socialize us to repress and deny our rage by characterizing it as unchristian behavior. The consequence of embracing this view is that it renders Black Christians in particular (and all Christians in general) able to express only positive feelings, while masking and controlling all others. Certainly, given the unspeakable, oppressive, destructive forms of organized evil under which people of the African Diaspora have been forced to live for generations, we hold *more* than just positive feelings that need to be expressed.

Our psychological and physical survival has included a need to learn to deny, repress, and minimize our true feelings in public spaces to such an extent that it has become difficult to recognize the amount of injustice that we repress and its connection to some of our problematic issues that are physiological, psychological, and spiritual.

Theological interpretations of anger have failed to unpack the space between being angry and "sinning not," while Theology overall seems to overlook or misunderstand the spiritual ramifications of being human. These interpretations leave us with very limited response options, i.e., to disavow, dismiss, and/or downplay our pain and anger.

While we believe that Jesus is both God and man, in practice we seem to have a hard time believing that Jesus had any real and deep human emotions. We don't take Jesus' tears or anger seriously, just as we don't take God's love for justice and for all human beings seriously.

Irrespective of what John 3:16 or I John 4:7-8 or Romans 5:8 or Proverbs 17:15 or II Corinthian 1:6-7 or Deuteronomy 27:17 say, our behavior belies our stated beliefs. Perhaps a theology that is so abstract is an anathema to the development of applied faith and emotional maturity. Failure to account for ethnicity and culture in the creation of an applied theology of humanness has led us down several paths that are unhealthy for Black people of faith. Western discomfort with our humanness has led us to preach the fruits of the Spirit in a way that creates an anxious attempt to display these Christian traits, rather than as a glorious statement of the ways in which, if unleashed, the Spirit will change our lives. Our failure to embrace our humanness has led us to deny and misunderstand our sexuality, thereby resulting in sexual violence against women, children, and LGBT populations. Failure to assess our humanness in the form of our psychological needs and expressions has created countless evils in the form of slavery, the Holocaust, violence against women, acts of White supremacy, and evil empires that oppress, repress, wage war, and silently sanction genocide.

Because we are not encouraged to embrace our humanness, we are forced to wear masks that separate, depress, stress, and deteriorate our mental health. We become guilt ridden by our hypocrisy in trying to be that perfectly emotionally controlled person of faith that we feel we should be. We believe that, as Christians, we must always remain in control of our emotions at all costs; thus, uncontrolled laughter and displays of unbridled joy or love or fear or anger are unacceptable.Perhaps it is related to the White Jesus with the lambs that we see in churches. Or could it be the church's tendency to focus solely on scriptures that speak of peace, unity and expressions of love as the sole or foremost virtues that we should reach for. Maybe it's the interpretation of "meekness" that leads us to believe that Christians are called to always remain calm, soft spoken, and far away from any expression of anger and certainly never rage. Whatever the reason, I have recently come to the conclusion that we are no longer angry— but enraged; and that the tenets of what we have been taught to be consistent with our Christian faith have not only *failed* to support our humanness, but proven to be deadly. What we need in this turbulent time is a new theology, based on a hermeneutic that recognizes the needs and reality of the lives and experiences of God's Black people.

Why is there a need to create a just theology of anger?

Because we have been students of a theology that lacked our voices at its inception, the model for Christian conflict resolution that we have learned is only and always characterized by the avoidance of discord, harsh words, or expressions of anger. Perhaps within a certain historical context, this was legitimate behavior appropriate to their lived experiences. But those who interpreted and fashioned this theology have never stood where we who are Black stand throughout the world. Therefore, while this interpretation of Christian anger may prove appropriate in the context of White historical experience, it is totally inappropriate to ours. When assessed within the context of Black life, it becomes ridiculously clear that the unspoken rules that we have set for discussions on race relations, justice, poverty, or any other topic of life in which a group of people are involved in daily and unjust suffering are totally inappropriate. It is quite unrealistic to expect that, as people living under these conditions, we could even *discuss* the issue of ongoing unacknowledged trauma in the lives of those we call "family members" in a calm and anger-free manner! If people in unspeakable pain and suffering are to have a truthful conversation, it cannot begin by imposing the conditions that our interactions must remain calm, quiet, and free of conflict! If such a discussion were seen to have those dynamics, its authenticity would certainly become suspect. A theology that teaches us to repress our justifiable rage is not a theology that embraces the truths and ramifications of our humanness. It is not a life-affirming or justice-building theology. We can no longer accept the accepted criteria of what defines Christian behavior; for it has meant the need for temperance in all things—especially if you are Black. It has intertwined itself with racist thinking, resulting in "Black Christian behavior according to Onesimus" and a poorly exegeted interpretation of Ephesians 6:5 and Colossians 3:2. The lack of a Black-adequate theology of holy Black rage has been a pernicious factor, disabling White Christians and other justice-seekers from seeing the real horrors of daily Black existence. And what is even more disturbing is its role in deadening their abilities for empathy, moral and intellectual clarity, and spiritual discernment on matters of racism.

How else has the present theology negatively affected Black expressions of anger? It has suggested scriptural interpretations that limit the parameters of what can be seen as godly actions against evil and on behalf of justice. It has focused us on a model of servanthood and sacrifice, one that ignores concepts of justice and elevates the concept of Martyrdom (when it comes to the disenfranchised).[11] As women and persons of color have entered into theological dialogues, these insufficient interpretations of scripture and of what constitutes true Christian behavior have given rise to new critiques and new and liberating theological understandings, ones that shine a spotlight on a flawed/inappropriate theology.[12]

The lack of a theology of Holy Black Rage has also aided in the development of unhealthy personality traits among many Black people (especially in the U.S.).

Acquired psycho-socio-cultural behavior stands in the way of our acknowledgment and true expression of the presence of a "Holy Black Rage." For Black (and Latinx) people, Biblical interpretations of appropriate behavior management have become connected with negative cultural/racist stereo-types, thus inducing behavior that is psychologically skewed toward denial. We struggle with fear and anxieties in an ef-fort to disprove the stereotypes of us as the loud, angry, un-controlled, aggressive, trouble-making Black woman or man. But, in order to live out a viable theology of Black rage, we must be willing to raise our voices in public places and trigger discord in discussions involving "race." We must be willing to take the risk of realizing our greatest fear: that we *are in fact* the angry ones in the discussion, those whose words have given rise to conflict and unease. We have been raised to avoid conflict, avoid antagonism, modulate our voices in public spaces, and be ever accepting and even-tempered, especially in the academy and in integrated leadership groups. But these are new and unusual times, where we are once again being forced to embrace and react to our reality and raise questions about how Black people of God must respond.

And this presents a psycho-social challenge. In order to do what is needed, we must be willing to leave discussions still angry, to allow others to have hurt feelings, and to stop our-selves from trying to take away the White pain necessary for growth and healing. We must be willing to learn to sit with our anger and not deny it as ungodly. We must learn how to cope with a lack of closure, for ours will be a battle to undo thousands of years of evil in the form of racism and xeno-phobia. We must be able to form a support group to whom we can go when others do not want to hear our story, admit responsibility, and commit to resolution.[13]

And as we reanalyze and restructure our Christian think-ing, we must include all areas of our Christian lives, includ-ing prayer and ritual. I include a brief excursus on prayer and ritual here because I believe that certain Western inter-pretations have served to weaken a Black sense of commu-nity, psychological and mental empowerment, and face-to-face connection with the Holy Spirit. The typical Christian/ Protestant practices of prayer and ritual have not served Black communities well in that they have disallowed ideas that contained even the verbal expression of anger to God; and altered the expectations of real, felt responses from the Holy One that would motivate people to movement. Prayer and ritual have served as a critical factor in the lives of people of the African Diaspora. For people of the African Diaspora (especially those enslaved), reaching out to God in prayer and ritual has been our greatest boon. It has been the *one* power that we were allowed to possess. But it was allowed as a safe option, because enslavers were content that *its* power had been sufficiently neutralized so as not to prove a danger to the continuation of their evil racist behavior. This situation is yet another example of the results of a lack of a theology of holy rage. For one for whom there are no available options for "bearing one's burdens," prayer is an indispensable tool. However, the form of prayer offered to those enslaved was one in which they were allowed to "tell Jesus all of their troubles" but were encouraged to let it end there. The manner in which prayer was presented as an option assumed a safe trajectory. One was to pray for help, guidance, and the ability to withstand. One was greatly encouraged to pray for one's enemies as the major response to injustice, malice, or abuse. Moreover, one was expected to pray only prayers of forgiveness, couched in love, placing the trespasser ahead of oneself.

I cannot recall a time when "imprecatory prayers" were used as a fit example of how to pray for one's enemies. Even when Psalm 137 was used during Black History Month preaching – the concluding verses were always left out. I cannot recall hearing any sermon or other Christian teachings that highlighted some of David's imprecatory prayers as an acceptable manner in which to pray.

Few Christian preachers tell their flock that in Psalm 69:24, the Great David once prayed:

"Pour out your indignation upon them, and let your burning anger overtake them."

Or that, while crying out to God for inward spiritual correctness, David also prayed these words:

> Lead me, O Lord, in thy righteousness because of mine enemies; make thy way straight before my face.

> For there is no faithfulness in their mouth; their inward part is very wickedness; their throat is an open sepulcher; they flatter with their tongue.

> Destroy thou them, O God; let them fall by their own counsels; cast them out in the multitude of their transgressions; for they have rebelled against thee. (Psalm 5:8-10)

Writer Benjamin Kandt [14]sites 22 reasons why we as Christians should pray imprecatory prayers, giving as an overall reason the fact that we are called to be involved in the coming of God's Kingdom.

Not only was the direction of prayer presented in a disabling way for abused and oppressed Black people; the very nature of prayer was likewise so presented. The act of prayer was presented as an intellectual exercise unrelated to transformation and detached from responsibility for any personal obligation in making one's prayer requests come to fruition.

Nor was there any expectation that God would speak and give a new vision and direction to obtain freedom and justice. Women such as Harriet Tubman and men such as Nat Turner must have proven a great surprise and disappointment to the majority of the Black-enslaving White Christian community of that time! Public expressions of reaching out to God were categorized and scripted into written and distributed liturgy, and anything not scripted was deemed inappropriate. The problem here is that this approach left no room for the free movement of the Holy Spirit in those in attendance. Through the many Africans from diverse religious cultures who were brought to this country, a variety of African American and Afro-Caribbean liturgies were birthed. Ring shout, synchronized and spontaneous spiritual dances, shouting, free physical movements such as the lifting and waving hands or calling out, pouring of libations, and other expressions of Africanized displays of spiritual worship and devotion were outlawed in this new, Church-sanctioned way of worship.

Applied theologies of prayer have suggested prayer as a personal experience that is an end in and of itself, rather than exploring the many and theologically justifiable ways in which, for those oppressed, prayer can and must be legitimately interpreted as a catalyst for achieving justice and community. There was no sense of the urgency of community prayer gatherings since each person was encouraged to seek God for themselves. Many Evangelical theological teachings have suggested that the move toward a deeper, meditative prayer life is diametrically opposed to any form of social justice action.

This theology presupposes that the true spiritual life is lived in opposition to any socio-political goals on behalf of injustice and evil. In doing this, it overlooks or purposefully ignores Jesus' bold and clear statement of his purpose found in this important New Testament declaration text:

> The Spirit of the Lord is upon me,
> because he has anointed me to bring good news to the poor.
> He has sent me to proclaim release to the captive,
> and recovery of sight to the blind,
> to let the oppressed go free,
> to proclaim the year of the Lord's favor.[15]

It is certainly likely that, coming from a culture that is community-based, Africans expected prayer/interactions with God/the Greatest Spirit to have ramifications not just for the one who was praying, but for those who were part of that person's community. Prayer/interaction with the Spirit was expected to be deeply spiritual and involve interaction with an actual tangible spirit. For many of the African Diaspora, prayer time was to be an unusual time, when anything could happen to the one who knelt in prayer (called upon the Spirit in ritual) and as a response to the prayer/interaction/

time of spiritual manifestation. The cultural foundation of this theology included the possibility that the faithful could and would be indwelt and that those who were "indwelt/possessed" would experience an unusual and holy time with God that would overwhelm, empower, and free them to dance, shout, cry, prophesy, or exhibit other forms of physical release! These expressions of the Spirit served to uplift both the one upon whom the Spirit fell, as well as those who participated by being a present part of the faithful community.[16] Sadly, somewhere along the line, people of the African Diaspora were taught to deny this freedom and unity, and given a new spirit—whose power was containable, abstractly understood, quietly and individually experienced, and completely removed from things loud, unexpectant, and fear-provoking.

But a story is told in the second chapter of Acts that does not support the Western-based theology of the Spirit that has replaced African religious thinking. A Black way of re-telling the story in present context, would go like this:

Jesus' followers are gathered together in one place waiting for a sign from God. They are longing to become involved with some manifestation of the presence of God's Spirit.

Their leader who had called them, taught them, fed them, and protected them, healed the sick, and raised the dead and set off a wind of disruption in both the political and religious *status quo* was now gone, killed by the empire that they had hoped that he would overthrow. This brings to memory the jailing of Nelson Mandela, the Killing of Steven Biko, the assassinations of Malcom X and Martin Luther King. And they, like us, were left in deep despair, unable to direct our anger and feeling a life-threatening void. Without a miracle-working new kind of Messiah—what would they do?

> So, they huddled together—in reality, hiding out—hoping that they would receive further instructions despite the fact that they had witnessed their leader's death with their own eyes. And, lo and behold, while they stood there, something strange and frightening and absolutely unexpected began

to occur! Like when Nelson Mandela walked out of the prison after 27 years and into the presidency of South Africa. Like when declared leaders all over the African Diaspora continued the struggle for liberation, running on empty and faith in God. And those in the story of Acts were suddenly confronted with strange and frightening things, things that they had never seen nor heard before in quite this way.

As promised, a new phase of Spirit-Christianity was to begin, and it sounds to me like it began more like African than Traditional Western expectations would allow. The Spirit came loudly. The Spirit came in ways that were unexpected, outside of decorum, and—good God Almighty!—it was frightening. The Spirit came like an uprising, with the outcome of getting the people's attention. The Spirit came with what looked like danger—fire on people's heads. The Spirit came with what felt like some form of miraculous confusion—people speaking in languages they had never learned. This awaited Holy Spirit came and the confusion, the danger, the loudness of a cacophony of voices all speaking at one time engaged those on "the outside of the church." The experience of this spiritual interaction caused them to talk and debate about spiritual things.

When it is time, and direction is needed, the Spirit of God comes in like a mighty wind, like a fire, like a battle axe— something that cannot be ignored. The spirit comes in ways that make the truth impossible to ignore, and the struggle real and clear. And in the end, God's purpose was fulfilled 3,000-fold.

This is the visible way of the Spirit that is absent and dis-avowed by many Western ideas of the Holy Spirit, so remote from the possibilities of what prayer and ritual could do for those enslaved.

It is important to note that Western thought and teach-ings about spirituality, the movement of the Spirit and prayer, were *not* the only teachings available to Christians. Histori-cally, the Eastern Orthodox and Oriental Orthodox churches stood alongside the preeminent Roman Catholic church, and

Orthodox theology and teachings stood in contrast to Catholic (and later Protestant) theologies. Church history includes eastern Orthodox churches such as the Russian Orthodox, Armenian Orthodox, Greek, Serbian and Bulgarian Orthodox churches, and Oriental Orthodox churches that include the Coptic Church of Egypt, the Ethiopian Orthodox Tewahedo church, and the Malankara Orthodox Syrian Church, among others.

John Cassian[17] is often said to be one of the greatest early monastic writers. He is also noted to be the founder of "contemplative prayer." This form of prayer is distinctly different from the way in which Protestant churches have taught prayer. It is not an asking prayer, but a *listening* and *seeking* prayer. In this method of prayer, the goal is to listen *to* and *for* God. Cassian attributes his knowledge of this form of prayer to his time alone in Africa with those third- and fourth-century Christian ascetics who are known in Christian history as "the desert fathers and mothers."[18] (Notably, many of them were North Africans.[19])

Present ideas about Christianity fail to raise issues pertinent to Black Christians seeking to follow a Christ-like lifestyle while suffering on-going and sanctioned racism.

Present theologies have left us with a need to ask and answer many important questions from within our own unique Black context. A theology that does not focus fully on the relevant issues—such as poverty, racism, justice, liberation, and following Jesus while living in dangerous, unjust, and traumatic circumstances—cannot prove sufficient to meet our needs.

Spending time in South Africa helped to clarify this for me. There I heard the voices of African clergy, scholars, and social activists from all over the African Diaspora speak about racism and the legacies of Apartheid. The realities that they raised forced me to see the need to engage in a time of culturally based theological reflection. One of my reflections involved seeking a full theological understanding of Black anger. This understanding was then related to Christian concepts of forgiveness and unity (between the races) juxtaposed against life within the evil empire of Apartheid. Within this context, it was then—and is now—clear to me that the way in which Christians have been approaching these issues has been from within a woefully lacking framework. I believe that we need a new theology. Our present theological approach is neither correct, nor expedient, nor Biblically accurate.

Our new theology must answer the question of what *a just model of forgiveness* is, and how—and if—it can be lived out by those in the midst of genocide. The lived theological understanding of Black Christians has been too conciliatory—detrimentally so. We have tolerated too much and compromised our humanness too much. At this point in the struggle for justice, we must not only resist voices that ignore, downplay, or divert conversations about race and racism; we must learn to detect and challenge more subtle and difficult theological ideas that have been infiltrated by evil. It is past time that we, who have been injured, speak our pain and express our anger and rage, refusing to be ignored!

I have come to believe that there is a call to resistance against a form of evil that has wound itself into the basic thread of Christian thinking, and thus is most difficult to ferret out.

The theology that we have been given leads us to the conclusion that the answer to all issues is love and forgiveness, and that this *alone* is the trajectory that all interracial faith communications ought to take! But if we take this approach, once again, the onus of U.S. race relations is placed upon the tired shoulders of Black people, who have borne the brunt of racism since our feet first touched this Native American soil. The acceptance of the idea that love and forgiveness alone are the key to resolving the evils of systemic racism— without an insistence upon drastic change in unjust, racist, and violent laws, teachings and behavior—is suggesting that those oppressed must learn to be content in this situation and forgive the injustice even as it is allowed to continue. A succinct response to this thinking is found in the well-known protest slogan, "No Justice, No Peace." I submit that if "the church in the U.S." continues to focus only on love and forgiveness in the present racial situations; they have elected to align themselves with a form of evil that must not only be *resisted*, and *challenged*, but *destroyed!* Ongoing practices that support bigoted, unjust, and narrow Christian thinking must be reinterpreted and repented of. We who can discern evil must *right now* assume the responsibility of creating an occasion for this to be done.

Too many of us have been semi-content to be part of an interracial, ethnically diverse church in which there has been, at best, a very fragile peace. Black and White Christians have remained strangers to each other's deep core. Beyond the loss of the possibility of forming meaningful connections, Black people have literally suffered in the not knowing. This can no longer remain the case.

How have we reached this state in Black-White relations and the church? This happens when positive, life-affirming concepts such as love and forgiveness are eclipsed by evil and diverted into actions that result in what theologian Dietrich Bonhoeffer called "cheap grace." [20] This is what happens when a type of flawed thinking that writer Ward Churchill terms "pacifism as pathology" guides our interactions.[21] Churchill states that "Forgiveness without need for repentance is an evil form of injustice. It is an anxious creation that poses as forgiveness, while continuing to victimize those wronged, and overlook even the possibility of a need for reparation."

Because of this flawed theological stance, Christian models of forgiveness as acted out are in fact unjust and thus ungodly. A flawed theology of anger has served to block Black Christian insistence upon reparations and repentance as critical initial factors to be addressed in opening real cross-cultural dialogue. We Black Christians have struggled to follow the example of Jesus, even when our churches were bombed, our children repeatedly murdered, and our people dying from benign neglect and overt racist policies. And while we have struggled to be "Christian," we have been too willing to allow those who are White, self-confessed Christians to neglect the hard and never-ending work that is required to live according to Kingdom principles.   We have literally compromised our very lives in the hopes that our White brothers and sisters would finally realize that God has always clearly stated that Black lives matter. It is now time that we *insist* that Black lives matter, with all the rage that is appropriate to force *serendipitous racists*[22] into a position to *have to state* this as a fact! Historical prophets have lived and died hollering out the truth... Harriet Tubman, Fredrick Douglas, Rosa Parks, Daisy Bates, Fannie Lou Hamer, Ella Baker, and even "the best-known colored woman in the U.S.," Mary Burnett Talbet, used her voice to make this truth known. Black prophetic writers like Zora Neale Hurston, Margaret Walker, and Lorraine Hansberry spread the news and introduced the world to the lives of Black people. Amiri Baraka, Richard Wright, Ralph Ellison, and James Baldwin, who introduced us to Beale Street and warned of "the Fire Next Time," while Langston Hughes asked the terrifying question, "What happens to a dream deferred?" and in his poem, *Warning*, instructed, "beware the day they change their minds." The frustrations of living under the oppressive rules set for Black lives was there, and being voiced even in 1919 when Jamaican American poet Claude McKay opened the "Harlem Renaissance" with a declaration defining an aspect of Holy Black Rage in his poem, "If We Must Die." And yet people would not hear.   Poet Nikki Giovanni gave voice to a sentiment about Black Life and others' interpretation of it that would later be echoed in 2020 by Black Princeton University Professor Imani Perry.[23]

In 1876, the African Methodist Episcopal Church formed, seeing the need to protect and support Black people who, despite no longer being enslaved, continued to suffer degradation and abuse in the United States. God's Black voices united to form protective, empowering organizations for the protection, support, and advancement of Black people. In 1910, The Urban League formed. In 1911, the AKA and Omega Psi Phi were established at Howard University. In 1913, Delta Sigma

Theta was established at Howard University, Black news-papers protested the inaccuracies of the hit movie, *Birth of a Nation*. Even as far back as the 1900's, U.S. academic behav-ior mirrored that of the populace and no credit was given for any achievements of Black people. Consequently, once again America was informed by Black prophets of the day. In 1905, Black Puerto Rican scholar Arturo Alfonso Schomberg estab-lished a research library to serve as an archive of the history of people of the African Diaspora. In 1915, Carter G. Woodson established the Association for the Study of African-American Life and History, its research goal being the promotion and preservation of Black scholarship and achievement.

Perhaps none of these voices served as a clue that things were patently unjust and inhumane for Black people living in the United States (and elsewhere)? Seemingly, not even the on-going needs expressed by groups of Black professionals were enough to clue the country in to the fact that something was drastically wrong in every facet of Black life.

In 1923, at Howard University, renowned Black Scholar and "father of Afro-American History," Carter G. Woodson, taught the first college course on this topic in the United States. Still, no one was listening. But the prophetic voices of Black people continued to rise in educational self-affirmation and holy zeal in support of ourselves. In 1947, John Hope Frank-lin's seminal book, *From Slavery to Freedom*, outlined the story of African-American Life that laid crucial information open for all to see. This should have served as a point of reversal and reimaging in the minds of White scholars and non-schol-ars. It did not.

The 1960's continued to give birth to new and living proph-ets who continued to give testimony to the injustice of racism in the lives of U.S. citizens with the instigating pedagogy of the Black Power Movement—Malcolm X, Kathleen Cleaver, Maulana Karenga, Elaine Brown, Frankye Adams-Johnson, Stokely Carmichael, Angela Davis, H. Rap Brown—voices of angry protest and indignation.

And as the racism continued, then as now, the voices from the other side of justice declared these Black prophets to be agitators; and the stories of Black America to be embellished, isolated incidents. Injustice was once more seen as justified and the fault of those being victimized.

The year is 2020, and we are now standing on a precipice that is not only socio-political, but spiritual. This is the defining moment for our country and our faith! Injustice and death have been tolerated for too long and are an affront to God and all things of the Spirit!

As we look around at this nation under quarantine, I can't help but believe that one of our unique experiences is that we are not just angry , we are justifiably enraged—and it is an anointed and holy Black rage that we are called to live out as "our living sacrifice, and reasonable service."

Endnotes

1   Ron Porambo, *No Cause for Indictment: An Autopsy of Newark* (Brooklyn, N.Y.: Melville House, 2007).

2   Lily Rothman, "What Martin Luther King Jr. Really Thought About Riots." *Time* Magazine, April 28, 2015.

3   William H. Grier & Price M.Cobbs, *Black Rage* (New York: Basic Books, 1968).

4   Jeremiah Wright, Jr., "Foreword" in Melinda Contreras-Byrd, *The Great Shift: Psychospiritual Manual for Survival and Transformation in the Trump Era* (U.K.: Cambridge Scholars Publishing, 2018). pp. ix-xii.

5   Melinda Contreras-Byrd, *The Great Shift Psychospiritual Manual for Survival and Transformation in the Trump Era.* (U.K. Cambridge Scholars Publishing, 2018).

6   Miguel A. De La Torre, *Burying White Privilege: Resurrecting a Badass Christianity* (Grand Rapids: Wm. B. Eerdmans Publishing, 2019), pp. 24-25.

7   James Cone, *God of the Oppressed* (New York: Orbis Books, 1975).

8   James Cone, *A Theology of Liberation* (New York: Orbis Books, 1970).

9   Black Excellence and Abundance Channel , YouTube," Other Towns Like Black Wall Street", November 22, 2019.

10 Margaret Walker, "We Have Been Believers" in *Poetry: A Magazine of Verse*, Vol. LIII, No. 6, 1939.

11 Melinda Contreras-Byrd, "A Living Sacrifice," *The Other Side Magazine*, 2002, pp. 20-23.

12 Jacqueline Grant, *White Women's Christ and Black Women's Jesus: Feminist Christology and Womanist Response* (New York: Scholars Press, 1989).

13 To read more about this issue, see: Melinda Contreras-Byrd, *The Great Shift: Psychospiritual Manual for Survival and Transformation in The Trump Era* (Cambridge Scholars Publishing, 2018).

14   Benjamin Kandt, "22 Reasons to Pray the Cursing (Imprecatory) Psalms."
      praypsalms.org, July 28, 2017.
15   Luke 4:18-19.
16   It should be noted that African people have diversity in their religious expres-
      sions and theologies. For further reading on this topic, see: John S Mbiti, *In-
      troduction to African Religion* (Portsmouth, New Hampshire: Heineman Educa-
      tional Publishing, 1975); Ephraim Isaac, *The Ethiopian Orthodox Tawahido Church*
      (Trenton, N.J: The Red Sea Press, 2013); Laurent Magesa, *What is Not Sacred?*
      (New York: Orbis Books), 2013.
17   St. John Cassian, *St. John Cassian on Prayer* (Scarsdale, N.Y.: Cistercian Publica-
      tions, 2007).
18   John Chryssavgis, *In the Heart of the Desert: The Spirituality of the Desert Fathers
      and Mothers* (Bloomington, Indiana: World Wisdom, 2008).
19   Mark Ellingson, *African Christian Mothers and Fathers: Why They Matter for the
      Church Today* (Eugene, Oregon: Cascade Books, 2015).
20   Dietrich Bonhoeffer, *The Cost of Discipleship* (Austin, Texas: Touchstone Pub-
      lishers, 1995).
21   Ward Churchill, *Pacifism as Pathology* (Oakland, California: AK Press, 1998).
22   A word I created to refer to those who espouse and create in accord with racist
      ideas and behavior that have been learned, modeled, denied, vehemently em-
      braced, and never challenged, but passed on.
23   Imani Perry, "Racism Is Terrible: Blackness Is Not," Atlantic Magazine, June 15,
      2020

Melinda Contreras-Byrd, M.Div., Psy.D.

Dr. Contreras-Byrd is a New Jersey state licensed psychologist with over 35 years of clinical practice. Dr. Contreras-Byrd's general areas of expertise involve issues of class, gender, ethnicity and faith, while her clinical areas of expertise are depression and anxiety. She has worked as a school psychologist in urban and suburban districts and as a clinical psychologist for juvenile offenders, homeless men, and adult substance abusers.

Dr. Contreras-Byrd has directed programs for bilingual preschoolers and the intellectually gifted. She has been a professor of Psychology, Christian and Pastoral Counseling, Black Studies, and Multicultural Counseling. For six years she served as the Special Services Advisor to the Office of the Dean of Students at Princeton University, developing, imple-menting and/or supervising programming directed at meet-ing the needs of Asian, Black, Latinx, and Native American undergraduate students. She also served as Director of the Third World Center (now renamed the Carl Fields Center).

For six years she served as a consultant psychologist and clinical supervisor for LifeTies, Inc. of Trenton and Ewing, New Jersey, working with teen populations with backgrounds of abuse and neglect, and those who were "medically fragile" or gay, lesbian, bi-sexual, or trans-gendered.

She received her undergraduate degree from Rutgers University, her Master of Divinity degree from Princeton Theological Seminary, and her doctoral degree from Rutgers Graduate School of Applied and Professional Psychology.

Lastly, Dr. Contreras-Byrd has appeared on local radio and television stations and has served as a lecturer, a preacher, and a workshop facilitator or keynote speaker for numerous corporations and community, religious, and educational organizations throughout the United States and Latin America. She has been a consistent presenter for The Transatlantic Roundtable on Religion and Race, and The Samuel DeWitt Proctor Conference. She presently serves as adjunct professor in the D.Min. program of the New Brunswick Theological Seminary.

Her first book was: *The Great Shift: A Psycho-spiritual Manual for Survival and Transformation in the Trump Era* (Cambridge Scholars Publishing, 2018). She was awarded a grant from the Louisville Institute enabling her to conduct research into the factors that inform the self-care decisions of Black and Latino pastors in the United States. Information from this research is presented in her second book, titled, *Saving the Lives of Black and Latinx Pastors: A Self-care Study,* published in 2019 by Africa World/Red Sea Press. In 2020, she edited a book, published by Desakajo Publishers, titled *Black Women and Girls Matter: Voices of Resilience, Resistance and Resolve.*

Melinda Contreras-Byrd is a poet and an ordained Elder of the African Methodist Episcopal Church, and joins her husband, Rev. Vernon R. Byrd, Jr., in pastoral ministry at St. Matthew A.M.E. Church in Philadelphia, Pennsylvania.

CHAPTER TWO

The Prophetic Power of Black Rage to Liberate Public Policy

Charles Boyer, M.Div., D.Min.

Abstract

This article will include an analysis of current Black rage as expressed towards unjust public policy. It will examine how unjust laws fuel Black rage through oppression, inequitable enforcement, and systemic racism. Then the analysis will shift to a scriptural learning regarding public policy by looking at Old Covenant laws, to the legal reformation brought about by Jesus, to the Old Covenant policy critiques of the Apostle Paul. This framework will provide space for something new, namely, a theological understanding of Black rage that can transform policy.

>>

The current genocide of unarmed Black people at the hands of police has taken our rage to unprecedented depths. Contemporaneous with this essay, Black America has just witnessed a Black man named Jacob Blake being shot in the back seven times by Kenosha police in front of his children. Black activists, organizers, politicians, and clergy are all filled with rage. It seems monthly we have a new assault, a new frivolous use of force, and a new dead Black body on display. Wisconsin is in an uprising, which the right-wing media calls riots while it celebrates a seventeen-year-old white teen who shot and killed two protesters. Donald Trump has tweeted that he is sending troops to Wisconsin to maintain law and order, while making no mention of justice for Jacob.

The strange fruit this nation has produced from its founding once created mourning; now it is growing the grapes of wrath and the fruit is vitriol. Generation X and the succeeding generations have existed in the claws of mass incarceration, the drug war, stop-and-frisk, racial profiling, and militarized police. We remain targets of an unjust system of police abuse and imprisonment. This reality has left us consumed with rage for as long as we have known we are Black in America.

In a *Time* Magazine article in 1965, James Baldwin said that, "To be a Negro in this country and to be relatively conscious is to be in a rage almost all the time." We cannot escape this rage. It is as present with us as our blood.

Not only do we find ourselves amid uprisings over the taking of Black lives, but we also find ourselves in the grip of a global pandemic that disproportionately seeks our lives as well. Our scorn is as complicated as our fear, isolation, and health in crowded protests. The passion in the streets often erupts into fire and destruction as a natural response to the violence of structural racism and the death it has inflicted. What is critical for this generation is what has been crucial for our ancestors, channeling our anger as a prophetic rage.

Our rage must not be a mere philosophical, theoretical, or even theological exercise. Rage must produce a tangible transformation. Most importantly, our rage must never disconnect from the anger in the streets. We must embrace rage. We cannot condemn rage or try to thwart or cool it down. We should not oblige the police chief, the prosecutor, or the may-

or to offer a calming prayer or call for peace. But instead, we must affirm our rage. We must confirm and articulate what anger means, and we must demand what that anger is demanding. Historically, Denmark Vesey and Nat Turner show us that even divine rage sometimes expresses itself violently.

Our anger and our rage should fuel us to prophetically declare the damnation of systemic sin. Yet, the prophetic role is not solely vocal but also visionary. Therefore, the prophet reimagines and advocates for God's revealed alternative realities. Cornel West writes that both Elijah Muhammed and Martin Luther King, Jr. "understood one fundamental truth about Black rage: it must neither be ignored nor ignited." He goes on to say that they "knew how to work with Black Rage constructively, shape it through moral discipline, channel it into a political organization, and guide it by charismatic leadership."[1] The Black prophetic tradition is uniquely anointed, equipped, and positioned to heal our trauma by channeling our rage through God's passion for justice.

The Black community is suffering from inadequate health care, subpar schools, addiction, violence, poverty, and disenfranchisement. How can these needs be addressed, and their voice be heard? We can become the prophetic voice for the people when we voice the collective pain of the Black experience and advocate for systemic and cultural change. Sustained and consuming fire demands change even when the cameras aren't on. This is the genuine difference between prophets and pulpit opportunists. Fueled by Black rage, we must theologically reflect and prophetically advocate for change in the halls of power and change the policy that creates that rage.

Black rage is the equal and opposite reaction to unjust public policy. The outrage expressed in the streets is the rage most Black people feel but do not express externally or publicly. Black Christians seek peace, nonviolence, and reconciliation, yet Black rage is an unquenchable fire shut up in our bones. That rage consumes us daily. We try to contain it, but the trauma weighs on our mental and physical health. Doc Rivers, head coach of the Los Angeles Clippers, expresses our outrage perfectly in just a few words: "It's amazing, we keep loving this country, and this country does not love us back."[2]

Far too often we run to condemn those who are burning things down rather than prophetically translating their passionate cry that arises from the flames. It is a passion that only knows how to express its desire to burn down the structures of oppression by burning down its physical structures.

King quotes Victor Hugo in an essay on riots in the Atlantic, "If the soul is left in darkness, sins will be committed. The guilty one is not he who commits the sin, but he who causes the darkness."[3] To be clear, public policy made by politicians who respond to and are supported by a white racist society creates the darkness. In a speech at the London School of Economics, Malcolm X rightly defined Black rage as "reactions against police brutality." The destruction of property is not Black people destroying their community, but the property owned by whites in neighborhoods occupied by Blacks. Malcolm goes on to say:

> And when you see the Blacks react, since the people who do this aren't there, they react against their property. The property is the only thing that's there. And they destroy it. And you get the impression over here that because they are destroying the property where they live, that they are destroying their own property. No. They can't get to the man, so they get at what he owns.[4]

Even with his commitment to nonviolence Martin Luther King, Jr. understood that Black rage was the natural reaction to white terror. King understood that the passion and fury that led to property destruction was the backlash against the violence of poverty:

> I think that we've got to see that a riot is the language of the unheard. And, what is it that America has failed to hear? It has failed to hear that the economic plight of the Negro poor has worsened over the last few years.[5]

It is uncomfortable for us to admit that there are peaceful pillars of protests by day but violent fiery protests by night.

We must stop seeking white people's approval by surgically disconnecting our collective pain from our collective rage. And while it is true that white supremacists and white left-wing anarchists are present and agitating, it is also true that our people have never needed agitation aside from oppression to burn shit down. At what point does America stop burning *us* down?

Since people of faith should seek to minister to the angry oppressed people in the community, who may be burning down physical structures, we can best join them by burning down *systemic* structures. If we are to change our reality, we must channel the fire and burn down the white power structure that controls our political destiny. The word, "politics," from the Greek *polis*, means *affairs of the cities*. Politics is all the activities around decision making in and about groups regarding power and resources. Other people are deciding our political reality. Systemic racism is administered, governed, and maintained by the very politicians who seek our votes. As a people, we have never had the privilege of being divorced from political realities with life or death consequences.

Our current policing structure emerged out of a political response to runaway slaves. The "drug war" started as a political tactic to control and warehouse Black bodies. Mass incarceration and law-and-order campaign slogans were a white backlash to the progress of the Civil Rights and Black Power movements.

Our health-care system is the result of political decisions that made health care an income- and class-based privilege rather than a human right. As a result, we are disproportionately contracting—and dying from—the coronavirus, and Black mothers are more than three times as likely as a white woman to die giving birth. Our health policies have violently attacked Black life.

New Deal policies intentionally excluded Black people after the Great Depression as they created the white middle class in America. The net worth of the average white family is over ten times that of the average Black family. It is public policy that brutally imposes economic segregation like redlining, predatory lending, and lower property values.

It is policy and politics that ferociously dictate that our children must go to under-resourced apartheid schools based on zip code. It is policy and politics that have placed the most toxic environmental sites in Black neighborhoods, leading to higher levels of asthma and lead poisoning.

All of these laws and systems have been the results of public policy authored by politicians and political power brokers. Our political policy making is the manifestation of systemic sin and the oppressive nature of unchecked power to *go to and fro seeking whom it may devour* (1 Peter 5:8). Our rage is fueled by our social reality, which is insidiously shaped for us by others. Where we find ourselves economically at birth, where we are educated and live, are choices made for us. By the time we have agency, we have already been placed inequitably behind those whom society has privileged for generations.

When those policies dare to boldly expose themselves on camera repeatedly in the form of police shooting an unarmed Black person with impunity, rage is inevitable. Yes, we express our outrage through peaceful protests, boisterous and angry uprisings, and even violent riots. When Black people destroy property, it is the assured response to a political system destroying Black bodies as if we were still legally white people's property. This riotous response creates a crisis moment to which the political structure must respond.

In his book, *The Fire Next Time,* James Baldwin prophetically expresses the potential consequences of unsatisfied Black rage. After giving riveting perceptiveness into America's racist nature through a letter to his nephew, Baldwin gives us insight into the anger that consumed Elijah Muhammed and his followers. He sees this rage as misguided but a prophetic warning coming from beautiful Black people.

> And when I sat at Elijah's table and watched the baby, the women, and the men, and we talked about God's—or Allah's—vengeance, I wondered, when that vengeance was achieved, what will happen to all that beauty then? I could

also see that the intransigence and ignorance of the white
world might make that vengeance inevitable—a vengeance
that does not really depend on, and cannot really be
executed by, any person or organization, and that cannot be
prevented by any police force or army: historical vengeance,
a cosmic vengeance, based on the law that we recognize
when we say, "Whatever goes up must come down."........
If we do not now dare everything, the fulfillment of that
prophecy, re-created from the Bible in song by a slave, is
upon us: God gave Noah the rainbow sign, No more water,
the fire next time![6]

The Black rage expressed by protestors creates the political
crisis necessary to bring change. The spring of 1963 saw
roughly 758 demonstrations with over 13,000 arrests for
ten weeks. Although the protests targeted local businesses
and institutions, they forced the Kennedy Administration
to pressure local politicians and business elites to offer
some concessions to protesters. These mostly peaceful
protests were organized, targeted, and systematic. Many of
these demonstrations were led by Black faith leaders who
were enraged at the condition of Black people. The Justice
Department knew that legitimate grievances provoked the
sustained protests. The consistent nature of mass mobilization
created the public pressure necessary to overcome their
reservations about conceding to civil rights demands.
Politicians were afraid that the protests would bring economic
and social turmoil. Therefore, addressing the protests involved
more significant political risks than ignoring them.[7]

Peaceful protests were not the only protests to force political change. The Black Power Movement, often at odds
with King's Civil Rights Movement, was that emergent generation's expression of Black rage. King, although sometimes
critical of the Black Power Movement, realized the potency
and righteousness in its demand. In a September 1966 interview, King said, "I contend that the cry of black power is, at
bottom, a reaction to the reluctance of white power to make
the kind of changes necessary to make justice a reality for the
Negro."[8] In 1968, that rage expressed itself through violent

uprisings in more than 130 cities, as a response to King's assassination. Forty-three people were killed, 3,500 injured, and 23,700 federal troops, as well as 34,900 National Guardsmen, were sent to restore order nationwide. Black Power advocates were blamed for the violence and "associated with intense rebelliousness and even revolutionary anarchism."[9] The riots in response to King's assassination were the understandable expression of a people whose peace had been murdered. The Black Power Movement capitalized on this rage. The protests culminated in the National Black Political Conventions and had a profound influence on Black electoral politics.[10]

Rage precipitates a crisis. It demands a response. Prophetic rage is focused and intentional; it is strategic and visionary. It requires a moral and political reaction. It urges public officials to change policy, and it demands new officials. But, disillusionment happens when the rage is disconnected from prophetic intention and reflection. The prophet not only condemns the current state of affairs, but offers an alternative vision. The crisis the anger creates is leverage for the people, and it is context and content for the prophet.

The Black Lives Matter Movement is our current expression of Black rage. It can claim both Black Civil Rights and Black Power ancestry. It is *both* Martin *and* Malcolm. Many blame Black Lives Matter protestors for the violence. Although the charge is demonstrably false, prophetic proclamation should never condemn the rage of the unheard to console white fragility. Instead, the prophetic process theologically reflects upon the anger and gives it voice and representation in places it otherwise would not be heard.

Black theological reflection is the path to channel our collective rage divinely. It is a process in which Black rage prophetically engages the principalities and powers in the political space. James Cone, in *The Cross and the Lynching Tree*, discusses the unease people had with how he channeled his rage through theology and how Black theology was the only healthy outlet for his anger.

They were disturbed by the militancy of black theology—
the passion and anger that characterized its language about
black liberation. They felt that I was influenced too much by
the radical, separatist rhetoric of Malcolm X and Black Power and too little by the moderate, integrationist philosophy of
Martin Luther King, Jr.[11]

The horror and constant trauma of being Black, while
watching Black people being shot by police, traumatizes us as
the lynchings of the Jim Crow era traumatized our ancestors.
That terror, at many levels intimidating, gives way to anger
and rage. Cone expresses this anger intimately:

> Reading and writing about the lynching nightmare, looking
> at many images of tortured black bodies, has been my
> deepest challenge and the most painful experience I have
> had as a theologian. At times it was almost too heavy for me
> to bear. The more I read about and looked at what whites
> did to powerless blacks, the angrier I became. Paradoxically,
> anger soon gave way to a profound feeling of liberation.
> Being able to write about lynching liberated me from being
> confined by it. The cross helped me to deal with the brutal
> legacy of the lynching tree, and the lynching tree helped me
> to understand the tragic meaning of the cross.[12]

King, like Cone, channeled his rage theologically and used it
to passionately fuel the Civil Rights Movement and a public
policy agenda. When reflecting on King, Columbia Business
School professor Hitendra Wadhwa wrote, "Great leaders
often have a strong capacity to experience anger. It wakes
them up and makes them pay attention to what is wrong
in their environment or in themselves. Without anger, they
would not have the awareness or the drive to fix what is
wrong." Harry Belafonte recalled, "Martin always felt that
anger was a very important commodity, a necessary part of
the black movement in this country."[13]

Malcolm X was once considered the angriest man in
America. According to Cornel West, Malcolm saw "Black
coming-together as the offspring of the recognition of boiling
Black rage."[14] He prophetically demanded an acknowledg-

ment of Black humanity and dignity. It drove his culminating mission to report the United States to the United Nations for war crimes. His rage directed him in his last days to form the Organization of Afro-American Unity (OAAU). Peter Bailey, who worked for the political group, said Malcolm was "on a committed campaign to internationalize the movement." This mission was not an armed, chaotic response but a calculated, impassioned strategy to bring a higher public authority to bear against U.S. public policy.[15]

Kelly Brown Douglas, in *Stand Your Ground: Black Bodies and the Justice of God,* reflects upon her church channeling its anger through faith after the verdict in the Trayvon Martin case.

> There was an overall sense of anger and frustration. But what struck me the most in all of the testimonies was that no one lashed out at God. No one doubted God. No one blamed God. At the end of several of the statements, there was a proclamation of faith. The congregation affirmed each of the proclamations. The people were sure that what happened to Trayvon betrayed the purposes of God, and so their faith, like that of Tracy Martin, remained unshattered.[16]

Douglas goes on to write that, historically, "Black prophets engaged in the struggle to end the stand-your-ground-culture realities of their day." She demonstrates how Black prophets preached to abolish slavery, end lynching, and eliminate Jim Crow laws. According to Douglas, Black prophetic witness channels Black rage, suffering, and fear to a call for moral participation.[17] The Black church has always been political. The historical significance and political influence of Black faith are well documented. The Black abolitionist movement was fueled by Black rage against the scourge of slavery.

Bishop Richard Allen's biographer, Richard Newman, rightly describes Allen as a Black founder who established Black institutions and engaged in Black politics. Allen founded the African Methodist Episcopal (A.M.E.) Church and is widely recognized as a catalyst of the Black church movement. Often Allen would zealously and prophetically declare judgment as he compared the African struggle for freedom with that of the enslaved Jews of the Bible. Frederick Douglass called Allen the "Author of a new Declaration of Independence and Racial Equality."[18] Twentieth-century activists viewed Allen as the original Black liberationist. DuBois wrote that Allen played a part in "Afro Christianity becoming a liberationist creed." James Baldwin called Allen one of the great "poets" of Black aspiration.[19] Allen's church, unlike any other religious denomination, was born of the principles of social, economic, and racial justice.[20]

Sojourner Truth (1797-1883) fought for women's rights and against human bondage.[21] Being a former slave who eventually rose to national influence for her abolitionist speaking, Sojourner Truth was one of the most influential prophetic voices of the period. She often spoke to mixed congregations, urging the liberation of her people, saying that both Blacks and whites should "engage in the good work of emancipation."[22] Sojourner's message of human rights was a prophetic appeal on behalf of the oppressed. Her bold humanism had a broad appeal that called people of all backgrounds to a place of accountability. Sojourner Truth was one of the most influential speakers for the cause of abolition and women's rights. Although she was not formally educated, her public speaking was among the most powerful of all the antislavery causes.[23]

The esteemed abolitionist and preacher Frederick Douglass spoke vehemently against injustice and saw the work of abolition and religion as intertwined.[24] Abraham Lincoln called Douglass "one of the most meritorious men...in the United States."[25] Douglass had powerful oratory skills, which he used to fight for freedom. He had a tremendous influence on the American movement towards emancipation and civil rights.[26] Douglass was not only critical of America as a nation, but also of American Christianity. In a speech delivered at the Plymouth County Antislavery Society in 1841, called "The Church and Prejudice," Douglass issued a prophetic indictment of church-sanctioned racism.[27] Fredrick Douglass was the quintessential Black prophet. He practiced prophetic engagement directed at the nation and the church. At the same time, he was a diplomat, who had access to the most powerful leaders in the country and influenced them towards justice. The prophetic oratory genius of Fredrick Douglass helped lift up the consciousness of the nation.

Henry McNeal Turner (1834-1950) was a Bishop in the A.M.E. Church and a trailblazer of Black Liberation Theology.[28] He was the most radical political voice of the late nineteenth century.[29] Turner declared, "God is a Negro," setting the stage for Black liberation theology.[30] Turner was the precursor to Malcolm X and led the A.M.E. Church to "connect theology to politics and the world."[31] Turner was also instrumental in planting a spirit of revolutionary religion in independent Black churches in Africa.[32] In 1893, he delivered a robust, prophetic discourse about the United States Supreme Court's decision to rule the Civil Rights Act unconstitutional.[33] Henry McNeal Turner was one of the most revolutionary preachers in African Methodism.

Such ancestors are not uncommon amongst our ranks. Countless preachers and laypersons from our founding to the present day have engaged politically to strive towards liberation. However, despite such examples of how the church has been actively political, we have yet to tap the full potential of our congregations to organize so as to more fully shape our lived reality. These Black prophets used Black rage politically to leverage the authority and influence God granted them for the liberation of our people.

Unequivocally, our Black prophets have taken their cue from Jesus. The ministry of Jesus was one of prophetic advocacy and healing. Jesus' ministry interpreted Jewish religious and civil law through justice and mercy. Jesus challenged cultural, religious, and gender taboos, to prioritize people over practices. His care and compassion challenged rigid, punitive enforcement of the law. Jesus' policy work lived as he emphasized the primacy of only two laws:

> You shall love the Lord your God with all your heart and with all your soul and with all your mind. This is

the greatest and first commandment. And the second is like it: You shall love your neighbor as yourself. On these two commandments hang all the law and the prophets. (Matthew 22:37-40; NRSV)

Jesus reinforced the role of advocacy in the life of his disciples by saying that he would send them "another advocate":

And I will ask the Father, and he will give you another Advocate to be with you forever. This is the Spirit of truth, whom the world cannot receive because it neither sees him nor knows him. You know him because he abides with you, and he will be in you.
(John 14:16-17; NRSV)

The spirit of advocacy is what God expects to dwell in and among the church. Therefore, discipleship cannot be divorced from advocacy. It is as essential to discipleship as prayer, fasting, and worship. Christians must see themselves as advocates, socio-spiritual-political forces, and powerful agents of God's passion for justice in the world. The people must spread the Good News of Christ's vision for "the least of these." Evangelism and discipleship are not merely getting people to recite our creeds and confessions by heart. It is Kingdom building by changing people's lived social, spiritual, and political realities by the liberating Gospel of Jesus Christ. As the prophet Isaiah proclaimed:

He will establish and uphold it
with justice and with righteousness
from this time onward and forevermore.
The zeal of the Lord of hosts will do this. (Isaiah 9:7b; NRSV)

We, as a prophetic political constituency, sustained by Black rage, must advocate for our most vulnerable, care for one another, and give future generations an advantage. This work is our consecration as a body politic; in the Black Christian context, the body politic that is the body of Christ. Obey Hendricks writes in *The Politics of Jesus* that the passionate ministry of Jesus was a focused prophetic rage that reinterpreted the Mosaic law in favor of love and compassion for the oppressed.

Jesus models for us that we must be outraged by social practices and policies that favor any of God's children over others. We must be outraged by systematic exclusions, all types of elitism, and every hierarchical structure that allows only the chosen few to fully enjoy the riches of community. And we must use that anger to move us to righteous action. Our anger, our outrage, our righteous indignation must remain focused on the perversion of policies and traditions meant for good into laws and practices that do harm and evil. Not on particular groups or personalities, but on unjust policies and practices.[34]

Like any politician, the preacher has a constituency. The preacher's constituency, like that of Jesus, must include people who have been marginalized by systemic sin and do not have a "seat at the table." Preachers do not have to bend to political winds, because they are not subject to elections and term limits. The preacher's authority does not come by votes but by divine appointment. The preacher's words do not have to be poll-tested but are rooted in the truth of the Gospel of Jesus Christ. The preacher, therefore, has a responsibility to be a prophetic, nonpartisan, political power broker. Our first responsibility is not loyalty to a particular party, but rather to be impassioned and sustained by divine rage, to set the captives free.

It is the preacher's responsibility to challenge politicians to do right by the people. Preachers must passionately demand that state and federal politicians address the demands of Black rage. Preachers must insist that our government decriminalize the Black body and redefine public safety. Preachers must vociferously advocate for investments in public health, prevention, violence interruption, and poverty eradication rather than endless resources for prisons and police.

Imagine preachers intentionally organized around shared agendas who refuse to be co-opted by the power structure to denounce uprisings. This sustained collective rage would create a political crisis and influence the electorate in ways we have yet to explore. We can no longer give up our pulpits to political figures who coerce us without a specific community-driven agenda. Our collective rage demands that the preacher no longer wait on politicians to enact change. That passive approach relegates us to reactionary dissonance. The preacher has the power and political authority to be proactively prophetic. The reimagined preacher is one who will bring the change, the solutions, and the rage-informed agenda to the politicians.

Imagine our congregations as focused on changing political reality and channeling Black rage as we are on personal issues and prayer requests. Fredrick Douglass famously said, "I prayed for freedom for twenty years but received no answer until I prayed with my legs." People from various congregations mobilized by the power of Black faith have broken down the gates of hell. The lunch counter sit-ins, bus boycotts, and marches encompassed scores of congregations focused on change. Political realities will shift when local, state, and federal politicians are accountable to a community-informed agenda from coalitions of Black churches. It is here that the church pew moves from being otherworldly and inward-focused to being transformational. The laypersons are the most potent political constituency we have. It is the responsibility of "the pew" to act and be active in changing political reality.

Much of the organizing around abolition and civil rights took place in our churches. The intersection of Black faith and Black sacred space has always been a necessary dynamic for Black political power. This power is demonstrated by the role that Brown Chapel A.M.E. Church played as a sacred organizing space that led to the passage of the 1965 Voting Rights Act. Movement-building from the pews is a deep socio-spiritual engagement. Evangelism and discipleship understood in this context involve not only personal piety but also social sanctification through civic engagement. Congregations and communities are constituencies that are powerfully socially located. Every congregation is a body of people who meet regularly.

The people in the pews are the most potent force of political organizing.

The preacher, the pew, and the protestor must channel our collective rage. We will then change the political reality by populating the halls of power with clergy and community guided by God's passion for liberation, mercy, and justice. We take our power to determine our political reality by advocating for just agendas and holding political figures accountable. We must embrace the combined rage of protestors and preachers and produce protest-*ing* preachers, who will strategically advocate for change.

Black freedom is a socio-spiritual political endeavor. To be clear, our churches would not be targets of white political terrorism if the preacher and the pew were not powerful political forces that could mobilize the community. The Gospel-driven ministry of the Reverend Clementa C. Pinckney, a state senator, and the people from the pews of Mother Emmanuel A.M.E. Church, demonstrates how demonic forces are afraid of our political power. This church reimagined itself in light of its founder, Denmark Vesey and other ancestors. Emmanuel's martyrs are powerfully symbolic of Christianity in its purest form, shedding blood for the redemption and liberation of others. The Black church is politically radical by its very existence. Therefore, this moment demands *Sankofa*. We must look back at what God has done through the ancestors and reimagine our roles as community leaders, impactful people, theologians, preachers, pastors, and laity as political forces that can transform our current political reality as they did.

God calls us to politically engage the contemporary "principalities and powers in high places" (Ephesians 6:12). When Black rage emerges spontaneously and then is focused strategically, structures like slavery and Jim Crow fall. It is then that Black people ascend to positions once withheld from us. It is then that systemically racist structures are burned down, and restorative, compassionate, just systems emerge. Then we can politically bring forth the Balm in Gilead, feed the hungry, clothe the naked, visit the sick, and set the captives free. Jacob Blake, unlike any before him, embodies the Black experience at this moment. He is criminalized, a fruit of the Black church, a father, a brother, a son, an uncle, and a friend. His struggle with police was an expression of his rage. The uprising in Kenosha is an expression of ours. The work of the prophet in the Black prophetic tradition is to submit to holy fire. As the prophet Moses said, "the Lord your God is a consuming fire" (Deuteronomy 4:24; Hebrews 12:29). Only divine intervention keeps the fire from consuming us.

Endnotes

1   Theresa Parry, *Teaching Malcolm X: Popular Culture and Literacy* (Routledge, 1995).
2   Kurt Helin and Dan Feldman, "Doc Rivers: 'We Keep Loving This Country, and This Country Does Not Love Us Back'," *ProBasketballTalk*, NBC Sports, August 27, 2020; https://nba.nbcsports.com/2020/08/26/doc-rivers-we-keep-loving-this-country-and-this-country-does-not-love-us-back/ (Accessed: August 31, 2020).
3   Martin Luther King Jr., "The Crisis in America's Cities," *The Atlantic*, March 31, 2018; www.theatlantic.com/magazine/archive/2018/02/martin-luther-king-jr-the-crisis-in-americas-cities/552536/.
4   Malcolm X, "Malcolm X on Racist Violence. Speech by Malcolm X at the London School of Economics, Feb. 11, 1965, to a Meeting Sponsored by the School's Africa Society," *World History Archives*, April 10, 2003; www.hartford-hwp.com/archives/45a/461.html.
5   Lily Rothman, "What Martin Luther King Jr Really Thought About Riots," *Time*, April 28, 2015; https://time.com/3838515/baltimore-riots-language-unheard-quote/
6   James Baldwin, *The Fire Next Time* (Vintage International) (Knopf Doubleday Publishing Group, Kindle Edition, 2013), pp. 105-106.
7   Kenneth T. Andrews and Sarah Gaby, "Local Protest and Federal Policy: The Impact of the Civil Rights Movement on the 1964 Civil Rights Act," *Sociological Forum* 30 (06 2015): 509-527.
8   "MLK: A Riot Is the Language of the Unheard," *60 Minutes Overtime*, 25 Aug 2013 [text of Mike Wallace's interview with MLK, September 27, 1966 for *CBS Reports*]; www.cbsnews.com/news/mlk-a-riot-is-the-language-of-the-unheard/ (Accessed: August 31, 2020).
9   Lisa Veroni-Paccher, "Black Power 1968: 'To Stumble Is Not to Fall, but to Go Forward Faster'," *L'Ordinaire Des Amériques*, no. 217 (12, 2014); doi:10.4000/orda.1624.
10 Ibid.
11 James H. Cone, *The Cross and the Lynching Tree* (Maryknoll, NY: Orbis Books, 2019).
12 Ibid.
13 Krissah Thompson, "The Unfinished Work of Malcolm ,." *The Washington Post*,

Feb. 19, 2015; www.washingtonpost.com/lifestyle/style/fifty-years-after-his-death-malcolm-x-speaks-to-the-current-moment/2015/02/19/4dba5ca4-091e-4303-b3ee-6a655c583655_story.html.

14   Parry, *Teaching Malcolm X.*

15   Thompson, "Unfinished Work."

16   Kelly Douglas Brown, *Stand Your Ground: Black Bodies and the Justice of God* (Maryknoll, NY: Orbis Books, 2015).

17   Brown, *Stand Your Ground.*

18   Richard S. Newman, *Freedom's Prophet: Bishop Richard Allen, the AME Church, and the Black Founding Fathers* (New York: New York University Press, 2009).

19   Ibid.

20   Junius P. Rodriguez, *Slavery in the United States: A Social, Political, and Historical Encyclopedia* (Santa Barbara, CA: ABC-Clio, 2007), p. 160.

21   David Henry. Bradley, *A History of the A.M.E. Zion Church* (Nashville, TN: Parthenon Press, 1972), p. 108; quoted in Gayraud S. Wilmore, *Black Religion and Black Radicalism: An Interpretation of the Religious History of Afro-American People* (Maryknoll, NY: Orbis Books, 1983), p. 121.

22   Margaret Washington, *Sojourner Truth's America* (Urbana, IL: University of Illinois Press, 2009), p. 249.

23   F. B. Carpenter, *Friends Intelligencer.*, vol. 37 (Philadelphia: [p.m.], 1880), p. 709.

24   Julius Eric Thompson, James L. Conyers, and Nancy J. Dawson, *The Frederick Douglass Encyclopedia* (Santa Barbara, CA: Greenwood Press, 2010), p. 120.

25   Connie A. Miller, *Frederick Douglass: American Hero and International Icon of the Nineteenth Century* (Xlibris, 2008), p. 235.

26   Frederick Douglass,"The Inhumanity of Slavery" [excerpt] in Jeffrey Lehman and Shirelle Phelps, *West's Encyclopedia of American Law* (Detroit, IL: Thomson/Gale, 2005), Encyclopedia.com; http://www.encyclopedia.com/doc/1G2-3437701508.html (Accessed: December 16, 2011).

27   Frederick Douglass, Philip Sheldon Foner, and Yuval Taylor, *Frederick Douglass: Selected Speeches and Writings* (Chicago: Lawrence Hill Books, 2012), p. 4.

28   Columbus Salley, *The Black 100: A Ranking of the Most Influential African-Americans, Past and Present* (Secaucus, NJ: Carol Pub. Group, 1999), 147.

29   Charles Eric Lincoln and Lawrence H. Mamiya, *The Black Church in the African American Experience* (Durham, NC: Duke University Press, 2005), p. 205.

30   Mark G. Toulouse, *God in Public: Four Ways American Christianity and Public Life Relate* (Louisville, KY: Westminster John Knox Press, 2006), p. 158.

31   Ibid.

32   Wilmore, *Black Religion and Black Radicalism*, p. 169.

33   Henry McNeal Turner, Frederick Douglass, and Robert Green Ingersoll, *The Black Man's Doom the Two Barbarous and Cruel Decisions of the United States Supreme Court, Declaring the Civil Rights Act Unconstitutional and Disrobing the Colored Race of All Civil Protection; the Most Cruel and Inhuman Verdict against a Loyal People in the History of the World... Also the Powerful Speeches of Hon. Fredrick Douglass and Col. Robert G. Ingersoll; Also a Review by Bishop Turner; Also the Monstrous Decision of the Same Conclave*, Issued May 18, 1896 (Philadelphia: J.B. Rodgers, 1896), p. 3.

34   Obery M. Hendricks, *The Politics of Jesus: Rediscovering the True Revolutionary Nature of the Teachings of Jesus and How They Have Been Corrupted* (New York: Doubleday, 2006), pp. 165-167. [Kindle Edition; The Crown Publishing Group.]

Charles Boyer, M.Div., D.Min.

The Reverend Dr. Charles Franklin Boyer is a third-generation African Methodist Episcopal preacher. He is the pastor of Bethel A.M.E. Church in Woodbury, New Jersey, and the founder of Salvation and Social Justice, a non-partisan Black faith-rooted organization that believes liberation should precede legislation and prophetic vision should precede public policy. He earned his Master of Divinity and Doctor of Ministry degrees from Payne Theological Seminary. He has most recently authored several papers, including: "Liberating Youth Justice Theologically"; "Moving African Methodist Congregations Towards Faith Rooted Oversight for Prisoners"; "Health Rights Through Liberation Preaching and Teaching"; and "The Uncomfortable Truth: Racism, Injustice and Poverty in New Jersey."

Dr. Boyer is a leading faith voice in New Jersey for racial justice issues. His advocacy has led to the statewide adoption of racial impact analysis for sentencing, closure of youth prisons, voting rights restoration for people on probation and parole, the independent prosecutor law, and restricting solitary confinement. He works closely with the Black Legislative Caucus and is a co-convener of the United Black Agenda. He is New Jersey's leading religious figure in the campaign to abolish the drug war, end isolated confinement, and undo the criminalization of Black people. Rev. Boyer has been recognized as one of New Jersey's 25 Most Influential African Americans by the *South Jersey Journal*, a Game Changer by the NAACP, a Torch Bearer by the ACLU, a Movement Maker by NJ Working Families, and a Community Servant by NJ Citizen Action. He has been recognized by the NJ Work Environment Council and has received the Making Democracy Work Award by the League of Women Voters. He was named #4 on the "Twenty-Five People to Watch in 2019" by NJ Advanced Media for his work around police accountability and is a 2020 Jefferson Award recipient.

CHAPTER THREE

"The Time for Pious Words Is Over"

Jeremiah Wright, Jr., M.A., D.Min.

Abstract

This chapter looks at the litany of inexplicable and possibly unforgivable sins of White Supremacy, white privilege and the racist mind set. Following that litany which justifies Holy Black Rage, this chapter argues that the first prerequisite needed for understanding the theology of Holy Black Rage is the task of decolonization. The need to decolonize education, decolonize theological education and even yes to decolonize God is a "must" when beginning the task of addressing Dr. King's question, "Where do we go from here?"

This decolonization process will help to attack the additional two heads that I argue which need to be added to Dr. Martin Luther King's naming of the demon in his 1967 sermon at The Riverside Church. In that sermon Dr. King pointed out that we were not just fighting the demon of racism. He argued that we were fighting a three headed demon: racism, militarism and consumer capitalism.

This chapter argues that there are two additional heads that Dr. King did not recognize in his analysis: the demon of political respectability and the demon of self-hatred. Decolonization will destroy those two additional heads of King's three-headed demon. This chapter argues that there are five heads that have to be faced, fought and defeated simultaneously.

Ultimately this chapter argues that we need to renounce vehemently white exceptionalism, White Supremacy, white privilege and white racism. In addition we need to respond violently to tear down the notion that property is more important than people; and finally we need to rebuild vigorously a new world or the beloved community Dr. King argued for, preached about and lived to try to bring into existence. There can be no rebuilding, however, until first there is deconstruction.

>>

The title for this essay is a direct quote from Allan Boesak, the South African Theologian whose ministry helped bring about the end of the ugliness of Apartheid in South Africa. Boesak's powerful words are expressed passionately by the ordinary lay folk in Trinidad-Tobago as follows: "Done talk!" That beautiful patois says the same thing that Boesak is saying. The time for talking about that which requires a revolutionary response is over. The time for talking is "done!"

In 1961, James Baldwin said that to be Black in America, "...and to be relatively conscious is to be in a state of rage almost all of the time." Grier and Cobbs' classic book, *Black Rage*, was written seven years later in 1968. William Grier, the Black psychiatrist, wrote an eye-opening and shocking psychological examination of Black rage and Black expressions of that rage in the United States.

Grier's colleague, Price Cobbs, and he released their book shortly after the assassination of Martin Luther King, Jr. to explain to the world the violent reaction people on seven continents were observing as African-Americans expressed their emotions physically, vocally and unmistakingly by destroying property in every major city of the United States of America. Their work said in book form the same thing James Baldwin said in poetic form.

Black Rage was released shortly after the President's National Advisory Commission on Civil Disorders (or the Kerner Report) was released in February of the same year, 1968, seven years after James Baldwin prophetically stated what was obvious to Black folk and a curiosity or unknown mystery to white folk. The disconnect and the confusion and consternation in the white Christian community was even more pronounced. White Christians could not understand what had blown up in their faces in terms of race relations in this country.

The Kerner Report (paraphrased) showed that this country was rapidly dissolving into two different Americas – one white and one Black. From my perspective, Blacks in this country have understood that since the 1600's. The Kerner Report was putting in print that which Black America had known in the flesh for almost four hundred years in 1968. Neither Baldwin's prophetic word in 1961 nor the civil unrest that caused President Johnson to call together the citizens who studied the urban population segment of the country and produced the Kerner Report, neither King's "60 Minutes" appearance in 1966 where he said "Violence is the language of the unheard" nor the massive display of Black rage following King's assassination, neither James Forman, the former Executive Director of the Student Nonviolent Coordinating Committee (SNCC), and the delegation of Black church men and women disrupting the services of the Riverside Church in New York on communion Sunday, May 4, 1969, placing the **Black Manifesto** on the communion table nor their pouring the communion wine on the floor of the sanctuary caused the masses of Black citizens in the country to be heard by most white Christians and far too many Black Christians.

It seems as I write this chapter that the murder of George Floyd and the resulting rage displayed in this country and across the globe is causing the voices of the unheard to be finally heard and is now or has now created a climate in which some serious thinking of our theological understandings of Black rage is being done; and I have been asked by the editor of this volume to offer my perspective on *holy* Black rage.

The 1985 *Kairos Document*, written by a group of Black predominantly lay Christians and signed by Black pastors and theologians, was yet another wakeup call in the Christian community that was a "shot heard around the globe." Black Christians in South Africa in the *Kairos Document* were saying that the time for pious words was over. They were saying "Done talk!" They were agreeing with the Mk by suggesting that perhaps holy rage expressed in violence was the only language that racist white Afrikaans could hear or understand. Pious pleas had been ignored since 1948. Pious prayers and imprecations had gone unheeded. Perhaps it was time for holy rage to be expressed violently by the destruction of property.

The Mk, better known as the uMkhonto we Sizwe in the Xhosa language, was the armed wing of the African National Congress (ANC). The Xhosa words are translated "Spear of the Nation." The Mk was formed right after the Sharpeville Massacre in March of 1960. The Mk was founded by Nelson Mandela to respond to the brutal reality of a South African government and its murder of unarmed Black South Africans.

The Mk was founded with the express mission of destroying property not killing people. Ironically, the first bombing of white owned property by the Mk was carried out on the very day that Albert Luthuli was receiving the Noble Peace Prize in Geneva. Chief Luthuli was receiving his prize for his staunch stand of non-violence in waging the struggle against Apartheid in South Africa; and on the day he stood to receive his reward in the public ceremony, wearing his ANC chieftain hat as he took the stand to deliver his acceptance speech, Mk was blowing up that which white racists treasure the most in this world – their property.

Blacks in South Africa learned from the rage and revolts of Blacks in the United States, the Caribbean and South America. They learned that white racists care more about property that they do about people!

To the horror of many Black Christians, most white Christians in the USA and in the Union of South Africa, after the advent of the Mk, the tactics of the African National Congress followed the strategy and the pattern of the tactics of the Stono Rebellion in South Carolina, the Diasporic African slave rebellions and revolutions of Gabriel Prosser, Denmark Vessey and Nathaniel Turner. The thinking was this: if you violently destroy the property of slave holders, White Supremacists and Europeans who believe in exceptionalism you will get their attention much quicker than trying to sit down at a table and negotiate in some civil manner of respectability politics. Mk set out to destroy property not people. Of course the white media neglected to point that out as they reported on the activities of the Mk, the ANC and the anti Apartheid forces in South Africa.

The holy rage of the Mk and the holy rage of African descended persons both on the continent and in the diaspora is saying that it is time to stop talking and start acting. It is time to cease mouthing pious expressions and it is time to go for the jugular which is the property of white racists. Remember! Africans in this country were legally classified as property from 1787 until 1865. Through the convict lease system they were still property. Prisoners were still property after the passing of the 13th Amendment. The 13th Amendment did not free prisoners in this country. Prisoners are still slaves according to the Constitution of the United States of America!

Rage and rebellion against these egregious laws are saying in the patios of Trinidad-Tobago, "Done talk!"

What is the theology that undergirds holy Black rage? What are its sources? Is it justifiable in the eyes of God? This book asks for the perspectives of men and women of the gos-

pel. Perhaps after finishing its last chapter, the reader will
have an answer to these questions. I can assure you that the
reader will at least have a glimpse of how complex and serious a discussion this volume has generated. Let me offer my
perspective on these questions in this brief essay.

All theology is contextual. Having said that, let me speak
from my context as an African-American born into a country that was founded on racism, built on the backs of African
slaves under the flag of White Supremacy and white exceptionalism. The context out of which I speak is that of an African-American male who was the same age as Emmitt Till was
when he was murdered by white racists on false pretenses,
accused by a white woman who recanted her accusations in
2017. My perspective is informed by Charles Mills' *The Racial
Contract*. My perspective is formed by the horror with which
I view the Christian church's Doctrine of Discovery and my
perspective is informed by growing up Black in a white man's
world.   Minister Louis Farrakhan, when he was Louis X the
calypso singer, put it this way, "A white man's heaven is a
Black man's hell!"

Conservative Christians who believe firmly in the politics of respectability cling fiercely to the myths on which this
country was founded. Dr. Benjamin Chavis calls those Black
conservative Christians "nervous negroes." They don't want
to offend any of our white brothers and sisters – especially
those in the Christian community – so when you ask them for
theological solutions they immediately run to Europe or to
England to quote the great white divines of our faith.

I heard that argument for over twenty-five years as I listened to my primary mentor in the field of the History of Re-
ligions, Dr. Charles Long, argue with Dr. James Cone about
using Niebuhr, Moltmann and Bultmann to talk about Black
religion, Black theology and Black liberation; and not using
the voices of the unheard, his own Black ancestors, brothers
and sisters. I, therefore, unashamedly do not quote any European of English sources for my theological foundation. I also
only take a glance at biblical sources in my theological foun-

dation for holy Black rage because as Willie Jennings points out, that biblical narrative is someone else's story. In fact, the Christian story historically is a story inside of the Jewish story; and I have no desire to use the Exodus narrative as my theological foundation because to do so I would have to talk about Yahweh as the liberator and the conqueror.

As a conqueror, the Hebrew narrative concerning Yahweh shows him to be a murderer and a genocidal maniac. How else do you explain the "conquest" of Canaan? I guess you explain it in the same way you explain the Europeans' "conquest" of the western world as their "promise land!"

Completely ignoring the command of Yahweh to go take over somebody else's land and kill everything in that land, men, women, children, and leave nothing or no one standing who can "piss against the wall," in trying to write about "holy rage" I could talk about the rage that Yahweh expressed when his own son was lynched. Matthew talks about the sun going out at midday, the moon refusing to shine and the dead being raised from their graves as an earthquake caused them to walk the streets of Jerusalem. Was that an example of holy rage? Or was the resurrection and the earthquake that caused the "gate keepers" to quake and become as dead men holy rage? Is that a biblical source for holy rage?

Or is the scene in the Garden of Gethsemane on the night that Jesus was arrested a theological source for holy rage? One of Jesus' disciples never did give up his shank. He stayed strapped and when the Temple Guards came to arrest Jesus, at least for one in the group it was "on like neck bones." It went down like four flat tires and he cut off the ear of one of the Temple Guards. What that holy rage?

I would like to think of Peter as being the one who exhibited holy rage; but his denial of the Savior and his cursing and swearing like Richard Pryor and Nikki Minaj in Caiaphas' courtyard makes me ask was that cowardice or bravado? The biblical justifications for holy rage are very thin; so I will look to the mother continent combined with the lived experience of Africans in diaspora as my theological sources for holy rage.

Starting on the mother continent, I would have to look at the Muslim example as my first instance for the formation of a theological framework out of which to operate when it comes to understanding and exercising holy rage. The Arab Muslims were carrying Africans across the Sahara Desert into slavery in the 6th and 7th Century. That is nine hundred years before the Christians Portuguese got in on the act and started carrying Africans into slavery. That is also seven hundred years before the Doctrine of Discovery where the Pope gave permission for the Portuguese armies to take the land of the people in the southern hemisphere; and if its indigenous inhabitants did not convert to Christianity, the Discovery Doctrine said it was alright to kill them. In the same Doctrine, the Spanish Conquistadors were given permission to claim the land of the indigenous people in the Caribbean and the land which became the United States with the same impunity. It said in effect, take their land for the Queen of Spain and convert all the indigenous people to Christianity. If they did not convert, kill them. A conscious response, to use James Baldwin's term, to those historical facts would certainly be reasons for holy black rage.

I could start with the 1619 Project by pointing out that the so-called "Christian conversions" by the Portuguese in their colony of Angola were not really conversions at all. I could start with King Leopold of Belgium and the murders in the Congo that were precursors for the Rwanda nightmare. Where do I start?

Clayton Jones, the brother of William Augustus Jones, wrote a book whose title says it all way back in the 1980's. His book was titled *Enough Is Enough*. The time for pious words is over. Done talk!

Or do I start on the Mother Continent with the Berlin Conference where the white European powers had the arrogant audacity to carve the continent up into fifty-four different countries over which they had complete control—the birth of racist colonialism in the "Modern Era." Is that where I start to get my theological foundation for holy rage? Or do I start with the Trans-Atlantic Slave Trade which has direct implications for me personally in terms of what Europeans did and Englishman did in North America and in the State of Virginia in particular. My parents and grandparents are from the State of Virginia. My grandfather's mother was a slave. Is that where I start?

Or do I start with the odd twist that the English Colonies invented in their "brand" of slavery? For the first time in human history, slaves were no longer human beings in the U.S. "brand" of slavery. We were chattel. We were property. Is that where I start? Enough is enough! The time for pious words is over. Done talk!

Or do I stay on the continent and look at the Zionism of the European Jews and the Apartheid of Palestine? Is that a good theological place in which to begin an understanding of God and what God sees and feels as God watches those created in God's image turn into beasts who would actually believe that one's skin color makes them superior to others who are not of that color? Is that a good place to start?

Or do I start in 1948 – seven years before Emmitt Till was lynched – when Apartheid became the official law in South Africa and Zionism became the official law in Palestine? Where do I start? What does God have to say about this human behavior? Is that enough to cause holy rage?

It is my belief that God is not pleased. It is my belief that God does not want us to bow to the idols of White Supremacy and racism, capitalism and militarism. Dr. King named the demon we fight in his 1967 Riverside Church sermon as racism, capitalism and militarism. Fifty-two years later I have discovered there are two other heads to that demon that King did not name. They are the politics of respectability and self-hatred. Enough is enough! The time for pious words is over. Done talk!

History has shown us that Mk was right in its mission. When you destroy a white racist's property, laws change. When you destroy the property of those who put profit above people, the language of the unheard gets the ear of those who turned a deaf ear to those of us who are melanin kissed by nature's sun.

Dr. King asked, "Where do we go from here?" After Emmitt Till in 1955, after the Montgomery Bus Boycott in 1955, after the Sharpeville Massacre in 1960, after the sit-ins of the Civil Rights Movement of which I was a part in the 1960's, after the murder of Medgar Evers in June of 1963, after the murder of four Black girls in the Lord's Day bombing of the 16th Street Baptist Church in Birmingham, Alabama in September of 1963, after Bloody Sunday in Selma Alabama on March 7th 1965, after King's lynching in 1968, after the murder of Hector Pieterson and the Soweto Uprising by Black students in 1976, after the *Kairos Document* in 1985, after the Rodney King attempted police lynching in 1991, after the murder of the Charleston 9 in Emmanuel AME Church in Charleston, South Carolina in 2015, after I was ordered out of South Carolina by a politics of respectability AME Bishop in 2015 for daring in a public prayer service held in an AME Church, honoring the murdered Black Bodies to name racism as the demon that had killed the Emmanuel 9 in their AME church the night before – the "Nervous Negro" Bishop was more concerned about the disfavor of the white city officials who were present in the audience when I said that, than he was about the death of the nine unheard voiceless who were prematurely present with the Lord in heaven because of the white hatred here on earth,... after the Charlottesville attack on Black bodies in 2018, after the murder of George Floyd in 2020, enough is enough! The time for pious words is over. Done talk! Yes; but where do we go from here? What is the theology that informs our action going forward?

I would submit to you that we have to decolonialize our educational system. We have to decolonialize our theological education system. We have to deconstruct the notions of white exceptionalism, White Supremacy and the reality of white racism, all of which ignore the poor and the darker color people on the face of this earth.

I submit to you that our theology of holy rage says we need to renounce vehemently, yes! My theology says that we need to respond violently and "tear the roof of the sucker" – property not people; but then after we renounce vehemently and respond violently I want to suggest to you that we need to rebuild vigorously.

We need to construct something based on an understanding of our God who loves all of God's creation equally. We need to construct something new that has built into it *equity* – not just equality. My theology says after expressing our holy rage it is time to demonstrate our holy righteousness with the understanding that "if God be for us who can be against us?"

Rev. Dr. Jeremiah A. Wright, Jr.
Pastor Emeritus
Trinity United Church of Christ
Chicago, Illinois

Jeremiah Wright, Jr., M.A., D.Min.

In his bibliographic inclusion in "The History Makers,, Dr. Jeremiah Wright Jr. is characterized as a "preacher par excellence." Notably the pastor emeritus of Chicago's Trinity United Church of Christ where its membership grew from eighty-seven adult members to a congregation of nearly 10,000. Under his leadership, Trinity adopted a motto coined by his predecessor that is descriptive of Rev. Dr. Wright himself, "Unashamedly Black and Unapologetically Christian".

He is a social activist, an outspoken community leader, giving voice and telling a risky truth about issues seldom spoken of in the church. His fiery, relentless style is appropriate to his name, and he speaks prophetically both inside and outside of the church. A man committed to his people and his God, his uncompromising prophetic style coupled with a surprisingly diverse wealth of knowledge have converged to make him a highly sought-after speaker both in the U.S. and internationally.

Rev. Dr. Wright is the recipient of numerous awards, including seven honorary doctorates and three presidential commendations. An accomplished musician and author, Wright has written four books, numerous articles and countless sermons and was voted one of Ebony Magazine's top fifteen preachers. In addition to involvement in national and international ministries, he serves on several boards of directors and committees.

His educational credits include a B.A. and M.A. from Howard University, an M.A. from the University of Chicago Divinity School and a Doctorate of Ministry from United Theological Seminary, where he studied under the eminent, late Dr. Samuel DeWitt Proctor.

Among his publications are: *What Makes You So Strong*, published by Judson Press, 1993, *Africans Who Shaped Our Faith*, published by Urban Ministries, 1995, and *Sermons of Hope: Good News For Today's Family*, published by Judson Press, 1995.

CHAPTER FOUR

Holy Rage Transformed:
A Call to Righteousness and a Demand for Reparations

Iva Carruthers, M.A., Ph.D, M.T.S.

Abstract

Representing the Spanish monarchs Ferdinand and Isabella in their quest for "discovery of the New World," Columbus set sail with the following mission and prayer:

> Today I will launch the ship and prepare to depart Thursday in the name of God . . . . This I pray to our Lord and your Highnesses will appoint persons of great diligence in order to bring to the Church such great numbers of peoples, and that they will convert these Peoples, just as they have destroyed those who would not confess the Father, Son, and Holy Spirit . . . to grant larger realms and dominions, and the will and disposition to spread the Holy Christian religion . . . . Amen.

The prayer petitions at the top of the ship were not the same as those at the bottom of the ship. Surely, they weren't praying to the same God.

This article will explore theological ideation of righteousness and justice from the lens of an African worldview and the implications they continue to have. The ideas of Maat, Ubuntuu, and Sawubona will be examined in a theological fame that informs an historical and contemporaneous examination of "justice" movements of people of African descent in the diaspora. The goal of the article is to deconstruct "justice and righteousness" in Western biblical scholarship and in Christian theology and praxis. It is to offer a foundation for further understanding of Holy Rage in the context of the pan-African quest for liberation, historically and including up to the Black Lives Matter movement.

>>

EPIGRAPH

And they shall declare: "Our hands did not shed this blood, nor were we witnesses to it. Absolve, O Lord, your people Israel, whom you redeemed; do not let the guilt of innocent blood remain in the midst of your people Israel." Then they will be absolved of bloodguilt. So you shall purge the guilt of innocent blood from your midst, because you must do what is right in the sight of the Lord. (Deuteronomy 21:7-9; NRSV)

CONTEXT

The alignment of a people's God talk (i.e., theology) and a people's culture (sociology) is a marker and a forewarning of a people's capacity to live into the fullness of God. And in one sense, people of African descent in the United States for 400+ years have been living with Holy Rage in a country whose theology and sociology are profoundly incongruent with what it means to do "what is right in the sight of the Lord."

Through it all, people of African descent have possessed a Holy Rage, propelled by a Holy Defiance, and tempered by a Holy Hope that has traversed centuries of inhumane physical, mental, and spiritual white hegemony and viciousness.   It is in the invisible space of sacred remembrance that the Holy Rage of a people is tamed by Holy Hope. It is in the hearing of that divine inner voice that transforms violent fury into Holy Rage. And just as Deuteronomy forewarns those who carry bloodguilt, it also warns those who are victims of it:

> But take care and watch yourselves closely, so as neither to forget the things that your eyes have seen nor to let them slip from your mind all the days of your life; make them known to your children and your children's children. (Deuteronomy 4:9; NRSV)

This reflection is offered to energize a Holy Rage Transformed as a hermeneutic framework grounded in our African identity of what it means to be human, as epitomized in the expressions "Black Lives Matter" and "I am a Man" and "Ain't I a Woman?" This reflection is intended to jolt us into Pan-African spiritual remembrance of an understanding of righteousness in relationship to justice, invoking our sacred responsibility for the demand for reparations. This reflection affirms the genre and power of liturgical and creative worship and education that fosters internal healing and connectivity to our African selves, like that of the annual *Maafa* commemoration at St. Paul's Community Baptist Church, in Brooklyn, NY, begun under the pastorate of Rev. Dr. Johnny Ray Youngblood, or the Umoja Karamu service of remembrance begun by Dr. Jeremiah A. Wright, Jr. at Trinity United Church of Christ, Chicago, IL. In short, this reflection is but an example of the wisdom, healing, and discernment that awaits us if we more fully embrace our Africanity to inform our theology and ministries.

In yet another epic period of American history, an existential nadir of suffering and pain upon our people is occurring. This period is characterized by the convergence of disparate consequences of the COVID-19 pandemic, continued and worsening state-sanctioned police violence against people of African descent, and the use of the U.S presidential authority to re-entrench pillars of white racism and hegemony in the institutional life of this nation.

All of this is converging in an era of neo-eugenic technologies that make public health policies a convenient instrument to serve the narcissistic tendencies of persons and a culture that could slither into acts of genocide, ethnic cleansing, and racial purging. We are at a crossroads that requires us to fully undress those who claim a Christian tradition and cultural hegemony that uncouples righteousness from justice. It is time for us to not just argue the case for African humanity but to raise the question about others' lack of humanity despite their claim of religion. It is more than implicit bias, fear of the other, and institutional racialized policing at work that explains why a young black man (Jacob Blake of Kenosha, WI) is shot seven times in the back at close range, as an officer is holding his shirt; while, at the same event, a white teen, Kyle Rittenhouse, having just shot dead two people, can run through the streets with an AR-15 rifle, past police officers(who were being told by others that he had just shot people), not being stopped, much less arrested, and allowed to go home to Illinois, even though arrested later.

That being said, our theological reflection, quest for justice, and mobilizing efforts are informed by how it is we're still here and what God has given us to work with to change our condition. This moment in history has become a *Kairos* moment, like no other, where the demand for reparations has not just taken root in the U.S. but has blossomed in particular ways of public discourse and political actions that have promise. At the federal and local levels, new possibilities are foreshadowed by the U.S. Congressional effort to pass HR-40, under the leadership of Congresswoman Sheila Jackson Lee, as well as the exploration by over 200 municipalities of policies and remedies being framed as reparatory justice or reparations programs.

Now, more than ever, thoughtful and historical reflection through the lens of Black liberative and womanist theologies has the potential to transform a moment and a movement towards a necessary reckoning born out of centuries of Holy Rage. But we cannot afford to be beguiled by the semblance of reparations, betrayed by the enticements of handlers, nor defeated by the forces of despair.

Sacred memory must frame our understandings and order our agenda and next steps. The faith agenda for reparatory justice and reparations must privilege a principle that true reparations cannot be reduced to a mere financial transaction. Cecil Cone's early admonishment of first-generation Black liberation and womanist theologies warrants much greater interrogation, especially by scholars and preachers of African descent who covenant to contribute to a movement for reparations *and* a global reset for righteousness and justice.

AFRICAN FOUNDATION OF CHRISTIANITY

Cecil Cone thus declared: "When the slaves were introduced to Christianity, they brought with them their African 'pre-understanding.' Thus it may be said that Africans were not converted to Christianity but that they converted Christianity to themselves."[1]

It was this Christianity to which the African father of Christianity, St. Augustine, referred:

> That which is known as the Christian religion existed among the ancients, and never did not exist; from the beginning of the human race until the time when Christ came in the flesh, at which time the true religion, which already existed began to be called Christianity."[2]

It was this form of Christianity to which Princeton- and Columbia-trained historian of Christianity Alvin Boyd Kuhn declared:

> This astonishing declaration was made in the early 4th century of our era. It can be asserted that if this affirmation of the pious Augustine had not sunk out of sight, but had been kept in open view through the period of Western history, the whole course of that history would have been vastly altered for the better.... It held the kernel of a great

truth the common knowledge of which would have been a stumbling block in the way of the perpetuation of priestly power over the general Christian mind. It would have provoked inquiry and disarmed the ecclesiastical prestige of much of its power....Every child born to Christian parents in eighteen centuries has been indoctrinated with the unqualified belief that Christianity was completely new, and the first true, religion in world history; ....All previous religion was the superstitious product of primitive childishness of mind. Christianity was the first piecing of the long night of black heathenism by the benignant gift of God.... Augustine shatters this illusion and this jealousy preserved phantom of blind credulity.... there has always existed in the world the true religion. It illuminated the intellects of the most ancient Sages, Prophets, Priests and Kings. It built the foundation for every national religion, the tenets of which consisted of reformulations of its ubiquitous ageless principles of knowledge and wisdom.[3]

As we engage Holy Rage in this period of racialized trauma, death, and lamentation, with a lens of liberative and womanist theologies, we know that the consequences of dismembering must be countered by acts of healing remembering.

To that end, I am arguing that the distinctive African view of righteousness, as an inseparable aspect of justice, must not be forgotten and is at the heart of our understanding of how it is that for 400+ years, a nation can claim to be "a nation under God, as a functioning democracy with liberty and justice for all" and still not confess to the most egregious acts of violence and harm that it continues to inflict upon native and African peoples in its territories. We must free ourselves from a canon that separates righteousness from justice, that holds captive our sacred memory and causes us to believe that the basic precepts of Christianity were borne out of a western worldview to which Black people were molded. The fact of the matter is that Christianity was born out of ancient African precepts and worldview, a fact that awaits our rediscovery as a part of our healing from the *Maafa* and will give us the power to contribute to a global reset for a more just world.

Cone's notion of converting Christianity back to ourselves suggests a quest to rediscover that which we once knew—an epistemological and theological journey of *Sankofa* as an instruction for moving forward.

THE GOD OF RIGHT: RIGHTEOUSNESS AND JUSTICE

W. E. B. DuBois understood Holy Rage. He concludes *The Souls of Black Folk* with a faith reflection on the God of Right in the struggle of his people:

> Around us the history of the land has centered for thrice a hundred years; out of the nation's heart we have called all that was best to throttle and subdue all that was worst; fire and blood, prayer and sacrifice, have billowed over this people, and they have found peace only in the altars of the God of Right.[4]

It is this God of Right that has power to transform Holy Rage under the worst of circumstances. To be sure, the prayers at the top of the ship have never been to the same God as the prayers at the bottom of the ship. By the time Christopher Columbus set sail in 1492, the Catholic Church had over a century of blood on its hands in the establishment of the Trans-Atlantic Slave Trade System. Representing the Spanish monarchy of Ferdinand and Isabella's in its quest for "discovery of the New World," Columbus set sail with the following mission and prayer:

> Today I will launch the ship and prepare to depart Thursday in the name of God…This I pray to Our Lord and Your Highnesses will appoint persons of great diligence in order to bring to the Church such great numbers of peoples, and that they will convert these peoples, just as they have destroyed those who would not confess the Father, Son, and Holy Spirit…to grant larger realms and dominions, and the will and disposition to spread the Holy Christian religion… Amen.[5]

Unlike that which is represented in Columbus' prayer as emblematic of Empire, the foundation of Christianity does not separate righteousness from justice.

> Take away from me the noise of your songs;
> I will not listen to the melody of your harps.
> But let justice roll down like waters,
> and righteousness like an ever-flowing stream.
> (Amos 5:23, 24; NRSV)

And neither does African spirituality separate the two; our Holy Rage which is transformative is grounded in a belief in a God of Right. At this time, we must endeavor to further free ourselves and the world from a theological worldview that: (1) is a-historical in the understanding of its roots, (2) is grounded in the hegemony of Empire and white supremacy, and (3) privileges a "balanced dualism" in the interests of the powerful and the Empire.

Over the past 400+ years, in response to white supremacy and racial oppression, belief in this God of Right has been ever present underneath many struggles of liberation and the various paths to Pan-Africanism. Belief in this God of Right shaped the call and activities of persons in the United States like David Walker, Nat Turner, Denmark Vesey, Gabriel Prosser, Harriet Tubman, Sojourner Truth, and Jarena Lee. Early advocates of Pan-Africanism such as Henry Highland Garnet, Alexander Crummell, Martin Delaney, James Holly, Bishop Henry McNeal Turner, and Edward Wilmot Blyden were empowered by this belief in the God of Right. It is this "soul factor" or "faith factor" of a spiritual dimension, that gave power to the Zumbi of Brazil, the Maroons of Haiti and Santa Domingo, the Garifunas in Nicaragua, and the Palengues of Peru. This faith factor also gave life to the revolutionary liberation movements in Africa. Movement reflections from Tanzania, Kenya, Angola, Mozambique, and South Africa are replete with references and petitions to the God of Right.

MAAT—RIGHTEOUSNESS AND JUSTICE

Today, Christians, including most Black Christians, talk about ancient Israel, Greece, or Rome, ignoring the stolen legacy of ancient Africa's contribution to those civilizations, including religion. Early Christianity was birthed in the context of African religious thought and spirituality. And, at the center of African sacred belief was/is an understanding of the complementarity of righteousness and justice—MAAT. It was in the crucible of MAAT that Moses was socialized in KMT (Egypt).

A God of Right was embedded in early precepts of Christianity. Right and Justice were inextricably connected by the principles and belief in MAAT. In short, MAAT consists of seven principles of human behavior: Truth, Balance, Order, Harmony, Righteousness, Morality, and Justice.

MAAT is surely oppositional to a theo-socio worldview of hegemonic Empire based on the Doctrine of Discovery and Manifest Destiny, the prayer of Columbus, and the Papal Bulls that justified enslavement of African peoples.

Theopile Obenga, African anthropologist/linguist, declares that "MAAT is the leading concept in the heart of Classical Egyptian society." It is characterized by five spheres of reality: the divine, the universe, governance, human community, and human being. Each of these realities has five dimensions of meaning: religious, cosmic, political, social, and anthropological.[6] They are interrelated concepts which, when adhered to, manifest themselves as peace and justice in the human community. Obenga declares MAAT to be linguistically and conceptually present in many African languages, including Coptic, Kongo, Yoruba, and Nuer.

Egyptologist J.H. Breasted noted: "The social, agricultur[al], and industrial world of the Nile dwellers under the Empire was therefore not at the mercy of an arbitrary whim, on the part of either the king or court, but was governed by a large body of long respected law, embodying principles of justice and humanity. The purpose of the law was to actualize MAAT on earth as it is with God; the king was the intermediary to make that happen. The sacred texts refer to "putting MAAT in place of injustice."

The sacred iconography shows the king presenting the symbol of MAAT to the gods. In the context of divine rule, the king as god was charged to transform the spiritual belief in MAAT as awareness of the will of God into the actualization of MAAT as evidenced between the relationships between people on earth.

In short, there was no separation between religion and the law, since divine power and authority both established and maintained/governed the social order. The core beliefs of right doing and right living—ethics and morality—were the responsibility of individuals and of society in general, manifesting the inseparability of human and divine justice. Herein lies the intersection of righteousness and justice through an African linguistic and hermeneutic lens; a both/and, not an either/or paradigm. The interrelatedness (intersectionality) of the divine or sacred and its manifestation in both individual and societal relationships was an embodiment of MAAT and the conjoining of righteousness and justice.

However, what emerged in the evolution of Western Christian thought was a "balanced dualism." Balanced dualism sanctioned the belief that there was no contradiction between slavery and Christianity, and then sanctified that belief through the sacrament of baptism and theologies of salvation. The Dutch Reformed Church, the Church of England, and Roman Catholics shared this common Christian concept of "balanced dualism," which privileged practical solutions in the interests of the Empire and the few over the ideal of governance for the common good and the people. Balanced dualism sought to resolve tensions between choices that may be ideally undesirable but practically necessary.

Thus, baptism became a form of reinforcing the slave system and temporal order, rather than a rite celebrating human freedom and equality. In fact, the assumption that Africans lived in an inhuman, uncultured, and degenerate state of moral imperfection justified the belief that there was no contradiction between slavery and Christianity.

The Soul of the Enslaved

The Christianity of slavocracy was dualistic in that it theologically separated earthly freedom from spiritual liberation; it viewed the sacrament of baptism as birth into heavenly salvation with no implications for earthy human and civil rights. It saw the relationship between the slave master and the slave as divinely ordained and perpetual, so that manumission of the slave depended solely upon the will and agency of the master.

By the 18th century, converting slaves into Christians was regularly done by giving each slave a Christian name while sprinkling salt on the tongue and baptizing with holy water with the following words:

> Consider that you are now children of Christ. You are going to set off for Portuguese territory, where you will learn matters of the Faith. Never think any more of your place of origin. Do not eat dogs, nor rats, nor horses. Be content.[7]

Any debate about the soul of the enslaved was forestalled by the western Christian mindset, which theologically separated righteousness from justice, and biblical hermeneutics and exegesis followed suit. Such hermeneutics and exegesis were concerned with salvation only for the master, due to the separation of righteousness from justice during the period of the Transatlantic Slave Trade System, which morphed into a justification of the Church's agency to selectively decide between individual salvation and communal justice.

Similarly, today in the U.S., religious design, participation, and sanctions still undergird white supremacy and the hegemony of Empire. The shift from a democracy of "cultural pluralism" to one of "genetic meritocracy" has been accompanied by a shift to the marketing of a "theocracy of Christian dominance" as a "democracy of religious freedom" by the re-

ligious "right" (or is it the religious "fake"?) from the pulpits
to the Oval Office.

In short, what has emerged are "dominion" theologies and,
by extension, Christian theologies of the last days and prophecy, manifested as evangelical racism and Zionism. These dominion theologies, over the past nearly 40 years, have gone
from being marginal to playing a significant role in conservative evangelical circles. They call for conservative Christians
to strategically take over the political and cultural institutions
of society. The so-called "Seven Mountains Dominionism"
identifies those areas of takeover as: religion, education, media, entertainment, business, and government. This justifies what is euphemistically called an "end-time transfer of
wealth," setting the stage for Jesus' return. Thus:

> "Kingdom Theology" is a whole new theology.... What
> we're doing is setting up a network by which we can spread
> propaganda...so that the systems of the world will collapse
> because of their inability to survive, and what will be left
> will be a system the church has built....a Christian culture
> that will have dominion over the world.[8, 9]

And to that end, today, we have the BLITZ Project, begun in
2015, driven by the Congressional Prayer Caucus of the U.S.
House of Representatives, outlining a state legislative agenda
under the banner of "religious liberty protection acts" or the
Religious Freedom Restoration Act, which is actually a form
of protection against pluralism and diversity, "clothed" in the
"armor of God."

The dominion theologies (over and against liberation
theologies) foster greater inequity by the concentration of unfettered corporate wealth and profit acquisition, further jus-
tifying support for land grabs in some areas and sustaining
environmentally unsafe land use in other areas; defunding
of public education in favor of commodification and privat-
ization of headcounts and a prison industrialized system of
cell counts; and a forecasting and recognition that the demo-
graphic shift in the browning of America was a coming threat
that required a possible declaration of the obsolescence of the

fundamental tenets of democracy towards what B.F. Skinner called a "genetic meritocracy." Please note, all of this was afoot 50 years before Black Lives Matter. Today, we see the evidence of its agenda unfolding in public health policy and the dismantling of the U.S. postal system, while hate speech is becoming an encouraged form of free speech.

These values are fast being normalized with zealous abuse of U.S. presidential authority, using coded and non-coded racial hate speech, labeling African nations as "shithole" nations, asylum seekers to the "democracy" as vermin to be caged because they are "infesting" the nation and fostering an environment that intentionally confounds human rights discourse around anti-Semitism, Zionism, and Palestinian rights. Equally, but likely more dangerous, is the manipulation of data and a disinformation health campaign that is associated with the management of COVID-19 and its impact upon our community.

HOLY RAGE AND THE DEMAND FOR REPARATIONS

I now turn to the question of reparatory justice and the demand for reparations as a step towards individual and communal healing and global transformation. We must recognize that, as people of African descent, our Holy Rage indwells in our deep spirituality that cuts across our shared experiences in the diaspora and on the mother continent. We are a part of a pan-African movement of repairing the breach, of healing from the continuing trauma and harm.

Reparations is a *process to remember, repair, restore, rejoin, replenish, set right, make amends, and reconcile*. Reparations can never be singularly reducible to monetary terms. To do so makes a mockery of the real significance of reparations as an end in a process of distributive justice, human atonement, and redemption.

In December of 2007, a group of faith leaders, made up primarily of persons of African descent, was convened under the auspices of the World Council of Churches and the World

Alliance of Reformed Churches. This was an international conference commemorating the 200th Year of the Abolishment of the British Transatlantic Slave Trade. The summary statement drafted from that consultation included the following:

> We believe that reparations are essential for the healing of peoples who were once enslaved. Reparations go far beyond a financial figure; rather, reparations are about recognizing the wrong that has been done. It is a process that compels confession, contrition, restoration and reconciliation; it also involves a process or truth-telling that sets rights, makes amend/ and restores breached relationships.... The Trans-Atlantic Trade in Africans and colonialism has impacted all peoples. Collectively, therefore, we need to destroy the power and institutional relationships of contemporary beneficiaries of the historic and corporate sins and crimes against humanity....[10]

In 1894, Ms. Callie House and Rev. Isaiah H. Dickerson, along with four other pastors, launched the reparations movement, incorporating the National Ex-Slave and Mutual Relief Bounty and Pension Association. And with each generation thereafter, efforts have persisted to advance the call and cause to amend for the wrongs, repair the damage, and reckon with the past to right the future. People of faith are uniquely called and positioned to stay the course.

Callie House, called Mother of the Reparations movement in the United States, said:

> We deserve for the government to pay us as an indemnity for the work we and our fore parents was robbed of from the Declaration of Independence down to the Emancipation.... My whole soul and body are for the slave movement and are [am] willing to sacrifices [sacrifice] for it.[11]

Since that time, momentum on the part of people of African descent the world over for the demand of reparatory justice and reparations has ebbed and flowed. Specific to U.S. history, a short chronology is as follows:

- The National Negro Congress (NNC) [under the leadership of Max Yergen and John Davis] who submitted A Petition to the UN on behalf of 13 million Oppressed Negro Citizens of the US of A in 1946
- The national Association for the Advancement of Colored Peoples(NAACP), [under the leader of Walter White and Roy Wilkens] who submitted An Appeal to the World in 1947
- The Civil Rights Council (CRC) We Charge Genocide: The Historic Petition to the United Nations For Relief From a Crime of the United States Government Against the Negro People [under the leadership of William Patterson] in 1951
- In 1962, Queen Mother Moore's Reparation Committee filed a claim in California.
- In 1963, Rev. Dr. Martin Luther King declared: "While no amount of gold could provide adequate compensation for the exploitation of the Negro American down through the centuries, a price could be place[d] on unpaid wages."

In May 1969, James Foreman, supported by other African American faith leaders, walked down the church aisles at the historic Riverside Church in New York City and read a "Black Manifesto" that had been adopted in April of the same year by the National Black Economic Development Conference in Detroit. The Manifesto demanded $500 million as a "beginning of the reparations due us as people who have been exploited and degraded, brutalized, killed and persecuted"

In 1989, U.S. Rep. John Conyers took the question of American slavery to the heart of the national political process with the proposed House Resolution 3745 to establish a study commission on American slavery. In 1999, Rep. Conyers proposed House Resolution 40, requesting a formal apology and establishment of the commission.

Now, in 2020, Sheila Jackson Lee, who accepted the mantle from the late Congressman Conyers, has taken a bold leadership role in the effort to pass HR 40 and in so doing has framed the reparations claim as "Why We Can't Wait." It is to this call and the cries and stories from ancestors buried in the oceans and soil to whom we owe a great debt, paid only by our vigilance of remembrance and demand for reparations, from generation to generation.

My Christian belief and African spirituality in the God of Right teaches me that each generation is bequeathed the shared memories, experiences, and spiritual fortitude of their forebearers. Our legacy can never be stolen or destroyed as long as some remember; our humanity can never be denied as long as some seek restitution; our living and dying will never be in vain as long as some carry the spirit of Godly resistance and purpose for generations yet unborn. In my presentation on *The Black Church and Reparations*, presented in Durban, South Africa at the 2001 United Nations Conference with a Pan-African view, I noted that "A stolen legacy, whether this generation or the generations of my fore parents, is stolen nonetheless. How can the victims not seek restitution? How can the victims owe the victors?"

May our Holy Rage Transformed continue to beckon and conjure our souls towards righteousness and justice, the demand for reparations, and the reset of a new global way forward that honors the whole of God's Creation.

Endnotes

1   Cecil Cone, *The Identity Crisis in Black Theology* (Nashville, TN: African Methodist Episcopal Church Publishing, 1975), p. 42
2   St. Augustine, *Retractions*, I, xiii.
3   Alvin Boyd Kuhn, *Shadow of the Third Century: A Reevaluation of Christianity* (Surrey, British Columbia Canada: Eremitical Press, 1949), p.3.
4   W.E.B. DuBois, *The Souls of Black Folk* (Greenwich, CT: Fawcett, 1961), p. 190.
5   John Henrik Clarke, *Christopher Columbus and the Afrikan Holocaust: Slavery and the Rise of European Capitalism* (New York: A & B Publishers Group, 1998), pp. 100-101.
6   Asa G. Hilliard, III, *SBA: The Reawakening of the African Mind* (Gainsville, FL: Makare Publishing Co., 1997), pp 12-16.
7   Thomas Hugh, *The Slave Trade: Story of Atlantic Slave Trade 1440-1870* (New York: Simon Schuster, 1997), pp. 64-65.
8   Bishop Earl Paulk of Decatur, Georgia, quoted in the Atlanta Constitution, March 3, 1987, A4, as cited by Gayraud S. Wilmore, "Black Theology at the Turn of the Century: Some Unmet Needs and Challenges," in Dwight N. Hopkins, ed., *Black Faith and Public Talk: Critical Essays on James H. Cone's Black The-*

ology and Black Power (Maryknoll, NJ: Orbis, 1999), p. 243.

9   Iva E. Carruthers, Frederick D. Haynes, and Jeremiah A. Wright, Blow the Trumpet in Zion: Global Vision and Action for the 21st-century Black Church (Minneapolis: Fortress Press, 2004), p. 18.

10   Mary Frances Berry, My Face is Black is True: Callie House and the Struggle for Ex-Slave Reparations (New York: Alfred Knopf, 2005), p. 171.

11   Ibid.

Iva Carruthers, M.A., Ph.D., M.T.S.

Dr. Iva E. Carruthers is General Secretary of the Samuel DeWitt Proctor Conference (SDPC), an interdenominational organization within the African American faith tradition focused on justice and equity issues. SDPC is both a 501c3 and a United Nations Non-Governmental Organization. As founding CEO and a trustee of SDPC, she has steered the organization as a unique, influential, and esteemed network of faith-based advocates and activists, clergy, and laity. Former director of the Black Theology Project, Dr. Carruthers has a long history of teaching, engagement in community development initiatives and social justice ministry, fostering interdenominational and interfaith dialogue, and leading study tours for the university and church throughout in the United States, Caribbean, South America, and Africa.

Dr. Carruthers is Professor Emeritus and former Chairperson of the Sociology Department at Northeastern Illinois University and was founding President of Nexus Unlimited, an information and educational technology firm. She was appointed to the White House Advisory Council on the Internet, "National Information Infrastructure", Mega Project, and the educational software she developed was awarded a ComputerWorld Smithsonian Award. She is also founder of Lois House, an urban retreat center in Chicago, Illinois.

Dr. Carruthers is a frequent guest speaker at various national and international forums, including U.N. Civil Society Forums. She currently serves as a Life Time Trustee for the Chicago Theological Seminary; a trustee for The Kwame Nkrumah Academy, Chicago; for the American Baptist College, Nashville; for Shared Interest, New York; and for Bread for the World, Washington, D.C. She is a member of the National

African American Reparations Commission and is working on initiatives related to the U.N. Decade of People of African Descent.

Dr. Carruthers is co-editor of *Blow the Trumpet in Zion: Global Vision and Action for the 21st Century Black Church* and has authored and edited a number of articles and publications in the areas of sociology, technology, and instructional technology. Her many study guides on African American & African history were developed as a co-producer of a multi-year educational television program. She was a delegate to the 2001 UN World Conference Against Racism, Racial Discrimination, Xenophobia and Related Intolerance, and her publication, *The Church and Reparations*, has been distributed by her denomination, the United Church of Christ, in several languages.

She received the B.A. degree from the University of Illinois; the M.A. and the Ph.D. in Sociology from Northwestern University; a Master in Theological Studies degree from Garrett Evangelical Theological Seminary; and a Doctor of Humane Letters, Meadville Lombard Theological School. Awards and postdoctoral fellowships received by Dr. Carruthers include Northwestern University Center for Urban Affairs, The Russell Sage Foundation, University of Chicago, Adlai Stevenson Institute for International Affairs, and The National Endowment for the Humanities.

She was inducted into the National History Makers; was a recipient of *Ebony* Magazine's year 2001 Outstanding Mother Award for Mentoring; and noted as a Chicago area social justice pioneer in the Women Alive! A Legacy of Social Justice Exhibit.

CHAPTER FIVE

Interpreting a Theology of Black Rage in the Context of the Lives of Black Women

Bishop E. Anne Henning Byfield, M.Div., D.Min.

Abstract

The discussions around Rage and the Black Community do not always include the Rage of Black women. This article examines the definition of Black women's anger in the context of race, scripture, tradition, and contemporary theology. I examine these theological perspectives to determine if there was an absence of or bias against Black women in tradition and contemporary theology. My findings demonstrate that there is a bias against the depth of Black women's rage by limiting it to specific acts or statements, not to a systemic form of injustice, abuse, and mistreatment. A plan of action is articulated to speak to the complexity of the circumstances impacting children and adults.

>>>

1. Introduction: We Are Called Women!

We are called women because we were taken from someone's rib to live on our inner power, fired in the belly of survival, and developed in the arsenal of strength. We have feasted on the fountain of faith, and learned that if we are strong enough to enhance life, bring forth life, support life, then we are strong enough to live and lead.

—Anne Henning Byfield, *The Essence of My Existence*

In the movie *Akeelah and the Bee,* Akeelah is challenged by Dr. Larrabee to say that she wanted to win the National Spelling Bee. After his prodding of Akeelah to acknowledge it was all right to want to win, she did. Dr. Larrabee helped Akeelah to mute her negative inner voices, which gave her permission to acknowledge her true emotion to win.

Akeelah's negative inner voices reflect what happens in the lives of Black women. In most instances, we are not permitted to experience an inner range of emotions and we are taught to temper any such emotions as ambition, adventure, or anger. Instead, we are taught the Smile Syndrome. If we cried as girls, we were tickled and played with until we smiled. If we were spanked, we could not cry. Everyone with a Black momma has heard: "Suck it up, Stop all that crying before I give you something to cry about!" If we were wronged, we could not show emotion, especially if we were angry. Good girls either had to smile or could not show any facial expression, despite their current emotional reality.

2. DEFINING BLACK WOMEN'S RAGE

Smiling under white supremacy and dominance, and life under Black patriarchy—both are burdensome and painful. Both are demeaning and confine Black women to a double inferior status. The burden becomes a triple threat when we Black Women endure mistreatment by White women. Under these circumstances, the result for Black women is anger, depression, anxiety, poor health, and isolation. Black women are often shut out of the integrated political activism and general leadership when we live our truth, and even when we do not. We walk a complicated journey when White men, White women, Black men, and often Black Women criticize our reactions, personhood, and choices in life as they defend and validate their own choices. Black women are compressed in extraordinary ways.

"We are Black women born into a society of entrenched loathing and contempt of everything Black and female. We are strong and enduring. We are also deeply scarred" (Lorde & Clarke, 2012, p. 151).

This entrenched loathing and scarring among Black women is demonstrated in every aspect of our lives and is intolerable and insufferable. Rage is a by-product of this loathing and scarring, and it is often the main product. We live in a world filled with systems of domination, including white supremacy, and in such circumstances, the wrongs to which anger points are often obscured. (Lloyd, 2019).

This anger is considered understandable when expressed by Black men. The scars of Black male anger, in many circles, is found understandable and acceptable. But this same anger is neither understandable nor acceptable from Black women. Black men have the right to rage and assail against the ills of our society. For Black women, to exhibit this rage, in polite or not so polite society, shows weakness and is embarrassing to us. Gentil, refined, and well-trained women do not show rage and must also diminish any feeling of hurt or anger about anything.

The description as an "angry Black woman" is one of the most insidious assaults we can receive aside from physical or sexual assault. It stereotypically places us in an untenable position. Whether we react or not, we are stressed, our blood pressure is raised, and we second guess what we feel, who we are, and what we said or didn't say. In fact, someone will invariably ask why we have to act out, respond in kind, or "be so angry."

Black Women are expected to accommodate this demoralizing treatment and embrace, adapt to, and assimilate into the unprotected behavioral nonsense. Any refusal to accommodate, embrace, adapt, or assimilate defines and redefines us as an angry Black woman. This is the stereotype that many people have about Black women: This is how they are, and this is who they are.

"The result of knowing we are expected to be strong while also being among the least considered, lowest-paid people in society is heightened levels of emotional distress that include frustration, anger and resentment" (Thomas & González-Prendes, 2009).

As much as others want to see us as nonexistent, invisible, and subservient personas, the greater tragedy is that we have to fight to not to see ourselves in this way, and to accept the scorn of our right to be angry. We must define it is as rage, self-define our rage, own how we feel and refuse to let others shame us because they are uncomfortable with our rage, and with us. We must also address the elephant in the room, the misguided interpretations of the Bible.

3. THE THEOLOGY OF RACE, SCRIPTURE, TRADITION, AND CONTEMPORARY

For many, the Bible inspires, guides, and establishes spiritual formation. It is replete with stories of faith. The Hebrew Bible in particular also contains stories of rage, revenge, and laments. We are taught life principles through the Bible, including negative ones. Slaves in the post-biblical era were kept in a subservient role by means of selected texts in the Bible. The curse of Canaan in Genesis 9:18-29 was used to justify a lie that God had cursed all Blacks and made them subservient because Ham saw Noah's nakedness. While we have fought against and corrected this lie that we were created to be subservient, we have not denounced the false theological perspectives that gave rise to the assault on Black Women.

In fact we, continue to affirm various verses as the basis of the subservice of women particularly when a woman steps out of some pre-defined role.

Dr. James H. Cone in his stellar work, *A Theology of Black Liberation,* raised our consciousness when he affirmed that there can be no theological work if we do not understand that God created us. A theology of Black liberation is critical, and we must denounce any philosophy espoused by the White Church that denies this truth of our place in God and in society. Initially, the Black community did not widely receive Dr. Cone's theology but over time his theology has become an accepted norm that germinated from his seminal work.

Dr. Jacquelyn Grant Collier, together with Dr. Delores Williams, Dr. Katie Canon, Dr. Stacy Floyd Thomas, and others have affirmed Dr. Cone's work but questioned the perpetuation of sexism by Black male leaders specifically in the church and generally in the wider society. Justice in the wider society must include justice by the Church and by Black men. Initially, the Black religious community did not widely appreciate the contributions of Black women. The community systematically criticized the personhood of Black women and upbraided them for their so-called radical theological perspectives, as well.

Many years ago, a Bishop invited Dr. Jacqueline Grant Collier to speak at a National Women's event. He was excited to have a scholar as the featured presenter. I suggested that he read some of her material before the invitation. He did not. Her sermon addressed the blatant sexism in the church, and she posed this undergirding question: "What if, someone mistreated your daughter?" During the sermon, quiet deafened the room but for a few responses by women. After the sermon ended, the Bishop publicly chastised her and privately reprimanded me for bringing her, although he had clearly asked me to do so. The next day, a different Bishop, known for his inclusion of women in ministry, asked me what I thought about the sermon. I responded that the better question would be, "What did *you* think?" He explained that his initial thought rebuffed her remarks and deemed them inappropriate for the venue; but his wife posed this same question to him: "But what if it were your daughter?" He said he then responded that his immediate reaction would be to do all that he could to see his daughter's gifts realized. Then I answered his initial question with my own question: "Why could he only do the right thing in the context of his own daughter's treatment?"

The visual in each observer's mind ought to see the collective violence that society has heaped on women, whether in the Bible or today. Congresswoman Alexandria Ocasio-Cortez has declared that, "We must be able to declare that this violence directed toward women is evil and that I am also someone's daughter" (Ocasio-Cortez, 2020).

Women in the Bible express their anger but are rarely defined by it. Jael, the "Certain Woman" in Judges 9, Jephthah's daughter, and Rizpah were angered at how men treated them, but their revolutionary actions are not always recognized. Jael and the "Certain Woman" killed the enemy. Jephthah's daughter surrendered to murder by her father on her own terms. She used her powerlessness in the limited power that she did have. Rizpah is an example of a woman who used her powerlessness against the system in the murder of her sons. We cannot have polite conversations about the woman in Judges 19 labeled as a concubine who left her abusive husband to eventually be raped and murdered, and which resulted in the murder of other women and men. Job's wife and Herodias, however, are identified as angry women because their stories do not fit our carved-out neat scenarios. These two negative descriptions are regularly held up as examples of Black women's rage.

The churches acquiesced to traditional white Europeans' interpretations of anger in the Bible, which identifies anger as harmful and good sense as making one slow to anger. These taught beliefs make it difficult to see anger as real in human dynamics for other than White—and sometimes Black—men, in whom it is justified and accepted, but not for women in

general and Black women in particular. This oversimplifica-
tion makes it difficult for Christians to respond to the victim-
ization of women by the rage of violence, abuse, misuse, and
political and social disengagement. Women in particular are
told that it is inappropriate to respond to such forms of vic-
timization and are redirected to pray and forgive. The recent
example of this comparison is the justification of Justice Kava-
naugh's over-the-top anger at his Senate confirmation hearing, where Christine Blasey dared to allege and Senator Kamala Harris dared to question him, the senators, and others
about the allegations of sexual abuse.

The Church applauded and the world marveled at the
ability of some of the Emmanuel Nine families to forgive the
murderer so quickly. I had serious concerns about how the
families of the victims dealt with the shock and anger. Later, at a Connectional meeting, a Bishop and I (who was not
yet a Bishop at the time) were asked to meet with a few of
the family members, who were pained at the showing of the
Emmanuel Nine video, and the continuous attention to their
presence. They were angry and did not know how to respond
to either the murders or to the attention to it. We were clear
with them about their needs and rights to be honest with what
they were feeling.

The Church fails when it says, "Get over it, anger is not
God's way, and don't give the devil a place to grow." For
years, the Church told sexually abused women to accept his
apology, to forgive, for that is the Christian way. This counsel was given with no thought about the consequence to the
abused nor any penalty for the abuser as a consequence for
his behavior. Anger is more than an emotional reaction to the
very obvious effects of violence—daily misuse, physical and
sexual assault, lack of opportunities for women, promotional
inequity, and misappropriations of gifts, not to mention hearing daily and incessantly about your lack of worth and that
God created you to be unworthy and subservient.

4. THE EFFECTS OF THE ABSENCE OF THEOLOGY OF BLACK WOMEN'S RAGE

It becomes easy to frame the argument that Black women are angry at men because of specific events; in fact, however, Black women are angry at the prolonged systemic treatment of Black women. It is disingenuous to expect Black women to continue to be respectful, and polite, and to operate within a European dialogue that kills and abuses us. Our so-called correctness made some significant changes but not to the depth and core of white supremacy and male dominance. Politeness has not changed our circumstances, but has only served to quell our ability to honestly respond to injustice.

Rage is replacing our politeness. Dr. Brittney Cooper, the author of *Eloquent Rage* defines rage as a political response rather than just an emotional response that we should quell or suppress. It is the acknowledgement of rage that keeps us honest. Cooper suggests that our rage is over more than racist systemic oppression, it is all of it. (Cooper, 2019; Cooper, 2017).

Limiting rage to discussions about singular causes does not dismiss the whole range of causes. Much like the arguments in the wider society, the beneficiaries and perpetrators of racism cannot absolve themselves by saying, "We never had slaves." Accusing the victim of anger when she is assaulted neither justifies the assault nor releases the assaulted one from the consequences of the assault. When women are called angry because of an assault, this response fails first to address the assault, and secondly serves to divide and alienate the possibilities of healing.

Our anger has had destructive appellations and connotations: "Aunt Jemima", "Mammy," and "Sapphire". These appellations are enhanced by Black men portraying a Black woman. Black women have either embraced with humor or rejected in frustration Black men in female dress who propagate the stereotype of outrageous Black female behavior.

In more instances than not, Black men portray their female caricatures with large or disproportionate bodies and with personalities or personas that exhibit rude, finger snapping, eye rolling, loud and insulting behaviors towards everyone, especially to Black men. Adding injury to their already insulting depiction of Black women is the significant financial profitability that Black men receive for creating these demeaning images of Black women while Black female actors suffer to land highly-paid, quality roles.

The Amos and Andy Show and *The Flip Wilson Show* are the earliest television renditions of this phenomenon that I can remember and I didn't like the portrayals then. Something about it offended me and, while family and friends laughed, I could not. It was years later that my mother told me she always left the room when these shows were on. We have since been inundated with the Wayans, Wesley Snipes, Jamie Foxx, Eddie Murphy, Martin Lawrence, and, of course, Tyler Perry. Tyler Perry has built his empire playing *Madea* and, although he has been very benevolent to the community, the image continues.

The generational impact that these actors will have on how all of society perceives Black women has yet to be told. Some of these men have said in various interviews they were told, "Put on the dress or lose the part." Others, such as Eddie Murphy, created these roles themselves. The movie *Norbit*, which particularly depicted Black women as violent, was justified since the purpose of the story was to show that Black women could also be abusers. Yet she was created as larger-than-life, with all of the caricatures rolled into one personality. Jamie Foxx and Martin Lawrence depicted some of these demeaning Black female caricatures that are now a part of syndicated television programming.

Daily our children observe the lack of balance in how women are portrayed in church, theater, work, politics, family, and by saturated sexualization images in Hip Hop music. Black women have succeeded by utilizing their gifts, education and experiences while many are virtually under attack for their hair choices, husband or lack thereof, career choices, or because they are LGBTQ. Our scrutiny suggests that there is something missing or inapt about our place in leadership. When no other indictment lands, the biblical identification of the subservience of women remains. It is no wonder we are angry.

In writing this essay, I realized that the notion of not wanting to be labeled an angry Black woman had diminished my own rage. I have preached about Biblical women and written about their emotional spectrum in their biblical narratives. Yet, I found that I had not used the words "anger" or "rage" as I explained their stories. It was obviously more comfortable for me to use the words, *hurt, sad* or *reaction* rather than *anger* or *rage* to explain their actions. By failing to explain their emotions as rage or anger, I had to admit my own suppression of any thought that I too was an angry Black woman.

My first remembrance of this kind of assault was in the seventh grade, when my male teacher told me I had too much mouth and would never get married because I was too strong as a woman. Although my mother wreaked havoc on him and told me I could be whatever I wanted to be, I remember well. The church nurtured me and used my gifts, but there was a subtle expectation that I was never to be first.

Once, I posed the following question on social media: "Why was it so difficult to consider that Bill Cosby could be guilty of some allegations since he had already admitted to others?" Not only did my timeline blow up, but a colleague wrote, "We hear your anger, Black woman." I was furious and did not know how to handle the remark. I thought, "If I call him on it, would it further suggest that I was an angry Black woman even though I wasn't when I wrote the post; but in truth I became angry? But If I did not respond, would I give substance to the allegation; or should I have exercised the third option and just delete it?" The posted response was a well-articulated public assault.

As a Bishop, there have been a few incidents where I was pulled out of line or denied entrance into the room because the greeter or usher said, "This here is for the Bishops." I usually laugh, but one time it was a woman, and for some strange reason I felt compelled afterwards to talk with her. Someone had severely chastised her for questioning me and I had compassion. I did not have the same compassion after I talked to her. I encouraged her by saying that we all make mistakes, etc. She responded, "You didn't identify yourself as a Bishop." I responded, "You didn't ask me or ask the brothers to self-identify, so you made a false assumption that I was not a bishop." It quickly became apparent that she felt I was out of place as a Bishop and for thinking that it was my job to help with her false assumptions.

The nomination of Senator Kamala Harris has again brought this issue of rage to center stage, especially with the church. It highlights the differences between how Black women and Black men are treated in public and personal arenas. Immediately, we heard the negative statements about her ambition, whether she is qualified, too white, not really Black, married to a white man, moved up too quickly, and didn't deserve to be chosen. She has been sliced and diced into small bite-sized pieces. The 45th President of the United States called her "nasty," which is his primary and favorite word that he uses to put down powerful and empowering Black women.

Sadly, many church leaders have bemoaned her selection. One denominational leader said. "We just lost the race because he put a woman and a former prosecutor on the ticket." Another leader has said it will be difficult for him to sell a woman to his congregation citing that she is too outspoken, married to a white man, and it is not clear that she is saved. Unfortunately, Black women have also told me that they can't vote for her for various reasons. Some have said they will vote for President Trump or not vote at all.

Some have embraced her leadership and recognized that no candidate comes without some baggage and focused on the greater need to change the present toxic leadership. She is well prepared, qualified, and grounded in Black culture. Many of the attacks have been on her ethnicity, denying her blackness and rehearsing past decisions. However, she comes to this moment more prepared by training than President Barack H. Obama was, and certainly much more prepared by training, experience, and integrity than the current president.

It has been exhausting to watch. While many have celebrated her nomination, the attacks against her are on auto pilot. Once again, a significant portion of the Church has responded with either passive acceptance or pronounced negativity; while others have embraced her. Political choices are deeply personal but when she is rejected because she is a Black woman the systemic assault on Black women continues.

This time many Black women have responded to the attacks, and the rage of Black women (and some Black men) is articulate and clear. The public has over-scrutinized her for simply being a Black woman who has had the audacity to live her best life in the political arena. The furor over Senator Kamala Harris is reminiscent of Senator Hilary Clinton's presidential campaign, as well as those of Governor Sarah Palin and Elizabeth Warren. But the uproar is always a little different when it is a Black woman. At least four other Black women have been severely criticized: Shirley Chisolm, Stacey Abrams. Barbara Jordan and Maxine Waters. Shirley Chisolm was called ugly and told that she was not pretty enough to be considered. Stacey Abrams was told that she was too fat and that she needed to fix her hair. Barbara Jordan, who was brilliant as a politician, was demeaned for her brilliance and her person. In the halls of Congress, many Republican leaders called Maxine Waters an angry Black Woman and the current president has bellowed more than once that she has a low IQ. Young people embraced her, calling her Aunt Maxine, because she stood her ground and fought back.

We have seen this assault repeatedly and experienced it as well. When Serena Williams questioned a bad call, she was attacked and given high fines. Tennis is a sport in which most players question a call, but not a woman and particularly not a Black woman. Many said she should have just shut up and called her an angry Black woman. Sandra Bland's murder occurred in part because a white Police Officer took offence at a Black Woman talking back to him. A national outcry over Breonna Taylor's death has lingered without the traction that her senseless killing deserves.

So we see little-to-no response from prosecutors or the public to the growing list of Black women killed by police. The names of a few include Kathryn Johnston, Korryn Gaines, Atatiana "Tay" Jefferson, Tanisha Anderson, Michelle Cusseaux, Charleena Lyles, Pearlie Golden , Kayla Moore, Duanna Johnson, India Kager, Aiyana Stanley-Jones, Rekia Boyd, Shelly Frey, Eleanor Bumpus, Mya Hall, Miriam Carey, Natasha McKenna, Kyam Livingston, and countless others.

There are not enough pages to list the names of women who have been murdered in domestic violence, who have been raped and killed, or who have endured other assaults of urban violence. The violence is not an exclusively American phenomenon; domestic violence and violence against women is very common in many other countries. It is, again, no wonder we are angry.

5. PLAN OF ACTION

I am particularly grateful to Dr. Brittany Cooper and her scholarship in the book *Eloquent Rage,* which mounts an honest, open assault on the systemic abuse of women. She joins others such as Bell Hooks, Audre Lorde, Dr. Eboni Marshall Turman, Dr. Patricia Hill Collins, Dr. Emile Townes Dr. Teresa Fry Brown, Dr. Renita Weems, Dr. Jaqueline Grant Collier, Dr. Delores Williams Dr. Stacy Floyd-Thomas, and Dr Mari Evans, in assuring me that our rage is not due for an apology. Though our rage may be problematic for others, it is not problematic for us.

In the words of Audre Lorde, "Black women are expected to use our anger only in the service of other people's salvation or learning. But that time is over." In her words as well, "We cannot use the master's tools to dismantle the master's house" (Lorde & Clarke, 2012).

There must be the acknowledgement that our rage is real and cannot be resolved by our own action. If we are able to use our anger in the service of other's people's salvation, we are able to confront the systems that attack us.   Acknowlegment begins the journey for empowerment for women and disempowerment of those who oppress.

Acknowledgment is not passive and the journey is critical for mobilization of the reality that Black women matter.

We salute Black churches who prepare Black boys for Black men's empowerment, as well as those who prepare Black girls for Black women's empowerment and our collective right to be angry at injustice. This problem will not end until the same theological and sociological principles that are implemented for the liberation of Black men are also used for the liberation of Black women. This effort requires that the barriers of race and gender be eradicated and fully addressed. It further requires the courage of each Black woman to identify her personal truth, to speak and not be silent, and to refuse to act based on someone else's expectation, particularly when the expectation is founded on racism and sexism. Though the global society yearns for the end of racism and classism, I pray that the day also comes when it moans and groans for the end of sexism.

Until then, I thank God that so many more Black women chose to speak and act than chose passivity and acceptance. Their legacy provided an impetus for us to continue to fight. Listing all their names is an impossibility, but we are here because they lived and fought. They represent the freedom we seek, and the essence of a poem I wrote years ago, *I'm Free*. It is the declaration that Black women have the right and will self declare, "We are free."   Let the rage continue.

I'm Free
By Anne Henning Byfield

The necessity of my sanity,
the level of my disintegration
causes a reassimilation of me.

I no longer yearn to be in order with you
if it means out of order with me.
Your definition of self,
your standard of perfect,
your identification for wholeness
causes a dissolution of my totality
I will no longer conform with your Identity
of what normalcy is
when it means I have to reject my own hair, my hips,
my beliefs. my faith, my thoughts, and my color.
I have no desire to be in acceptance by you
if it means rejection by me.
I have decided that I am in order with myself and with God
which may make me out of order with you.
I am free.
The Essence of My Existence
annehenningbyfield

References

Cone, J. H. (2011). *A Black Theology of Liberation—Fortieth Anniversary Edition* (40th Anniversary edition). Orbis Books.

Cooper, B. C. (2019). *Eloquent Rage: A Black Feminist Discovers Her Superpower.* Picador Press.

_____. (2017). *Beyond Respectability: The Intellectual Thought of Race Women (Women, Gender, and Sexuality in American History).* University of Illinois Press.

Henning Byfield, A. (2010). *The Essence of My Existence.* True Vine Publishing.

Lloyd, V. (2019). The Ambivalence of Black Rage. *CLCWeb: Comparative Literature and Culture, 21*(3). https://doi.org/10.7771/1481-4374.3550.

Lorde, A. (1984). Eye to Eye: Black Women, Hatred, and Anger In: Lorde, A. & Clarke, C. (2012). *Sister Outsider: Essays and Speeches.* Crossing Press, pp. 145-175.

_____ & Clarke, C. (2012). *Sister Outsider: Essays and Speeches.* Crossing Press.

Thomas, S. A., & González-Prendes, A. A. (2009). Powerlessness and Anger in African American Women: A Theoretical Perspective. *Researcher: An Interdisciplinary Journal*, 22(3), pp. 23-42.

Bishop E. Anne Henning Byfield, M.Div., D.Min.

Bishop Anne Henning Byfield, is an AME Bishop who serves the 13th Episcopal District and is the formerly served the 16th Episcopal District. She is currently the President of the Council of Bishops and Chair of the Social Action Commission of the AME Church. She is married to Ainsley for 44 years they have one son, Michael, and daughter in law, Adrienne. And four grandchildren. She holds a Bachelor of Science degree from Wilberforce University, a Master of Divinity Degree from Payne Theological Seminary, and a Doctor of Ministry Degree from Ashland Theological Seminary. She is the author of four books, a composer, and a poet. She is a 2020 recipient of the Samuel DeWitt Proctor Conference Beautiful Are Your Feet Award, and a Golden member of Alpha Kappa Alpha Sorority, Inc.

CHAPTER SIX

"For Three Transgressions of America, and for Four": Racism as "Wickedness-Beyond-the-Pale"

Brian Rainey, M.Div., PhD.

Abstract

The paradigm of "structural sin" as a theological explanation for white supremacy—and in particular, the Church's role in perpetuating that "sin"—is a "whitewashing," a soft-pedaling explanation for the brutal system that is white supremacy. Rather, the Hebrew Bible's portrayals of *wickedness-beyond-the-pale*, a wickedness worthy of God's pitiless judgment, better fits the profound evils of white supremacy Characterizing white supremacy as "sin" conveniently relativizes and subsumes the horrors of this phenomenon within a theological system in which "all have sinned and fallen short of the glory of God" (Rom 3:23). But white supremacy is a particularly evil monstrosity. Worse, the very idea that white supremacy is "sin" allows white Christians to manipulate Christian theology to demand "forgiveness" and "grace" from Blacks. Forgiveness for white

America should be left to God's grace, while Black America should unequivocally proclaim God's calamitous judgment on white supremacy as "wickedness-beyond-the-pale," without the derailing, distracting rhetoric of Black "forgiveness."

>>

It has become common in some Christian theological circles to conceptualize racism as a "sin." The US Conference of Catholic Bishops (USCCB) refers to racism as "particularly destructive and persistent form of evil" as well as "sinful."[1] White evangelical pastor and theologian Jim Wallis, who considers himself a progressive, calls racism America's "original sin":

> [R]acism must be named as a perverse sin that cuts to the core of the gospel message. Put simply, racism negates the reason for which Christ died—the reconciling work of the cross, first to God and then to one another. It denies the purpose of the church: to bring together, in Christ, those who have been divided from one another—particularly, in the early church's case, Jew and Gentile—a division based on racial ethnicity, culture, and religion. There is only one remedy for such a sin, and that is repentance. If genuine, it will always bear fruit in concrete forms of conversion and changed behavior, with both rejections and reversals of racism.[2]

Wallis is not the first to express such sentiments. Indeed, general Christian theological arguments against racism are very similar. Wallis appeals to Gal 3:28, where the Apostle Paul says "there is neither Jew nor Greek, neither slave nor free, there is neither male nor female; for you are all one in Christ Jesus." White, conservative pastor and theologian Timothy Keller appeals to the same passage, and others (e.g., Isa 19:25; 60:1–7; Gal 6:15), to make a similar albeit more eschatological argument. The "new creation" through Jesus Christ, the beginnings of which are present now, will be a world where there is no "racial, ethnic, and national strife, alienation, and violence" and will comprise "every tongue, tribe, people and nation" (Rev 7:9).[3] Others appeal to the Priestly notion in the Hebrew Bible that humanity has been made in the "image of God" (Gen 1:26–7; 9:6). Still others claim that racism violates the command—first expressed in Lev 19:18, then restated by Jesus and the Apostle Paul—to "love your neighbor as yourself" (Matt 19:19; 22:39; Mark 12:31; Luke 10:27; Rom 13:9; Gal 5:14). Many appeal to all three sentiments in their condemnation of racism.[4]

Many who call racism "sin," also acknowledge the existence of an "institutional" or "structural" or "systemic" component to racism. USCCB (as recently as 2018) argues that racism "can also be institutional, when practices or traditions are upheld that treat certain groups of people unjustly. The cumulative effects of personal sins of racism have led to social structures of injustice and violence that makes us all accomplices in racism."[5] The Southern Baptist Convention's 1995 *Resolution on Racial Reconciliation* apologizes "to all African-Americans for condoning and/or perpetuating individual and systemic racism in our lifetime" and claims to "genuinely repent of racism of which we have been guilty, whether consciously (Psa 19:13) or unconsciously (Lev 4:27)."[6] Liberal theologian Stephen Ray understands structural sin as a force that "works through structures to inscribe itself on the bodies and souls of persons and communities as ill-being and death.... it effectively shields itself from scrutiny and intervention by constructing ideological formations that take the presence of ill-being and death as simply the natural order of things."[7] USCCB emphasizes that, in their view, structural racism is a result of the "cumulative effects of personal sins" while Ray roots structural racism in historical events.

Optimistically speaking, it is possible that the conceptualization of racism-as-sin could render the horrors of racism more relatable to Christian communities by putting racism in theological terms that non-Black Christians will recognize and appreciate. By doing so, racism-as-sin has the potential to be a starting point for important conversations within churches about how racism manifests itself surreptitiously and unconsciously in our daily lives. Those who view sin as an affliction into which people are born involuntarily due to the Fall (the Augustinian concept of "original sin") might be receptive to discussing the implicit, profoundly psychological, and social embeddedness of racism. Indeed, some very important discussions *have* occurred as a result of seeing racism as sin, especially in those analyses that regard racism as *structural* sin.

Sadly, however, in my view, using the concept of sin to describe racism is just as likely to relativize and minimize Black oppression as it is to prompt Christians to urgent action. After all, some biblical texts claim that not one person is righteous (Psa 14:3; 53:3; 143:2; Eccl 7:20; Rom 3:10–18) and that "all have sinned and fallen short of the glory of God" (Rom 3:23). If racism is "sin" and "*all* have sinned," then what special urgency is there to eradicate the sin of racism? Racism-as-sin can be rationalized as no more urgent than any other "sin." Moreover, the relationship between personal sin(s) and structural sin is rarely explained, leaving the connection between the two obscure and open to theological obfuscation and abuse. Neither the USCCB letter nor the Southern Baptist Convention explain how personal sins of racism aggregate into institutional structures, leaving the door wide open for someone to render the observation that structural racism exists into an individualistic concept of sin—in short, domesticating it! What is to stop someone from disallowing anti-racist activism by asserting that racism is an inevitability, just like any other sin or simply a function of humanity's sinful nature? And since sin will only be fully defeated in the Eschaton, why bother? Better to focus on saving individual souls.

The notion that both structural and personal racism are a result of some vague accumulation of individualized human sinfulness seems to have led to a half-hearted, indefinite commitment on the part of conservative Christians to the idea that racism is structural. It also seems that this half-hearted commitment has had practical implications. In 1995, the Southern Baptist Convention claimed that they would dedicate themselves to addressing racism as a systemic issue. Twenty-five years later, Black Southern Baptist pastors are still begging the largely white leadership of their denomination to take structural racism seriously, as the Rev. Rick Armstrong pleads:

> [The Southern Baptist Convention's] Ethics and Religious Liberty Commission **must** encourage Southern Baptists to understand that **racism** is much more than an individual sin. Rather, Southern Baptists must embrace the reality of **structural, systemic, and institutional** areas of racism.[8]

Apparently, Southern Baptists were not very serious when they promised to tackle structural racism in 1995. And their weak theology of racism now indicates that they are not serious even in the era of "Black Lives Matter," as Rev. Armstrong's letter indicates.

Christians who are invested in white supremacy (consciously or unconsciously, directly or as white-adjacent) can subvert anti-racist social movements by claiming that the "sin" of racism is on a par with other things they deem "sins," such as abortion, homosexuality, or trans-gender and non-binary gender expression. Along these lines, some Christians have invented excuses for their slow response to institutional racism by claiming that Scripture is clearer on "social issues" than it is on structural or economic issues. For example, with respect to abortion, Russell Moore, head of the Southern Baptist Convention's Ethics and Religious Liberty Commission, the very commission that Rev. Armstrong begged to take structural racism seriously asserted that, while the use of the Bible to support economic justice and systemic issues is controversial, the Bible is clear on the need to oppose legal abortion.[9] This excuse is insupportable. The application of biblical texts to political issues like abortion rights and modern-day queer identities is also contentious. The Bible does not directly address either abortion or expressions of sexual orientation and gender identity as we understand them today. Yet Moore feels free to use contentious, controversial biblical passages to enthusiastically trumpet his own political viewpoints on social issues, while claiming that interpretative controversy around social *justice* issues warrants reticence and caution.

Though there is an abundance of shade to cast on conservative Christians, liberal Christians cannot get on their high horse, either. It seems that there is also a great lack of seriousness within liberal and mainline Christianity when it comes to tackling racism. Thus far, liberal and mainline Christian denominations and institutions are unwilling to put any full-throated moral force behind defunding the police or behind police and prison abolitionism—at least not on an institutional or denominational level. Liberal and mainline Christian institutions need to be very careful in this racial justice struggle lest they fall into old traps that have previously ensnared "progressively" minded Christians. In US history, when it comes to race, "moderate" positions are usually wrong. At the current moment, liberal and mainline religious institutions must dig deeper and even be willing to put their institutional prestige on the line for Black lives. As a case-in-point, my current employer, Princeton Theological Seminary, has had to come to terms with the fact that during the antebellum period, many of its own theologians, though anti-slavery, rejected the idea of enfranchising Black people fully in American society, instead promoting the recolonization of Black people in West Africa—a "moderate" position in the nineteenth century.[10] It may also prove useful to recall Martin Luther King, Jr.'s criticisms of the white "moderate" (which I read as "liberal") as he wrote from a Birmingham jail. Liberal and mainstream churches must flee from the temptation to champion "gradualist" and "slow" approaches to racial injustice, and instead preach the urgency of immediately and completely extirpating and eradicating the outrage of racism from society *right now*.

My harsh criticisms of conservative Christians, then, are part of a larger discussion about how all Christians should respond to the current anti-racist movement. What will distinguish authentic Christian responses from lip-service are the things churches and religious institutions are willing to put on the line, concretely, in this political climate. One thing that may help reorient Christians to bold action is a reconceptualization of racism as more than mere "sin." The word, "sin" does not do justice to the profound evil that characterizes racism. When we think about the horrors of slavery—oppressive, soul-crushing, uncompensated labor, appalling torture, rape and child sexual abuse, denial of dignity and humanity—does the word "sin" really capture the horrors? When we think about lynchings in the United States (i.e., publicly celebrated torture-murders), or the destruction of entire Black communities like Tulsa and Rosewood, does the word "sin" really capture the atrocities? When we think of the vicious slaying of Emmet Till, who was just a child, or the killing of four girls, also children, in a church bombing, or the brutality unleashed on civil rights activists, or the assassinations of Black leaders, does the word "sin" really capture the cruelty? When we think of the killings of Trayvon Martin, Tamir Rice, Ahmaud Arbery, Breonna Taylor, George Floyd, and so many more, does the word "sin" really capture these monstrous acts? Or do such biblical terms as "wicked" (Heb. *rasha'*), "depravity" (Heb. *zimmah*), "abomination" (Heb. *to'evah*), and "iniquity" (Heb. *'avon* or *'aven*) seem more fitting?

Additionally, when I see the sophisticated, deliberately constructed legal edifices that keep holding killer cops unaccountable, and the mental contortions that people go through to justify police and vigilante violence against Black people, I am reminded of biblical passages that excoriate scoundrels who "devise evil" in their minds. Interestingly, passages censuring those who "devise evil" often appear alongside condemnations of social injustice. Prov 6:14–18 lists a person who has "depravity on his mind" (*tahpukot belibbo*), one who "devises evil all the time" (*choresh ra' bekol-'et*), and a mind that devises iniquitous plots (*lev choresh machshvot 'aven*) along with people who shed innocent blood. Isa 32:6–7 calls "good-for-nothing" (*naval*) those whose "minds make up iniquity" (*libbo ya'aseh 'aven*) in order to "leave empty the throat of the hungry and deprive the thirsty of drink." These same villains (*kiylay*) "plot depraved schemes" (*zimmot ya'ats*) in order "to ruin the poor with deceitful words." Ezek 11:2–3 condemns the leaders of the people, who have slain so many in the city (11:6), as men "devising iniquity" (*ha-'anashim ha-choshvim 'aven*) and "counseling evil counsel" (*ha-yo'atsim 'atsat-ra'*). Zech 7:9–10 commands post-Exilic Jews, "Do not oppress the widow, the orphan, the resident alien, or the poor and do not devise evil in your minds against each other (*ra'at 'ish el-achiyv 'al-tachshevu bilevavkem*). Zech 8:15–17 exhorts, "Speak the truth to one another, render truthful verdicts for the general welfare in your gates, and do not devise evil in your minds against each other" (*'ish 'et-ra'at re'eh 'al-tachshevu bilevavkem*).

Stronger language than "sin" is needed in order to give racism its due as the monstrosity that it is. We would need to marshal all of the execratory vocabulary of the Old Testament to even get close to describing it. This level of evil cannot just be lumped into a category that encompasses literally every human moral failing from small lapses in judgment to mass murder, thereby relativizing and diluting the magnitude of racism's wickedness and humanity-crushing violence. Adding adjectives to the word "sin" — (e.g., "grievous sin" or "perverse sin") does not adequately describe the deep depravity of American racism, either. Racism, particularly anti-Black and anti-indigenous racism, is Sodom and Gomorrah–level wickedness — a kind of wickedness that cries out for destructive retaliation from a just God. The people of Sodom and Gomorrah never entered a unique covenant relationship with Israel's God, as Abraham's descendants did (Genesis 15; 17); nevertheless, they are accountable to God for their extraordinary wickedness because their crimes violate a universal sense of justice that applies to all peoples. Though the word "sin" (Heb. *chatta't*, Gen 18:20) is used to refer to the terrible crimes committed within Sodom and Gomorrah, the text specifically points out that the people of Sodom and Gomorrah are *also* wicked (*rasha'*, Gen 18:23–25). In addition, racism is Haman-level wickedness (Est 3:5–14; Est 7:6) — genocidal evil that deserves a fierce, but *strategic*, response from a persecuted and hated people (Est 8:1–17). Wickedness of this kind violates a universal sense of justice that every human being should possess regardless of what God they worship or what religion they follow.

Amos 1:3–2:16's oracles also speak to this kind of evil. These oracles pronounce judgment against foreign nations as well as against Judah and Israel, but the condemnations of foreign nations are more interesting. Here, God condemns these foreign nations not for the violent outrages they inflicted on Israel or Judah—because not all of these crimes were committed exclusively against Israel and Judah—but for what a modern observer might call indiscriminate "war crimes" or "atrocities" against their fellow human beings. Notably, one of those atrocities is deporting entire populations into slavery, which is a crime upon which the United States was economically and socially founded (Amos 1:6, 9). Amos's oracles clearly imply (or at least strongly suggest) that the crimes of these condemned nations transgress a kind of intuitive morality that God expects everyone—Israelite or not—to follow. Amos calls the transgressions of the foreign nations *pesha'*, which is often translated "transgression," but it really means "rebellious acts" against God, as the refrain that starts each oracle exclaims: "for three rebellious acts (*pish'eiyim*) and for four, I will not revoke [my imminent judgment]." Concerning the oracles of Amos 1–2, Biblical scholar Shalom M. Paul notes:

> The revolt implied here can be better understood as one against God.... All of mankind is considered a vassal of the Lord whose power, authority and law embrace the entire world community of nations. His sovereignty is not confined merely to the territorial borders of Israel and Judah. Offenses against him are punished directly, wherever they are committed and whoever the guilty party may be. The Lord enforces the law he authors and imposes punishments against his rebel vassals. His law binds all peoples for the God of Israel is the God of all the nations.[11]

Those who perpetuate unspeakable violence against other people on this level rebel against an intuitive, universal divine law. Their acts are not merely "sins" (as in acts that violate a moral code understood only by those who worship and acknowledge Israel's God); rather, they are acts that show contempt for God's relationship with *all* peoples. The vicious legacy of racism certainly falls under Amos's concept of *pesha'*. If racism constitutes rebellion against God's universal relationship with all of humanity, then racism is so wicked that people can rightly expect and even anticipate retaliation from God.

But sometimes Christians—and too often, Black Christians—do not want to go there. Christians frequently emphasize forgiveness and reconciliation, dwelling on passages that say to "turn the other cheek" or "love your enemies" or "forgive your brother/sister" or "seventy times seven" or "forgive them for they know not what they do" and/or "bless those who persecute you" (Matt 5:39, 43–44; 18:22; Luke 23:34; Rom 12:14). The result is that Black people are constantly in a state of "forgiveness" because the outrages of white supremacy are relentless. Worse, biblical commands to forgive can be—and frequently are—weaponized and turned around on Black people, turning forgiveness into an obligation that only shores up the status-quo and reinforces an unjust order. As *New York Times* opinion writer Roxane Gay puts it:

> Black people forgive because we need to survive. We have to forgive time and time again while racism or white silence in the face of racism continues to thrive. We have had to forgive slavery, segregation, Jim Crow laws, lynching, inequity in every realm, mass incarceration, voter disenfranchisement, inadequate representation in popular culture, microaggressions and more. We forgive and forgive and forgive and those who trespass against us continue to trespass against us....
>
> What white people are really asking for when they demand forgiveness from a traumatized community is absolution. They want absolution from the racism that infects us all even though forgiveness cannot reconcile America's racist sins. They want absolution from their silence in the face of

all manner of racism, great and small. They want to believe it is possible to heal from such profound and malingering trauma because to face the openness of the wounds racism has created in our society is too much. I, for one, am done forgiving.[12]

While many would distinguish between "forgiveness" and "absolution" (abstractly, at least), Gay is referring to what happens in practice when a white supremacist society expropriates acts of grace from Black people for its own purposes. Indeed, as Stacey Patton points out:

When black forgiveness is the means for white atonement, it enables white denial about the harms that racist violence creates. When black redemption of white America is prioritized over justice and accountability, there is no chance of truth and reconciliation. It trivializes real black suffering, grief, and the heavy lifting required for any possibility of societal progress.[13]

And this is one of the most disturbing legacies of the idea that racism is a "sin"; it reinforces the idea that white people are *entitled* to forgiveness; it gives them a basis on which to insist and demand that they be forgiven—while not forgiving others. As Patton also notes, "After 9/11, there was no talk about forgiving al-Qaeda, Saddam Hussein or Osama bin Laden. America declared war, sought blood and revenge, and rushed protective measures into place to prevent future attacks."[14] When a doctrine of forgiveness enables the perpetuation of injustice against marginalized people so blatantly, it is time for a reevaluation.

As a result, I am going to make the case for vengeance as a response to racism. I want to say explicitly that I do not advocate taking it upon *oneself* to avenge injustice. I do believe that vengeance, ultimately, belongs to God (Deut 32:35; Rom 12:19) and that vigilantism usurps God's role by making oneself the principal agent of vengeance. Rather, I am arguing that there is space within the life of a Black Christian for desiring vengeance, meditating on vengeance, asking God for vengeance, and—only when appropriate and after intensive discernment—for participating in God's vengeance. Scriptural passages that promote forgiveness need to be brought into conversation with passages that discuss and even celebrate vengeance.

One possible example of participation in God's vengeance comes from the 1980's—a story with eerie similarities to anti-Black violence that takes place today. On March 20, 1981, Michael Donald, a 19-year-old Black teenager, was tortured and lynched by members of the white-supremacist group United Klans of America in Mobile, Alabama. At first, in an all-too-familiar sequence of events, the police had no sense of urgency to solve Michael's murder. Only after a mass political mobilization, very reminiscent of the response to Ahmaud Arbery's killing, were the murderers pursued, tried, and sentenced. One was even sentenced to death. That was not enough for Michael's mother, Beulah Mae Donald, however. With the help of the Southern Poverty Law Center, she was eventually awarded $7 million in a civil suit against United Klans. Mrs. Donald ended up receiving the United Klans' only real asset, the property on which its headquarters sat, and her lawyers also made sure that the wages of United Klans members were also garnished to effect the settlement.

The conclusion of the criminal trial played out like the familiar "black forgiveness" trope, but Mrs. Donald's theological nuance is striking. One of the murderers, who testified against his fellow Klansmen, passionately apologized to Mrs. Donald on the stand, which, similar to the Botham Jean case (see below), prompted weeping in the courtroom. Even the judge and jurors cried. In response to the tearful apology, Mrs. Donald simply said, "I forgive you.... From the day I found out who you all was, I asked God to take care of y'all, and He has."[15] On the one hand, Mrs. Donald forgave those who murdered her son; on the other hand, she prayerfully asked God to "take care" of them—which I interpret as an invocation of God's judgment. She even went beyond the criminal courts, and relentlessly pursued those responsible in civil court.

Though my interpretation is contestable, Mrs. Donald, in my view, prayed for God's judgment and was therefore able to participate in God's vengeance. Circumstances allowed her to take an active role in bringing about a fitting punishment on the organization responsible for her son's murder.

Let us first look at the idea that vengeance belongs to God. The Apostle Paul says, "vengeance is mine, I will repay" (Rom 12:19) as part of a larger conversation about how members of his churches should treat one another, though he is also concerned about how church members should respond to outsiders (12:17–18). The chapter is about putting oneself in the right frame of mind so that one can discern God's will (12:1–3), and I am struck by how some of the Apostle's exhortations are contingent upon weighing what the right thing to do might be in one's own context:

> Bless those who persecute you; bless and do not curse... Do not repay anyone evil for evil *but take thought for* what is noble (*kala*) in the sight of all (*pantōn anthrōpōn*). *If it is possible, so far as it depends on you,* live peaceably with all (*pantōn anthrōpōn*). Beloved, never avenge yourselves, but *leave room for* the wrath of God; for it is written, 'Vengeance is mine, I will repay, says the Lord.' No, if your enemies are hungry, feed them; if they are thirsty give them something to drink; for by doing this you will heap burning coals on their head. Do not be overcome by evil, but overcome evil with good. (12:14, 17–21; NRSV)

Translations of Paul's words can encourage passivity in the face of appalling injustice. However, at *this* moment in history, after over four-hundred years of anti-Black oppression and violence, we should reflect critically on what the truly "noble" or "morally right" thing (Gk. *ta kala*) would be in our present context. Should Black people really be gracious when, to use the language of Romans 12, it is *impossible* for Black men and women to live "peaceably" in the United States? Are Black people required to bless those who repeatedly commit acts of wickedness beyond the pale? There are no easy answers to these questions; but to contend that the *only* correct Christian response is to reject vengeance, and embrace forgiveness is too simple. Would it alter the reader's understanding of the passage if we change the passive tone of "*leave* room for the wrath of God" to more active commands, such as "*give space* to the wrath [of God]" or "*provide a space* for the wrath [of God]" or (my personal preference) "*set a place* for the wrath [of God]" (Gk. *dote topon*)—which are all closer to the Greek text? The Apostle is correct about one thing: we, like his audience in the first century CE, do not have the power to avenge ourselves according to some tit-for-tat (or "evil-for-evil") concept of vengeance. But we can "set a place" for the wrath of God in our mental, theological, and even political lives in response to racism. To be sure, "providing space" for God's wrath in our lives must be tempered with discernment and careful consideration, but it cannot be excluded as some interpretations of this passage, and other forgiveness passages, seem to imply.

Second, the maxim "vengeance is mine" originally appears in Deut 32:35. This verse is part of what is known as the "Song of Moses," a poem that lists multiple calamities that will befall the Israelites if they violate the unique covenant they made with their God. In the Song of Moses, "vengeance is mine" is directed at an unnamed nation (probably Babylonia) to whom God will deliver the Israelites as punishment for their disobedience. This anonymous nation believes that it is responsible for the subjugation of Israel through its own power and refuses to recognize that they were successful only because Israel's God, in his sovereignty, allowed them to be. The Song indicts this nation as one whose "vine comes from the vinestock of Sodom, from the vineyards of Gomorrah; their grapes are grapes of poison, their clusters are bitter; their wine is the poison of serpents, the cruel venom of asps" (Deut 32:32–33; NRSV).

As noted above, Sodom and Gomorrah are infamous for violating principles that humanity, universally, should acknowledge. By comparing the nation to Sodom and Gomorrah, the author is making sure that the audience knows that this nation is going to get what is coming to it.

Then the Song celebrates God's impending destruction against this nation:

> I kill and I make alive;
> I wound and I heal;
> and no one can deliver from my hand.
> For I lift up my hand to heaven,
> and swear: As I live forever,
> when I whet my flashing sword,
> and my hand takes hold on judgment;
> I will take vengeance on my adversaries,
> and will repay those who hate me.
> I will make my arrows drunk with blood,
> and my sword shall devour flesh—
> with the blood of the slain and the captives,
> from the long-haired enemy.
> Praise, O heavens, his people,
> worship him, all you gods!
> For he will avenge the blood of his children,
> and take vengeance on his adversaries;
> he will repay those who hate him....
> (Deut 32:39b–43; NRSV)

It may be significant that this part of the Song characterizes the enemy nation as people who "hate" God, because the word "hate" (Heb. *sanē'*) can carry political connotations. The word can serve as a euphemism for the disloyalty displayed by a subject or ally.[16] The word "hate" recalls Amos 1–2, which accuses the foreign nations facing imminent judgment of committing acts of rebellion against God through their violent atrocities. It seems that in Deuteronomy 32, God's retaliation is so violent because Israel too has rebelled against God, at least partially, through their cruelty to others (32:33).

Thanks to Deuteronomy 32, we have even more Old Testament invective to hurl at the agents of white supremacy and white supremacist societies. We can now say that a white supremacist society is God's enemy, and that such a society is ruled by people to be classified as haters of God. A nation founded on chattel slavery and genocide, and which has refused to repent by extirpating every last trace of it, root and branch, cannot claim to be a "godly" nation. Such a claim is blasphemous, and a nation that hypocritically imprints "in God we trust" on its money and on public monuments in insincere public performances of religiosity is actually mocking God. Through its actions, the United States has demonstrated that it is an adversary of God, and those with power in this country have exposed themselves as haters of God.

The admonition "Vengeance is mine," then, is not necessarily a call to abandon the desire for vengeance. It is, in my reading, an invitation for Black people to *set a place* for God's wrath in our thoughts by wrapping ourselves in the graphic, slaughterous imagery of Deuteronomy 32 as if it were a cozy blanket. Yet, those who envelop themselves in the Song of Moses's bloody fantasy should remember that this is *divine, providential* vengeance that will happen in *God's* timing. Human beings cannot bring it about unilaterally. Acknowledging such a reality is different from claiming, in the name of forgiveness and reconciliation, that it is wrong to desire the suffering of those who perpetuate white supremacy (more on that below).

But the question remains: If the idea of vengeance is something that Black people can rightfully entertain in response to racism, what about those verses that command us to love our enemies, turn the other cheek, forgive, and bless those who persecute us? Does a desire for vengeance, or praying for vengeance, contradict exhortations to love our enemies and forgive? Some forgiveness passages even say that those who do not forgive others, will not be forgiven by God, in turn. Many Black Christians believe that these passages command them to forgive those who brutalize, abuse, and kill Black people. As a recent example, these verses seem to have inspired some of the relatives of Botham Jean, an innocent man gunned down in his own home by a cop, to publicly forgive his killer.

On the night of September 6, 2018, Botham Jean was sitting in his apartment, minding his own business and eating ice cream, when white Dallas police officer Amber Guyger burst in and shot him dead. Guyger claimed that, due to exhaustion, she accidentally entered what she (wrongly) thought to be her own apartment and, mistaking Jean for an intruder, opened fire. Many seemed unsympathetic to Guyger's excuses for her reckless, trigger-happy disregard for the life of a man who was just existing in his own home—especially the jury that convicted her of murder and sentenced her to ten years in prison. Considering the history of the US legal system, it was remarkable that Guyger was convicted of anything at all, and even more remarkable that she was sentenced to more than a slap on the wrist—though the sentence was still, for many, inadequate. But arguably, the most amazing part of the trial was that during the victim impact statements, Botham Jean's brother, Brandt, forgave Guyger on the stand, saying, "I don't even want you to go to jail. I want the best for you because I know that's exactly what Botham would want for you. Give your life to Christ. I think giving your life to Christ is the best thing Botham would want for you."[17] He even asked the judge to allow him to hug her, which he did for close to a minute. Even more incredibly, the trial judge, Tammy Kemp, who is Black, cried from the stand, approached Guyger, hugged her, and gave her a Bible. Kemp also recommended an absurdly lenient sentence of two years, which, thankfully, the jury rejected.

While many respected the fact that Jean's family was working through their grief in their own way, Jean's family—and especially Judge Kemp—were also criticized for being so forthcoming with these public displays of grace. Bertrum Jean, the father of Botham and Brandt, defended his son's actions in the courtroom by saying, "If you will not forgive, neither will your father forgive you. I don't want to see her rot in hell. I don't want to see her in rot in prison. I hope this will help her to change and recognize the damage, the hurt that our family's going through. So I wish her well and I will pray for her family and pray for her as well."[18]

I too believe that Botham Jean's family has every right to process their grief and heal in their own way. Even if I do not agree with or like it, this is their journey and, if this graciousness helps them heal, it is a good thing. I cannot fault Brandt Jean or any other members of the Jean family for choosing this path. And there is a great deal of evidence suggesting that forgiveness, as in letting go of the rage and hate that one feels toward someone who harmed you, has positive effects on mental health. I suspect that one of the reasons the Bible emphasizes forgiveness so much is because of the immense psychological benefits that come with forgiving. So I accept the necessity of forgiveness in one's own spiritual life, but take issue with the theological rationale offered for forgiving Guyger. And I certainly do not accept Judge Kemp's sickeningly saccharine performance of Black servility.

The idea that everyone must forgive unconditionally is based on the idea, found in many New Testament texts, that because God forgave us, Christians should forgive others — as Botham Jean's father, Bertrum, notes. But we can reframe the common reading of these forgiveness passages by looking more closely at a parable designed to illustrate that very idea. In Matt 18:21–22, Simon Peter famously asks Jesus how often one should forgive one's fellow sibling. Jesus responds that one should forgive "seventy times seven" and also responds through the so-called "Parable of the Unmerciful Servant" in verses 23–35:

> For this reason the kingdom of heaven may be compared to a king who wished to settle accounts with his slaves. When he began the reckoning, one who owed him ten thousand talents was brought to him; and, as he could not pay, his lord ordered him to be sold, together with his wife and children and all his possessions, and payment to be made. So the slave fell on his knees before him, saying, "Have patience with me, and I will pay you everything." And out of pity for him, the lord of that slave released him and forgave him the debt. But that same slave, as he went out, came upon one

of his fellow slaves who owed him a hundred denarii; and seizing him by the throat, he said, "Pay what you owe." Then his fellow slave fell down and pleaded with him, "Have patience with me, and I will pay you." But he refused; then he went and threw him into prison until he would pay the debt. When his fellow slaves saw what had happened, they were greatly distressed, and they went and reported to their lord all that had taken place. Then his lord summoned him and said to him, "You wicked slave! I forgave you all that debt because you pleaded with me. Should you not have had mercy on your fellow slave, as I had mercy on you?" And in anger his lord handed him over to be tortured until he would pay his entire debt. So my heavenly Father will also do to every one of you, if you do not forgive your brother or sister from your heart. (NRSV)

Unpacking the ethically problematic use of slavery to illustrate a point is beyond the scope of this essay, but, elsewhere in the Bible, slavery represents the covenant relationship God has with His people—as disturbing as the imagery might be (Lev 25:42, 55; Matt 25:14-30; Rom 6:22). Alternatively, based on my reading of Amos 1–2 above and other biblical passages (Gen 8:21–22; 9:9–17), the enslaved persons in this parable might represent humanity in general, with whom God also has a covenant relationship, though Peter's use of "brothers" in verse 21 suggests that the forgiveness here refers to forgiveness among believers. Either way, there are some interesting details that allow us to look at the conventional reading of this parable from a different angle.

The parable reminds us that forgiveness often just emboldens and empowers evil, hypocritical people. In the parable, the lord's forgiveness only affords the unforgiving slave the opportunity to mistreat someone else. If the lord (i.e., the enslaver) had just sold the unforgiving slave off, the slave who owed the smaller debt would not have wound up in debtor's prison. A key lesson of the parable is that forgiveness often just makes the forgiven more brazen. The Apostle Paul claims that feeding and giving drink to one's enemies will heap burning coals on their heads (Rom 12:20). But this is not always the case. I am not sure it is even often the case. Your enemies often just gobble up your food, guzzle down your drink, and, having been refreshed, take those very coals and heap them back on *your own* head, or, worse, on someone else's. As Gay and Patton argue above, our white supremacist society appropriates and manipulates public displays of "Black forgiveness" to support a narrative that focuses on white redemption, which only further perpetuates the inequality Black people face in the legal system and in media portrayals. Forgiveness is turned right around to harm Black people some more.

As if to drive this point home, Botham Jean's murderer, Amber Guyger, has recently appealed her murder conviction. Her lawyer argues that the circumstances of the case warrant a negligent homicide conviction, not a murder conviction, because:

> ...her mistaken belief negated the culpability for murder because although she intentionally and knowingly caused Jean's death, she had the right to act in deadly force in self-defense since her belief that deadly force was immediately necessary was reasonable under the circumstances.[19]

This language, indistinguishable from the numerous justifications offered in the past for police and vigilante killings of Black people, is a slap in the face. The Jean family was understandably upset by Guyger's abuse of their forgiveness, which they expressed through their attorney:

> After admitting her crime and asking Botham Jean's family for mercy—Guyger's actions in filing this appeal reflect someone who is not repentant but instead was hoping to play on the families [sic] sympathies at the time they were most vulnerable.

It would appear as though Guyger has deflected those "hot coals" the Apostle Paul was talking about right back onto the Jean family's head.

Then there is the behavior of the other enslaved persons in the parable. They witness the outrageous behavior of the unforgiving slave and take action against it. In telling the story, Jesus could have chosen to be more opaque about how the lord found out, simply saying, for example, "when the lord heard…" or "later, the lord found out…." Instead, Jesus makes it clear that the agency of the other enslaved persons is critical to bringing about the punishment of the unforgiving slave. The slave who was directly victimized and who was thrown into debtor's prison is not the one who sets the events in motion for the unforgiving slave to be punished. It is the other slaves, in solidarity with him, that do so. Of course, the lord in the parable represents God. And Scripture, inspired by God (however one understands that), has certainly provided us with a rich tradition that enthusiastically extols forgiveness and reconciliation. But like the unforgiving slave, the agents of white supremacy are the ones who have abused that tradition, and the divine grace that God has instituted—not angry Black people.

I have already referred to the stunning hypocrisy about forgiveness and reconciliation relative to 9/11. As another example, the US legal system that white people set up, defend, and champion is largely *unforgiving* towards Black people when they break the law, and was designed to be so. The so-called "war on drugs," being "tough on crime," and endorsing "law and order" are all expressions of a punishing, unforgiving regime that targets primarily Blacks and other minorities. Those who emphasize reconciliation and understanding in this context are often dismissed as "bleeding hearts" and "soft on crime." We live in a nation that sees state violence (more police, more prisons) as the main solution to social problems. And white people generally support and celebrate such a system, while lecturing Black people about forgiveness. Furthermore, one of the arguments for gun ownership in the United States is that people have a right to possess a firearm to defend themselves and their homes. Funny that no one brings up Jesus's commands to "turn the other cheek" and to "not resist an evil person" (Matt 5:39) when it comes to white people's desire to defend themselves and their possessions. Strangely, in gun-rights discussions, no one ever suggests that a better solution than a gun would be to offer your shirt to a home invader who takes your cloak (as per Luke 6:29). As Matt 18:31 puts it, we should be *greatly distressed* by the duplicity regarding forgiveness that we are witnessing from white Christianity.

To put it another way, the other slaves—who also represent God's people—intervene to stop the unforgiving slave's misuse and abuse of the forgiveness he received. When Black Christians witness Black people brutalized because of white supremacy, our proper role as a community is *not* to forgive. In fact, a public stance of forgiveness would be to do the opposite of what the other slaves in the parable do. Let the individual victims directly affected by each particular act of racial injustice make their own decisions about forgiveness, which is between them and God. Perhaps there is a reason Jesus does not tell us what happens to the victim of the unforgiving slave's mercilessness. Does he somehow get released? Does he die in debtor's prison? Does he himself forgive the unforgiving slave? Maybe the fate and response of the victim are shrouded in mystery because that kind of forgiveness is a matter for victims to work out in their own lives. In the story, the response of the victimized slave is immaterial to the solidarity expressed by the other slaves, and their mobilization to stop the unforgiving slave.

Similarly, the Black community's decision to call down God's vengeance in solidarity with victims of racial injustice is immaterial to the decision on the part of a victim of a particular injustice to forgive his/her individual perpetrators. Black people not directly impacted by a particular act of injustice, like Judge Kemp in the Amber Guyger trial, have no business indulging in melodramatic public performances of forgiveness. Moreover, Black people generally should cease giving theological explanations of "Black forgiveness" to the media. These performances and explanations will only be manipulated by a white supremacist media, society, and Church. Rather, Black people should publicly invoke divine vengeance in the face of white supremacist atrocities, because white supremacist Christianity has flagrantly abused Christian doctrines of forgiveness to camouflage their own mercilessness. Like the unforgiving slave in the parable, white supremacist Christian theology has turned the beautiful theological concept of forgiveness into a license for more cruelty. In response, we can unequivocally, and without apology, set that place for God's wrath in our anti-racist theologies. Greatly distressed at the manipulation of forgiveness by white supremacist Christianity, Black people can appeal to the true "Lord" with the hopeful anticipation that the perpetrators of racism will receive the suffering they deserve, until they pay "the entire debt" that they owe—whatever God decides that will look like.

White supremacist Christianity will continue to parrot and selectively fetishize Bible verses about sin and forgiveness in an attempt to minimize the scale of white supremacy's evil and to keep the focus on white people's needs and desires, rather than on justice for Black people. They will wag their finger in indignation at Black people when we finally decide we will no longer be manipulated by their misuse and abuse of forgiveness as a theological concept. But the glossed over details in the "Parable of the Unmerciful Servant" reframe every, single one of their selective proof-texts. The parable rebukes those who demand that Black people forgive while ignoring or minimizing the white supremacy around them. From the parable we learn that those greatly distressed by duplicitous abuse of forgiveness have every right to call upon God in pursuit of divine vengeance.

Let us return to passages like Matt 6:14–15, which lay down the rule that "if you do not forgive others, neither will your Father forgive your trespasses" (compare Mark 11:25; Eph 4:31–32). Passages like these suggest that those who do not forgive their fellow humans will not be forgiven by God, or at the very least that, because God has forgiven our "trespasses," we should forgive the "trespasses" of others against us Yet, as I have argued above, racism is not merely a "sin" or a "trespass." It is wickedness beyond the pale. It is an Amos 1–2 *pesha'*. It demonstrates hatred of God and renders those who perpetuate it enemies of God, worthy to be crushed (Deut. 32:39b–43). It is wanton depravity that even people who have never even heard the name of Jesus or Yahweh intuitively recognize as profoundly evil. And, indeed, many who do not recognize Jesus as Lord have a better track record with responding to racism than do *Christians*. To relativize racism as being on a par with other "trespasses," as common interpretations of these passages do, is to deny the horror of racism and to minimize Black suffering. Second, Black people have the right to take the role of the other slaves in the story and intervene when someone is abusing forgiveness, which is exactly what the agents of white supremacy do, both by perpetuating white supremacy itself and by demanding forgiveness from Black people while a much larger specter of *unforgiving white supremacy* rages around them.

Finally, desire for vengeance must come to terms with the practical, or the way God's Providence actually works in the world. Black people know from experience that we are not always able to perceive or see God's vengeance in our lifetimes. And more often than not, God denies us the opportunity to participate directly in His vengeance. It is very possible that we will continue to see Black people abused and killed and never see God's wrath in response—at least not in a way we can appreciate from our human vantage point. If so, how long should we remain in that space that we have provided for God's wrath? How long should we preach about vengeance? This is why discernment is critical. The multiple forgiveness passages in Scripture are there for a reason. At times, for one's own mental health, or for a community's survival, it might be best to deemphasize the desire for vengeance and just forgive. At the same time, we must acknowledge that there are times when we are justified, and perhaps even morally compelled, to emphasize the vengeance of God in response to injustice. The problem is that the emphasis on sin, forgiveness, and reconciliation in Christian circles makes it seem as though there is absolutely no place for vengeance in Christian life. Christians frequently claim that because of biblical commands to forgive, there is absolutely no place in our hearts and minds for, say, feeling a sense of satisfaction and even pleasure from the suffering of the unjust. But as we have seen, these tendentious readings are quite contestable. Therefore, I call on Black Christians to set a place for God's wrath, so that we, as a community, may discuss the appropriate times in which to ask God for it.

Endnotes

1   United States Conference of Catholic Bishops, Committee on Cultural Diversity in the Church, *Open Wide Our Hearts: The Enduring Call to Love* [Pastoral Letter against Racism] (Washington, D.C.: United States Conference of Catholic Bishops, 2018).

2   Jim Wallis, *America's Original Sin: Racism, White Privilege and the Bridge to a New America* (Grand Rapids, Mich.: Brazos, 2016), 163–64; iBook.

3   Timothy Keller, "The Sin of Racism," *Gospel in Life: Redeemer Churches and Ministries' Quarterly Newsletter*: https://quarterly.gospelinlife.com/the-sin-of-racism.

4   See, e.g., from a liberal Christian perspective, Dismantling Racism Task Force, St. Louis Association, Missouri Mid-South Conference, United Church of Christ, "Racism Declared as Sin": https://www.ucc.org/justice_racism_racism-declared-sin; and, from a conservative perspective, Keller's "Sin of Racism."

5   USCCB, *Open Wide*, 5.

6   Southern Baptist Convention, "Resolution on Racial Reconciliation on the 150th Anniversary of the Southern Baptist Convention": https://www.sbc.net/resource-library/resolutions/resolution-on-racial-reconciliation-on-the-150th-anniversary-of-the-southern-baptist-convention/.

7   Stephen Ray, "Structural Sin" in Keith L. Johnson and David Lauber, eds., *T&T Clark Companion to the Doctrine of Sin* (London: Bloomsbury, 2016), 424.

8   Rick Armstrong, "Letter to Southern Baptist Leaders June 4, 2020," Published June 27, 2020 on the weblog *SBC Voices*: https://sbcvoices.com/letter-to-sbc-leaders-june-4-2020-rick-armstrong/?utm_source=onesignal&utm_medium=-push. Emphasis original.

9   Emma Green, "Southern Baptists Wrestle with the Sin of Racism," *The Atlantic*, April 7, 2015: https://www.theatlantic.com/politics/archive/2015/04/southern-baptists-wrestle-with-the-sin-of-racism/389808/.

10   Historical Audit Task Force, Princeton Theological Seminary, "Princeton Seminary, Slavery, and Colonization" in *Princeton Seminary and Slavery: A Journey of Confession and Repentance* (Princeton, N.J.: Princeton Theological Seminary, 2019): https://slavery.ptsem.edu/the-report/colonization-movement/.

11   Shalom M. Paul, *Amos: A Commentary on the Book of Amos* (Minneapolis, Minn.: Fortress Press, 1991), 45–46.

12   Roxane Gay, "Why I Can't Forgive Dylan Roof," *New York Times*, June 23, 2015: https://www.nytimes.com/2015/06/24/opinion/why-i-cant-forgive-dylann-roof.html#commentsContainer.

13   Stacey Patton, "Black America Should Stop Forgiving White Racists," *Washington Post*, June 22, 2015. https://www.washingtonpost.com/posteverything/

wp/2015/06/22/black-america-should-stop-forgiving-white-racists/.

14   Ibid.

15   For the disturbing details of the story, see Jesse Kornbluth, "The Woman Who Beat the Klan," *New York Times Magazine*, November 1, 1987. https://www.nytimes.com/1987/11/01/magazine/the-woman-who-beat-the-klan.html

16   The language of love (and *not* loving) is often political and covenantal; see W.L. Moran, "The Ancient Near Eastern Background of Love of God in Deuteronomy," *Catholic Biblical Quarterly* 25 (1963): 77–87, esp. 80–81; see also Susan Ackerman, "The Personal Is Political: Covenantal and Affectionate Love (*'āhēb, 'ahăbâ*) in the Hebrew Bible," *Vetus Testamentum* 52 (2002): 437–458.

17   Katie Kindelan and Sabina Ghebremedhin, "Botham Jean's Brother on Courtroom Hug with Amber Guyger: 'She Still Deserves Love'," *ABC News*, October 4, 2019: https://abcnews.go.com/GMA/News/botham-jeans-brother-discusses-emotional-courtroom-hug-amber/story?id=66055688.

18   Doug Criss and Leah Asmelash, "The Problem with Always Asking Black People to Forgive," *CNN.com*, October 4, 2019: https://www.cnn.com/2019/10/03/us/black-americans-forgiveness-trnd/index.html.

19   Mallika Kallingal, Jennifer Henderson, and Kay Jones, "Attorneys for Former Dallas Police Officer Amber Guyger File Appeal in Botham Jean Murder Case," *CNN.com*, August 7, 2020: https://www.cnn.com/2020/08/07/us/amber-guyger-botham-jean-appeal/index.html.

Brian Rainey, M.Div., Ph.D.

Brian Rainey is Assistant Professor of Old Testament at Princeton Theological Seminary.

Dr. Rainey earned his M.Div. from Harvard Divinity School and his Ph.D. from Brown University. His areas of expertise include ethnicity in the Hebrew Bible and ancient Near East, including anthropological, sociological, and cognitive theories of "ethnicity" and their usefulness for the study of ancient societies. His interests also include modern Christian and Jewish communities and ways in which they bridge the gap between modern ethical concepts and the ethically problematic social context of the Bible. Other areas of study include Assyriology, biblical mythology, Christian theology, and the development of "monotheism" in the ancient world. His recent book, *Religion, Ethnicity and Xenophobia in the Bible: A Theoretical, Exegetical and Theological Survey*, was published by Routledge Publications in 2019.

CHAPTER SEVEN

The Transforming Power of Holy Rage

Bishop Frank Madison Reid, III, M.Div., D.Min.

Abstract

The purpose of this essay is to encourage, equip, and empower people to discover the transforming power of Holy Rage. Moses is adduced as an example of a person who allowed his anger to fuel his rage. His anger was inflamed against the oppressive treatment of his enslaved people. The result was the murder of an individual oppressor, not the dismantling of the institution of slavery. Later, when Moses encountered the holy presence of God, his individual life was transformed. Holy rage transformed reactive rage into a life-giving, life-changing, liberating, transformational movement. The deconstruction of institutional, cultural, spiritual, political, and economic White Supremacy requires Holy Rage. The Reconstruction of a nation built on freedom, justice, and equality requires a Great Awakening of Holy Rage. This essay will help us understand, rediscover, recover, learn from, and embrace the individual and institutional healing and transformative power of Holy Rage.

>>

INTRODUCTION AND PURPOSE

The purpose of this paper is to encourage, equip, and empower Black people, people of color, to transform divisive, destructive, and deadly rage into healing, liberating, and life-changing Holy Rage. This call to activate the principles and practices of Holy Rage is also a call for the "radical reconstruction" of individual people of color and the institutions, such as the Black Church, that were created to serve and give "power to the people." Will "Black Rage" become the tool kit of the thief who has come to steal, kill, and destroy our people (John 10:10)? Or will Holy Rage heal us, deliver us, and make us whole so we can recover all that the thief has taken from us for over 400 years?

I began writing "The Transforming Power of Holy Rage" after taking time to review the July 2020 issue of *Rolling Stone* magazine. The umbrella title for that issue is "American Uprising" and it contained many empowering articles: "Say Their Names," "Black Lives Matter," "The Disgrace of Donald Trump," "Why Policing Is Broken," "The Case for Radical Reform," and "George Floyd's Hip-Hop Legacy." Each article confronts us with thoughts and feelings of rage, revenge, and reactive violence. Each article reminds us that hurt people hurt people. Each article reminds us that the proper understanding and practice of Holy Rage can transform us, our communities, and the institutions we represent.

I began writing this essay about Holy Rage after praying over the 54 pictures and names of Black people shot and killed by police from May 16, 2010 through May 27, 2020 in the July 2020 *Rolling Stone* article, "Say Their Names." The written words are few but powerful. They are words that lead to passive or reactive rage. They are words that can open the doors of our hearts and minds to the transforming and proactive power of Holy Rage:

> The people pictured here are just a fraction of those killed over the past decade by officers who were sworn to protect them. Some are well known names: Tamar Rice, the 12-year-

old boy gunned down in Cleveland for playing with a toy gun at a park. Philando Castile, the school lunch supervisor who was shot because his 'wide set nose' resembled that of a robbery suspect. Other cases never made the national conversation, like Charleena Lyles, a pregnant mother of four who was shot by a Seattle police officer in 2017 after she reported a burglary in her home. In each of these cases, and in so many others, the officers were either not charged or not convicted of any crime.

I began praying, meditating, and writing about the transforming power of a holy rage, after weeks of prayer, planning, thinking, bible study, reading, and research. After re-reading the classic *Black Rage* by William H. Grier and Price M. Cobb and after reading a biography of Jarvis Jay Masters, titled *The Buddhist On Death Row* by David Sheff. After reflecting on my own experiences of rage and my recent experiences with Holy Rage, there was one more task I had to complete before I could begin writing this chapter. I needed to discharge a responsibility I had been given, namely, the drafting of a statement for the African Methodist Church on the police shooting of Jacob Blake in Kenosha, Wisconsin.

On Sunday, August 23, 2020 Jacob Blake, a security guard, stopped his car to break up a fight between two women, leaving his three children inside the vehicle. When the police arrived to intervene, they focused on Mr. Blake, as he prepared to enter the car where his children were seated in the back. They then opened fire shooting Mr. Blake seven times in the back. Jacob Blake is the grandson of a sainted and distinguished AME Pastor and activist, Rev. Jacob Blake, Sr., who served as Pastor of Ebenezer AME Church in Evanston, Illinois. Mr. Blake's cousin, Rev. Robert Blake, is the Pastor of Quinn Chapel AME Church in Detroit, Michigan. Four generations of Blakes have served churches and their communities across this country and now one of their family members lies in a hospital bed in critical condition because of the excessive and unwarranted use of force by the police.

Holy Rage in Kenosha, Wisconsin organized a peaceful protest. Reacting to White Rage with Black Rage led to the burning of businesses in a poor community. Unlike many in the media, both so-called progressives and conservatives, the Black church refuses to condemn the uprising in reaction to 400 years of White Rage and Terrorism—the handmaiden of White Supremacy. To condemn an uprising on the part of people who have been the victims of spiritual, social, political, and systemic White violence for generations would be an absurdity.

It is time to recognize that the uprisings of Black people in this nation—from the slave revolts, to the General Strike, to the Red Summer of 1919, to the destruction Black Wall Street, to the Civil Rights Movement, to the uprisings that followed Dr. King's assassination, to the uprisings of today—are the effect of white police terrorism, which I characterize as White Rage. Unrepentant, unjust, and strategic White Supremacy is the cause of these uprisings. Sadly, the reactionary rage of some Black people is the effect of an inner anger and anguish caused by being beaten down by individual and institutional racism for so long. In the words of the authors of *Black Rage*:

> Depression is anger turned on the self. It is instructive to pursue the relevance the of this truth to the condition of Black Americans. If you could for a moment be any Black person, anywhere, you would feel the waves of hopelessness that engulfed Black men and women when Martin Luther King was murdered. Black people understood the tide of anarchy that followed his death. (*Black Rage*, pp. 208 and 210)

Black rage has often led to uprisings or violence against ourselves, because it is an emotional rage. Black rage rises up like a quick-burning forest fire when fear and compromise with White Supremacy no longer pacifies Black people. Black rage waits for a spark, like Dr. King's murder, Freddie Gray's murder, George Floyd's murder, and Breonna Taylor's murder. Put the name of any Black person lynched, murdered, or imprisoned unjustly in the place where Martin

Luther King's name is in the previous quote. Then, you might be open to understanding that Black Rage and uprisings are the fruit of the seeds of hate sown in every Black person by an environment created and sustained by White Supremacy. Grier and Cobb make the following enlightening observation:

> It is the transformation of this quantum of grief into aggression of which we now speak. As a sapling bent low stores energy for a violent backswing, blacks bent double by oppression have stored energy which will be released in the form of rage—black rage, apocalyptic and final. (*Black Rage*, p. 210)[1]

As we prepare to move from our introduction and purpose into the body of this work, our purpose is to redirect the raging energies of anger, madness, and destructive passion into the transforming power of Holy Rage. Moses will be our guide on this heroic—and *she*-roic—journey. We will watch and reflect on how Moses' murderous rage, while still a privileged member of the oppressor's household (Exodus 2:11-15), transitioned in the wilderness when he had a life-changing encounter with the Holy One on holy ground. We will reflect on how, although a privileged member the oppressor's household, Moses' murderous rage was transformed by a wilderness experience when he encountered the Holy One on holy ground (Exodus 3:1-6). This wilderness transition was the bridge from Moses' Black Rage to the transformation (in the wilderness) that led to a liberation movement that has inspired powerless people all over the world (Exodus 3:7-10).

Within the particulars of this paradigm shift from rage to holy rage, there is teachable wisdom for Black people and people of color all over the world. This holy rage revolution is a global spiritual movement that has and will turn the world upside down as it radicalizes the 21st-century Black church. It will unleash a great global social force, a political and economic awakening, that will grow the church militant and empower the powerless.

Part I: The Rage of The Oppressed!
(A Reflection on Exodus 2:11-15)

Now it came to pass in those days, when Moses was grown, that he went out to his brethren and looked at their burdens. And he saw an Egyptian beating a Hebrew, one of his brethren. So, he looked this way and that way, and when he saw no one, he killed the Egyptian and he hid him. (Exodus 2:11-12, New King James Version)

BIGGER THOMAS'S RAGE IS THE RAGE OF THE OPPRESSED

Reading Richard Wright's book *Native Son* was my first conscious experience of the rage of the oppressed. Bigger Thomas's anger, Bigger's murderous Black rage, was the rage of the oppressed. His Rage was visceral, vibrant, violent— and yet vital. That rage, that anger, was an energy I thought I would never feel or experience. Sadly, I was wrong.

Native Son made me look at and listen (at) to my life in a new way. I was born in Chicago and raised on the Southside of the city. My mother and father lived on old South Parkway, now Martin Luther King Jr. Blvd. My father pastored a church in Evanston, Illinois and attended the University of Chicago for a graduate degree before transferring to Northwestern's Garrett Theological Seminary. My mother worked for the government until she became pregnant with me and then stayed home to raise her infant son and three other children. Both my mother and father were proud, strong, smart people. But they lived and raised their children under the shadow of White Supremacy and Black Rage.

Having read *Native Son* at an early age, I discovered through experience that there was a reason why Black children were raised to be "good boys" and "good girls." I came to realize that Bigger's destructive and fiery rage was socially "acceptable" as long as it was used for personal self-destruction or the destruction of other Black people. When their rage was taken out on a liberal White woman, this act of aggression was deemed socially unacceptable by the system of White Supremacy. White Supremacy: that idolatrous spiritual, emotional, cultural, political, and economic system of oppression that programmed rage into Black people to steal, kill, and destroy their lives, communities, institutions, and future.

BIGGER'S RAGE AWAKENS MY RAGE!

As I looked back over my young life at age 14, I discovered the seeds of the rage of the oppressed in me. I saw in myself the seeds of Bigger's rage. My sisters and I grew up never knowing that there was a difference between White and Black people. We came of age in a beloved and protective community in St. Louis, Missouri, where our father was sent to pastor in 1956. I remember the experience of being an invisible Black child on road trips with our father—and being denied service at White restaurants and restrooms. I remember seeing the rage come and go across my father's face.

Remembering the look on my Mother's face when she was disrespected by a White Supremacist department store made it clear, as I got older, that the rage of oppressed people was becoming my rage. White Supremacy had sown seeds of self-hate, division, distrust, and destruction in my life from its inception. This phenomenon is what sociologist Orlando Patterson describes as "natal alienation."

Would these seeds of White supremacy bear fruit of spiritual, physical, mental, and emotional self-destruction in another young Black Man? Would these seeds lead to a violent and deadly confrontation with a White person whose looks represent the privileges of White Supremacy? Would the seeds of White Supremacy cause me to turn against myself and descend into the pit of spiritual, mental, physical, and social death? Would this pit, this prison of rage, dug by the proponents of White Supremacy, enslave another person of color and make me a member of the living dead?

Grier and Cobb speak of how the history of White Supremacy has created an oppressed people who are living but dead, physically alive, but dead as a people, to the supposed benefits of being "free" in a so-called American democracy:

> Aggression leaps from wounds inflicted and ambitions spiked. It grows out of oppression and capricious cruelty. People bear all they can and, if required, bear even more but if they are Black in present-day America they have been asked to shoulder too much. They will be harried no more. Turning from their tormentors, they are filled with rage. (*Black Rage*, pp. 3, 4).

MOSES, A BIBLICAL EXAMPLE OF THE RAGE OF THE OPPRESSED!
(A Reflection on Exodus 2:11-15)

Long before the story of Bigger Thomas's rage, long before I was born and the seeds of White Supremacists's destructive anger and rage were sown in my life, the biblical story of Moses and how God used him to organize a people into a liberating freedom movement was well known.

Moses was raised as a child of the oppressed in the rich and powerful African nation of Egypt. This Pharaoh implemented a political policy of genocide against the people he oppressed. Fearful of being outnumbered, he demanded that enslaved midwives, Shiprah and Puah, kill every male Jewish child at birth. It was through these two fearless midwives that God orchestrated a plan to save the lives of these children. Moreover, God's plan allowed Moses's mother a portion of time to bond with her infant son. (Hebrews 11:23). When Moses grew too large to hide, God revealed to his sister and mother a plan that led to Pharaoh's daughter adopting Moses. After the adoption, Moses's mother became the servant of Pharaoh's daughter. Ironically, her servant's duty was to care for Moses.

Moses, a son of oppressed parents, had now become Pharaoh's grandson. This son of oppression was raised in the home of his oppressor to one day become a Prince in Egypt.

But as a beneficiary of this dehumanizing system of slavery, financial impoverishment, and terror, would Moses become conformed to this destructive system? Would he suffer a mental breakdown because of the tug of war between his oppressed self and his opportunity to become an oppressor of his own people? Would Moses escape the rage of the oppressed?

Moses, like African Americans, had to resolve this double consciousness. Would he ultimately decide to identify with the oppressed or the oppressor? Would Moses let this conflict of consciousness divide and defeat him, or develop his highest self? Reflecting on this inner conflict opens a door for us into a deeper understanding of the rage of the oppressed. As the story unfolds, we discover the answer to the question of what Moses did in this situation:

> Now it came to pass in those days, when Moses was grown that he went out to his brethren and looked at their burdens. And he saw an Egyptian beating a Hebrew, one of his brethren. (Exodus 2:11)

This text raises many questions. How did Moses know that the oppressed Hebrews were his brothers and sisters.? Why did the burdens of the oppressed trouble this man raised to become an oppressor? Did his birth mother tell him the stories of an oppressed people ready to be free? Did she tell him of the blessing of Abraham and the Prophecy in Genesis 15:13-16? There was something in Moses's history and experiences that activated this "reactive rage of the oppressed":

> So, he looked this way and that way, and when he saw no one, he hid the Egyptian in the sand. (Exodus 2:12)

Once the rage of the oppressed had been activated in Moses, he went out the next day and saw two enslaved men fighting. Seeking to be a mediator between his brothers who were manifesting another aspect of the rage of the oppressed, fighting each other instead of fighting for their freedom, Moses asked, "Why are you striking your companion?"

(Exodus 2:13). The response given was another example of the oppressed turning on each other instead of to each other: "Who made you a prince and a judge over us? Do you intend to kill me as you killed the Egyptian?" (Exodus 2:14a).

The response of Moses gives us great insight into one of the weaknesses of the reactive rage of the oppressed—fear:

> So, Moses feared and said, surely this thing is known! When Pharaoh heard of this matter, he sought to kill Moses. But Moses fled from the face of Pharaoh and dwelt in the land of Midian; and he sat down. (Exodus 2:14b-15)

The reactive rage of the oppressed is often an individual expression of suppressed rage. As such, this individual act of reactive rage leads to fear because, when Pharaoh orders the empire to strike back, it is the empire against an individual. (In this case, we see a situation in which an individual who stood up for oppressed people was betrayed by the people he tried to defend and protect.) Thank God, the experience of Moses is a liberating lesson for us today. The life of Moses shows us how to transition from the use of the reactive rage of the oppressed, to the embrace of a transformative rage that sparked a Promised Land movement that still inspires people today.

Part II: The Wilderness Transition:
From the Rage of the Oppressed to the Healing Release of an Overcomer!
(A Reflection on Exodus 3:1-6)

The rage of the oppressed activates what psychology calls the "flight or fight response." The rage of the oppressed either makes us flee from collectively facing the oppressor or fight other powerless and oppressed people. Until we face and overcome our fear of the oppressor and replace self-hatred with self-love, and condemnation with forgiveness, we will forever be restricted by the rage of the oppressed. Moses's encounter with the Holy One in the wilderness was a healing transition that would prepare him to embrace the transforming power of Holy Rage.   Healing and transformation *can* take place in the wilderness.

The wilderness experience of Moses is similar to that of generations of African American men and women who had a life-changing experience in the wilderness of White Supremacy. Richard Allen, the founder of the African Methodist Episcopal Church, expressed his wilderness transition experience in 1777 this way: "My dungeon shook, and my chains flew off." From the eighteenth century to the twenty-first century, many Black people found that the rage of the oppressed led us into the wilderness.   We discovered that our wilderness experience could be a place of empowerment, just as it was for Denmark Vesey and Harriet Tubman. Conversely, the wilderness transition can also be a place of narcissism, selfishness, addiction, spiritual imprisonment, and spiritual death. This transition experience can *develop* us or *destroy* us; it can either *conform* us or *transform* us.

Moses went from being a prince in the palace of power to being a shepherd in the wilderness. On the day he led the sheep to the backside of the wilderness, he came to Horeb, "the mountain of God." It was there that he encountered a messenger of God and was about to turn away from his divine encounter when God called him by name. Moses responded, "Here I am." God's next directions are key for Moses's wilderness transition: "Do not draw near this place. Take your sandals off your feet, for the place where you are standing is holy ground." (Exodus 3:1-5).

Moses was challenged to change by his extraordinary encounter with God's presence and power in the wilderness. It was in the wilderness that Moses met the God of the oppressed who gave him the beginning of a story that would become a new and timeless liberation narrative for oppressed people everywhere: "I am the God of your father—the God of Abraham, Isaac and the God of Jacob. And Moses hid his face, for he was afraid to look upon God." (Exodus 3:6).

The Moses who was afraid of Pharaoh's oppressive rage, fled to the wilderness. But this same fleeing Moses became encouraged, equipped, and empowered to discover a transformational shift from rage that hurts and kills people to a Holy Rage that heals and activates people to live the abundant life.

God moves to create something holy in the wilderness.

The street where George Floyd was killed was a wilderness of racist policing that became Holy Ground. Peaceful protestors experienced and expressed twenty-one consecutive days of Holy Rage.

The street where Breonna Taylor was shot in her own residence was a wilderness of White Supremacist terrorism that became Holy Ground, as peaceful protestors, policymakers, entertainers, the people of Louisville, and an entire generation expressed Holy Rage over the unjust handling of her case.

The street where Jacob Blake was needlessly shot in the back seven times in front of his three children was a wilderness of White rage that became Holy Ground as protestors took to the streets to advocate for systemic change.

Moses would soon discover that Holy Rage heals people, helps people help other people, and builds a movement that cannot be stopped.

May the 21st-century Black Lives Matter movement let the wilderness moments in our current season activate the Holy Rage that moves from protests, to policies, to power for all powerless people!

Part III: The Transforming Power of Holy Rage

Brings the People Out of Oppression

(A Reflection on Exodus 3:7-10)

The process that Moses and his people went through followed a progression: from the destructive and self-destructive rage of the oppressed, to the wilderness transition test, to the transforming power of Holy Rage. This is the way/process that brought them to the Promise Land—the land of freedom, justice, and equality.

Holy Rage is the process that Moses went through, and I believe that Holy Rage is the process that Black people, the Black Church, and the Black Lives Matter movement are being called to embrace to achieve radical results.

In Exodus 3:7-8 we are told: "And the Lord said: I have surely seen the oppression of My people who are in Egypt, and have heard their cry because of their taskmasters, for I know their sorrows. So, I have come down to deliver them out of the hand of the Egyptians, and to bring them up from the land to a good and large land flowing with milk and honey...." (Exodus 3:7-8a).

God is equipping Moses and us with some of the principles and practices of Holy Rage. The God of the oppressed is not satisfied with a big march through the wilderness. The God of the oppressed seeks a radical reconstruction that will form what Dr. King called "the Beloved Community." The principles and practices of radical reconstruction listed below are taken from Exodus 3:

1.   The oppression of the people must be seen.
2.   The voices of oppressed people must be heard.
3.   The sorrows and sufferings of oppressed people must be made known.
4.   Oppressed people must be delivered from the oppressor's system and brought into a new system of peace, power, and prosperity (reparations).

In Exodus 3:9-10, the God of the oppressed "ups the ante" and moves from the mission of Holy Rage to a liberation movement fueled by holy, healing, helping, and hopeful rage. The God of the oppressed lays the foundation for this movement in these verses:

1.   The time for deliverance and liberation is now.

2. Now the cries of the oppressed have been heard by the God of the oppressed.
3. Now God has seen the oppression inflicted on the oppressed by the oppressor.
4. Now God will send you, God will send us, to become empowering partners with the people to rise up together and walk out of oppression.
5. This is the power of Holy Rage.

CONCLUSION

Holy Rage is both an individual and a collective process of healing, help, and hope. We must continue to make sure that we are acting out of Holy Rage, and not the rage of oppressed people. We must remember that oppressed people have been negatively affected by the oppressor's system and strategies. The system of White rage and terror has trained Black people to take anger and Black Rage out on ourselves. We must remember that Holy Rage is an evolving process that makes individuals and movements better and not bitter.

After 40 years of serving oppressed people through their wilderness transitions, Moses had grown tired of their complaining and their self-destructive behavior. Sadly, Moses missed out on bringing his people into the promised land because he reverted to the reactive anger of the oppressed (Numbers 20:1-12). May we daily grow in the transforming power and peace of Holy Rage. May our rage become Holy Rage. May our anger become Holy Anger.

Finally, Myisha Cherry, Assistant Professor of Philosophy at the University of California, Riverside has written an article, "Anger Can Build A Better World," from which I would like to quote in closing:

> For those skeptical of anger's power and usefulness, it is important to note that anger at racial injustice does not cause poverty, inadequate housing, a police state, or dehumanizing practices. Anger responds to these atrocities. Many refuse to believe this, because to them, anger is always irrational, undemocratic, and synonymous with violence.

So, they fear it. However, anger is a legitimate response to wrongdoing. It challenges us to achieve political equality. And we can have anger without violence, and violence without anger. (*The Atlantic* online, August 25, 2020)

Endnote

1   William H. Grier & Price Cobbs, *Black Rage* (New York: 1968).

Bishop Frank Reid, III, M.Div., D.Min.

The Rev. Dr. Frank Madison Reid, III is an internationally known leader, a pre-eminent power speaker, a cutting-edge thinker, as well as a motivator who encourages and equips people to rebuild their broken lives and communities.

A native of Chicago, he is the 5th generation of his family to become a minister in the African Methodist Episcopal Church, and the second to become a Bishop. The Right Reverend Frank Madison Reid, III holds the distinction of being the 138th Elected and Consecrated Bishop of the AME Church and the Presiding Prelate of the Third Episcopal District.

Dr. Reid is a graduate of Yale University and the Harvard Divinity School. Dr. Reid became a part of the first class of Samuel DeWitt Proctor Doctoral Fellows at United Theological Seminary, graduating with a Doctor of Ministry Degree in 1990.

Bishop Reid is a servant leader whose ministry of over 30 years has been on the cutting edge of positive change. Under Dr. Reid's leadership, "The Bethel Outreach of Love" Broadcast was the first African Methodist Episcopal Church to have an international TV broadcast. For over 10 years, the broadcast was on Black Entertainment Television (BET). The broadcast has also been on the Armed Forces Network and is now seen internationally in Europe on Revelation TV and UC-TV, nationally on The Word Network, and regionally on WB-TV. Among his writings are his latest books:

- *The Nehemiah Plan: Preparing the Church to Rebuild Broken Lives* (Treasure House, 1993; ISBN:1560437669).
- *Restoring the House of God* (Destiny Image Publishers, 2005; ISBN: 1560433493)

CHAPTER EIGHT

In Defense of Black Rage

Lukata A. Mjumbe, M.Div., Th.M.

White Man: "You seem quite hostile."

Black Man: "I got a right to be hostile, man, my people been persecuted."

—Public Enemy, *Prophets of Rage* (1988)

In the face of police murder, state violence, mass incarceration, structural poverty and other oppressively enduring realities of institutional racism and white supremacy, it is easy to argue that the oppressed have "a right to be hostile." In this modern moment the hostility of the crowd has manifested in the form of a sustained, protest movements that have resulted in hundreds of thousands and even millions of dollars of property damage, looting of businesses, shooting of police officers and even the loss of life. The powerful protests of the very present moment have eclipsed any other in terms of size, scope and sustained mobilization. At the conflux of crisis, faith leaders, theologians and advocates motivated by a call to justice must consider not only what might be rationalized as *"a right"* but what can also be morally and politically justified *as "being righteous."*

As much as the rage of protest may be cast by activists as an ethically justifiable right, it is often religiously characterized as a pathological and morally repugnant wrong. Contemporary Church leaders have often been called upon to deliver reactionary condemnations of "Black rage" and to join the off-tune chorus of political and police powers urging the masses to "nonviolence and peace" above all else (in the tradition of Pax Romana – "the peace of Rome"). Proof texted precepts calling upon communities to be "slow to anger" (Proverbs 15:18, 16:32, 19:11) and reminders that "vengeance belongs to the Lord" (Deuteronomy 32:35, Romans 12:19) permeate the prose of those who are presented as the most pious in our Christian pulpits. While it is clear that the people of God are called to be guarded by a peace that "surpasses all understanding" (Philippians 4:7), in some quarters of the Christian church, rage in and of itself is too quickly and uncritically condemned as inexplicable sin.

It is my contention that the true "peace of Christ" that so frequently surpasses all understanding is a "shalom" that emphasizes being in right relationship with God, community and self. The content of the most reactionary religious reproofs of rage are often divorced from the urgent need to critique and repair the broken relationships which create the context for protests themselves. In the gospel of Matthew, the Christ reminds his disciples that when they do not stand with the poor, the imprisoned and the estranged that they do not stand with Him (Matthew 25:40-45). In the first century communities of "the Way," both Christ and his disciples confronted many types of crowds that were filled with emotion and even rage.

Without question, the lawlessness of many of the crowds in the Bible are violently reactionary, destructive and hostile to the will and Way of God. In other circumstances, however, the tenor and tone of the crowds seems confused and require a more thoughtful consideration (John 6:1-15, John 7:25-36). In still others fickle, fair-weather crowds shift trajectories by the time they get from Palm Sunday to Good Friday. In the face of the rage of a growing twenty first century protest movement, the Church must be mindful that our first century Christ frequently felt and expressed compassion over quick condemnation of crowds in crisis (Matthew 9:36, Mark 6:34). There are moments when the threat of the crowd seemingly provided political cover and protection for the Christ.

Students of the New Testament will recall that the opponents of Jesus, Peter, the Apostle Paul and other followers of the Way frequently feared that "the people might riot." In fact, the fear of "Black rage" violence was often put forward as the pretext for placing a pause on the plans to execute arrests. The fear of the riot ultimately delayed the crucifixion of Christ. One could argue that the unspoken, violent voice of the potential Black rage rioter helped create the space for Jesus to advance and fulfill his earthly ministry (Matthew 26:3-5, Mark 14:1-2). In fact, the Hebrew Bible offers earlier accounts of how raucous, protest uprisings inspired, directed and protected by God served as critical components of God's plans for the liberation of the people of God. We can and must principally ask, "How did God use the looting of the Egyptians before the Exodus and even the destruction of property in Jericho for the ultimate uplift of the people of God?" (Exodus 12:31-36, Joshua 6:1-27).

How can the modern protestor interpret the words of the God of Israel spoken to the young prophet, "See, today I appoint you over nations and over kingdoms, to pluck up and to pull down, to destroy and to overthrow, to build and to plant" (Jeremiah 1:10) in this day? One could argue that Black rage is often the voice that most clearly articulates the calls for justice to roll down like water and righteous like an ever-flowing stream (Amos 5:24). It is important to note that those who know the word of the Bible understand that there are many "words" found within scripture that can be and have often been manipulated in pursuit of wholly unholy political agendas. Yet, I am convinced that the most important struggle is and has been rooted and wrapped up in answering the question, "What is God calling us to see and do today?"

A Black Rage Tradition

There is indeed an authentic liberation tradition within Christianity that leads one to seek to reconcile revolutionary political commitments with the authority of holy scripture, and the Way of Jesus Christ. A full consideration of Black rage through a political-theological lens supports the connection of the modern political phenomenon of urban unrest, uprising and insurrection to an ancient and anointed process that has contributed to the struggle for liberation of oppressed people for thousands of years. Black rage is undeniably biblical, when both "blackness" and "rage" are properly understood. Indeed, Black Rage and its demand for justice for Black people can be and should be understood as being connected to the liberation of all people. Before any modern day Black Lives Matter movement argued that "when Black lives matter all lives will matter," James Cone, the father of Black liberation theology offered a theological description of blackness that transcends both skin color and racialized phenotypes. Cone argued "being **black** means that your heart, your soul, your mind, and your body are where the dispossessed are.»[1]

I am convinced that when the Church separates itself from the legacy of liberation that illuminates the unfolding of God's plan for God's people, it becomes isolated from the will and Way of God. The movement for Black lives has centered the pain and protest of the Black community. Tragically, the Black Church and many of its leaders fail to fully embrace the very people that our Lord may be shaping, preparing and anointing to proclaim Good News to the poor, release to the captive, sight for the blind and liberation for all who are oppressed (Isaiah 61:1, Luke 4:18). The fear of violent riots is not unique to a Black Lives Matter mobilization as it is clear that violence can be birthed out of both legitimate and illegitimate contexts. Context matters. There were and are times when anointed blessings can be birthed out of rage. This must be understood when Black rage of protest movements unasham-edly articulates its demands by any and all means necessary. Even the threat and the actualization of what is politically and simplistically described as "rioting," "looting," "destruction of property" and "mob violence" cannot be separated from the morally justified, authentic calls for justice. As disturbing as certain insurrectionary activities may appear and certainly can be in the modern context, believers should remember and respect our history. We have been here before.

Political protest rage of oppressed people in general and "Black rage" in particular should be historically and contem-porarily understood as a visceral, individual, often collective and yes, even a morally justifiable response to oppression that prioritizes the perceived interests of the oppressed over that of the oppressor. When it comes to Black rage protest, I believe that God's hand can be and is most likely in all of it whether that be in the form of guiding and directing, protect-ing and correcting. Black rage protests may not always be per-fect in the eyes of the Church. Yet the Church, at its best, un-derstands that Black rage is often a starting point of a critically important process of political and spiritual maturation that is connected to our own individual and collective histories and identities as believers in a radical liberator called Jesus the Christ. Black rage for many of us is where we begin. The rage of the oppressed is not now and has never been especially concerned about appearances, permission or the approval of those it deems responsible for its pain.

Baptized in Black Rage

Almost two decades before I was ordained as a pastor I was "born again" by being baptized in the fire of protest rebellion and rage. In the spring of 1992, hundreds of thousands of mostly Black and Brown people across the country stormed the streets following the Rodney King verdict which found four LAPD police officers not guilty of the brutal beating of a Black motorist that was captured on videotape. I marched. I protested. I raged. I was called a rioter, looter and thug "not in the tradition of Dr. King." As a younger man, "No justice! No peace!" became my daily mantra set to the beat of the "prophets of rage" that emerged within the hip hop culture of the 1980's and early 1990's. Primed through the prism of rap music, "Black rage" hip-hop represented the soundtrack of my daily life in my early 20's. I embraced the spirit of rebellion of the times fully digesting the controversial catechism of the most highly politicized rappers like Ice Cube, Tupac Shakur and Public Enemy whose "Prophets of Rage" track on the "It Takes a Nation of Millions to Hold Us Back" album boomed from stereo systems as the "CNN of the Black community."

During the 1992 presidential campaign, Sister Souljah, the one female member of the Public Enemy rap group publicly imagined the thinking of some of those who participated in the urban uprisings in Los Angeles. Speaking at a gathering of the Jesse Jackson's Rainbow Coalition, Souljah said, "I mean, if black people kill black people every day, why not have a week and kill white people?....So if you're a gang member and you would normally be killing somebody, why not kill a white person?....Unfortunately for white people, they think it's all right for our children to die, for our men to be in prison, and not theirs."[2]

Sister Souljah's message was as raw and uncut as an eighth century Hebrew prophet and the youth of my generation understood what she meant. She was clear about what she (and we) needed to be against. She was against racism and white supremacy. She was against the violence that was killing Black people every day whether that be from the outside or the inside. The sound of her passion, emotion and rage filled every sentence. As she said in her song "The Hate That Hate Produced," "Souljah was not born to make white people feel comfortable," and she did not. Sister Souljah was speaking the confrontational protest language of a new generation. At the time, we understood hip-hop as a "movement" that had the ability to "move the crowd." Even if it did not sound "right" to others, we felt that Black people had the right to be angry at the injustices that we saw all around us every day. Souljah was us. Souljah was me.

Rooted in our rage, young Black activists were incensed at how the words of Sister Souljah were later manipulated and attacked by then presidential candidate and Arkansas Governor Bill Clinton. Clinton was seen as a down home, "Black friendly" presidential candidate who had memorized the words of all three verses of the Black national anthem, "Lift Every Voice and Sing."[3] Appearing before the Rainbow Coalition soon after clinching the 1992 democratic nomination for president, Clinton condemned Sister Souljah saying, "If you took the words 'white' and 'black' and reversed them, you might think David Duke was giving that speech."[4] Clinton's speech, delivered before an audience that was supposedly populated by responsible Black folk was clearly heard as a dog-whistle to the conservative right wing of the Democratic party signaling where he would stand as President on the consistently racialized "law and order" litmus test. The speech later came to be known for Bill Clinton (and other politicians in the future who sought to condemn so-called "extremist factions" within the Black community) as his "Sister Souljah moment." Clinton's more recent attacks on the militant, Black liberation legacy of Stokely Carmichael (Kwame Ture) at the 2020 funeral of civil rights leader Congressman John Lewis, served as a reminder that not much has changed to this day.[5]

In 1992, I was ready to burn my Rainbow Coalition Membership card when I heard people clap for Clinton's southern twanged scolding. (I did not actually have a membership card but that's beside the point). Young activists were angry at Reverend Jesse Jackson for not being angry enough. Reverend Jackson and other supporters who applauded Clinton's rebuke seemingly embraced a false equivalency that sought to equate the resistance of the oppressed with the violent repression of the oppressor. In my view, Clinton's alleged affinity for barbeque and Black anthems did not qualify Clinton to be judged as our "first Black President" as some had rhetorically described him. [6]

In fact, dark sunglasses and playing the saxophone on "The Arsenio Hall Show" did not keep Clinton from losing my vote in 1992, the first time that I was eligible to vote in a presidential election. I distinctly remember defiantly writing in the name of the hip-hop DJ, "Eric B." of the New York rap group "Eric B. and Rakim" for the office of U.S. President on my ballot. I may have spoiled my ballot, but if nothing else, my write-in choice emotionally spoke to what I as a 21-year old voter was clearly against even if I was not yet entirely clear about what I was for. My Black rage was the starting point of the process of development that was beginning to take shape in what were perhaps predictably important ways.

Black Rage and the Three-Fold Path

Black rage is connected to an evolving process of growth and maturity. In 1967, a revolutionary Black nationalist organization known as the House of Umoja conceptualized a process of consciousness development for those within the Black liberation movement known as the "Three-Fold Path." The Three-Fold Path makes use of the traditional red, black and green Black liberation color scheme and identifies each color with a particular stage of development in an individuals' political consciousness. The process begins with what is called the "Red Stage" which is characterized as "Inspiration By Emotion." It teaches that most Black people predictably enter into the process of liberation consciousness development at the Red Stage where they are frequently focused upon what they are against. It is my contention that the Red Stage can be considered the "Black Rage Stage."

In a published description of the Three-Fold Path first published by the House of Umoja in the 1960's and revised by the Malcolm X Grassroots Movement in 2014, people at this stage are described as being "ready to shed and take blood to ensure that the life forces our ancestors have bestowed in us will continue. This is usually the stage of a new recruit or neo-phyte who has recently learned in a rapid way about the in-justices that Afrikan people have experienced. It is a very significant stage, but also a dangerous one. The person is ready to act, to do something about the conditions under which we live."[7] In real time, the manifestations of the Black rage of the Red Stage may involve what is simplistically labeled as "rioting," "looting" and "mob violence." Yet, this first stage can also be understood as being connected to an evolving developmental process through which the person(s) can potentially come to better understand the protracted nature of the struggle for liberation that has been seen around the world and throughout history.

Dr. Walter Rodney, a prominent Guyanese freedom fighter, historian and radical intellectual effectively analyzed and critiqued the fallacy of rebukes of Black rage by the powers that be and those under their influence. Rodney warned, "We were told that violence in itself is evil, and that, whatever the cause it is unjustified morally." Yet Rodney challenged, "By what standard of morality can the violence used by a slave to break his chains be considered the same as the violence of a slave master? By what standard can we equate the violence of blacks who have been oppressed, suppressed, depressed and repressed for four centuries with the violence of white fascists? Violence aimed at the recovery of human dignity and at equality cannot be judged by the same yardstick as violence aimed at maintenance of discrimination and oppression."[8] Those that are guided by Black rage may not be able to clearly articulate what they are fighting for, yet, they often are equipped to offer expert opinion on that which they are fighting against. The Church should listen intently.

In its more moderate rebukes of Black rage, Church leaders have sought to explain away uprising and insurrection by incessantly invoking the words of the Reverend Dr. Martin Luther King, Jr. who observed, "the riot is the voice of the unheard."[9] Yet this is ultimately an inadequate explanation for the full utility of Black rage and its function within the process of the development of individual and collective consciousness and commitment to Black liberation. Black rage must be considered as an essential dimension of the baseline vocabulary and syntax of an oppressed people that demands that it be heard, seen and felt by those individuals and institutions that they deem responsible for their collective suffering. Early in the process, the so-called "rioter" or "looter" may have yet to learn how to sustain the victories of the continuing struggle which are characteristic of the "Green Stage" - "Enlightenment By Reason" and the final "Black Stage" - "Sustenance By Knowledge." However, even though the Green and Black stages are more advanced within the larger framework of the process they are no more important than the Red Stage itself. In fact, both the enlightenment and knowledge of the Green and Black stages emerge from Black rage. Each stage in the process is important and balance is necessary as a person committed to liberation grows and matures over time.

When writing about the "violence" of the oppressed in the often quoted, classic liberation text "The Wretched of the Earth," Black liberation psychiatrist Franz Fanon can be understood to be referring to the utility of the process of Black rage which he describes it as "a cleansing force." Fanon argues that violence functionally realizes that demolition must often precede construction of a new people and new reality.[10] Black rage must be considered as an important step in a pathway that can lead to the liberation of both Black bodies and minds. Yet, Black rage misrepresented out of historical context is easily maligned, mischaracterized, misunderstood and is strategically disconnected from the broader individual and collective process of growth and development of oppressed people. This becomes very clear when one considers the various depictions of "so-called" Black rage contemporarily over the course of hundreds of years. There were clear examples of these depictions in the years immediately following my Black rage baptism.

Black Rage as Insanity

In 1994 criminal defense lawyers argued "Black rage" as a "temporary insanity" defense for Colin Ferguson, a 35-year Jamaican immigrant accused of the December, 1993 killing of six people and the shooting of 19 others on a New York subway train. Ferguson was charged and later convicted of walking up and down a subway train murdering white and Asian commuters with a nine-millimeter handgun. At the top of a hand scribbled note found within Ferguson's pocket after his arrest were the words *"Reasons for This"* and below were the words *"racism by Caucasians and Uncle Tom negroes."* This hand scribbled manifesto of sorts was offered by Ferguson's attorneys as the reason for the crime.[11]

Ferguson's lawyers grounded their supposedly innovative legal defense strategy on the research of a 1968 book titled "Black Rage" written by two Black psychiatrists William H. Grier and Price Cobbs that was published soon after the assassination of Dr. Martin Luther King, Jr. The book examined the mental health of Black people and the deeply embedded psychic stresses that are caused by racial discrimination. Grier and Cobbs had argued that the reality of the pervasive stench of racial hatred in the United States was a source of much of the racial conflict and predicted that racial explosion might erupt in the future.[12]Twenty-five years later, Ferguson's lawyers argued that their Black client had been driven insane by his experience with the reality of racism in America. They posited that Ferguson could not be held criminally liable for his actions. They passionately and publicly argued that the killings should be categorized in the same way as those offenses negated for criminal liability under the "battered woman defense," "post-traumatic stress disorder," and "child abuse syndrome."[13]

Without question there are Black men and women in need of serious psychiatric help as a result of the reality of racism. However, the general association of Black rage with an insanity defense, temporary or otherwise is deeply problematic and improperly frames the authentic and reasonable manifestations of Black rage. Ultimately, the legal defense of Black rage as temporary insanity did not work in the court room for Ferguson as it became clear that Ferguson internal mental health contradictions began to eclipse his attorneys efforts for serious consideration of external causality. His case unraveled within a few months after beginning and he would later fire his attorneys, abandon the temporary insanity defense and chose to represent himself as the victim of government conspiracy. [14]

In a moment that was painful to watch, one victim after the next identified Ferguson as the person who shot them as Ferguson referred to himself in the third person, "Are you this is the person who shot you?" Ferguson himself called a witness who stood before the court house claiming that a nefarious, mystery "Oriental man" had secretly implanted a microchip into the back of Ferguson's head while he slept on the train, "lasered him out" by a remote control device and then "commanded him to go up and down the aisle shooting people."[15] The controversial "Black rage" trial would be ultimately be overshadowed by the intersection of race and celebrity in the O.J. Simpson "trial of the century" that same year. While Simpson was found not guilty in 1995, Ferguson was ultimately convicted on six counts of murder, nineteen counts of attempted murder and was sentenced to 315 years and eight months to life in prison.[16]

Historically, the forces of white supremacy have concocted political and pseudo-scientific psychiatric arguments to simultaneously explain and scandalize those who dared to rage against the machine of racism. In 1851, a Louisiana doctor named Samuel Cartwright argued that Black slaves who decided to seek to escape from slavery suffered from a psychiatric condition he called "drapetomania." The term derives from the Greek δραπέτης (*drapetes*, "a runaway [slave]") and μανία (*mania*, "madness, frenzy").[17] As late as 1914, the third edition of Thomas Lathrop Stedman's *Practical Medical Dictionary* included an entry for *drapetomania*, defined as "vagabondage, dromania; an uncontrollable or insane impulse to wander."[18] Interestingly for our theological considerations of the functionality of Black rage, Cartwright sought to religiously rationalize and root his ridiculously racist claims in the Bible advising that when the negro was properly and benevolently maintained as a "submissive knee-bender" then he would be maintained in a state where he is "spell-bound and cannot run away."[19]

To understand Black rage properly we must understand that the urge to escape and resist racist oppression is not a sickness or a psychological disorder that needs to be cured. Black rage at its best is neither temporary or insane. Black rage is the first step of a process toward imagining and realizing Black liberation. Black religion and the influence of the Black Church must never be used to leave a community "spell-bound" and immobilized in its march toward freedom. The cancer of racism and white supremacy must be irradicated in order for the human family itself to be made whole. The legacy of the specious and pathological arguments of slave owners which claim that the leaders of slave rebellions like Nat Turner, Denmark Vesey or Gabriel Prosser had to be insane in order to want to rise up against their enslavers must be rejected historically and even contemporarily. What pathology would make them not want to be free? Without question Black rage can be understood as a sign of a person who is maladjusted to racism and discrimination.

In 1963, Dr. Martin Luther King, Jr. observed, "Modern psychology has a word that is probably used more than any ... It is the word "maladjusted." This word is the ringing cry to modern child psychology. Certainly, we all want to avoid the maladjusted life. In order to have real adjustment within our personalities, we all want the well-adjusted life." King contrasted the language of the psychological diagnosis with a prescription for an oppressed people, "...there are certain things in our nation and in the world (about) which I am proud to be maladjusted..... Through such maladjustment, I believe that we will be able to emerge from the bleak and desolate midnight of man's inhumanity to man into the bright and glittering daybreak of freedom and justice."[20] Admittedly, there is an irony in citing Rev. Dr. Martin Luther King, Jr. a champion of 'non-violent resistance" in defense of Black rage. Yet the consideration of the tradition of what Dr. Cornel West has called a much more authentically "radical King" leads us to remember King's counsel about violence in the last year of his life. In September 1967, speaking before the American Psychological Association King said, ""Urban riots must now be recognized as durable social phenomena. They may be deplored, but they are there and should be understood. Urban riots are a special form of violence."[21]

The Transformation of Black Rage

The words that King spoke at the end of his life about understanding the meaning of the riot resonated deeply for me at the beginning of my political and theological rebirth in Black rage. They have remained with me as I have grown from a youthful activist to middle-aged activist Pastor. My process was primed with Public Enemy and the "Prophets of Rage," that taught me:

> They tell lies in the books
> That you're readin
> It's knowledge of yourself
> That you're needin'
> Like Vesey or Prosser
> We have a reason why
> To debate the hate
> That's why we're born to die

It was years before I realized that the "Vesey" in the song lyric referred to the leader of what could have been one of the largest slave rebellions in the U.S. In examining the planning of the Denmark Vesey slave rebellion (Vesey was historically labeled "insane" and is contemporarily labeled by some as a"terrorist,"[22]), I came to realize that there needed to be more than a plan for a night of purging where thousands of enslaved people would kill every white man in Charleston in a night of rage. Vesey, like Nat Turner, Gabriel Prosser and so many others that would come before him and after him understood that minds had to be opened, hearts needed to be touched and communities needed to be organized for a protracted struggle.

Scholars have noted that the South Carolina slave rebellion leader led a late-night Bible study and prayer meeting in the swamps under the cover of darkness helping enslaved people from area plantations to understand that God was on their side. The secreted swamp service gatherings included a wide variety of co-conspirators undoubtedly including folks of different Christian denominations (Vesey had been both Presbyterian and AME) and others such as one "conjure man" named "Gullah Jack" who was a practitioner of African traditional religion.

Freedom struggle must be inclusive and often is not televised. Each swamp gathering included an offering where those gathered made contributions in the form of weapons and other resources. Freedom struggle requires investment and sacrifice. Some scholars have suggested that though 34 co-conspirators were arrested and executed alongside Vesey in Charleston ahead of the planned uprising on June 16, 1822 as many as 9,000 people who had been organized faded back into society to await the next opportunity to mobilize. Sustained freedom struggle requires organization and we are still learning that today.

The Emmanuel A.M.E. church that Vesey had built and co-founded in Charleston was burned to the ground soon after the rebellion was thwarted. It would be almost another 50 years before South Carolina was emancipated. In 2015, 193 years later on the anniversary of the planned Vesey uprising a young white supremacist entered into an evening Bible study at Emmanuel AME in Charleston and murdered nine people including the Pastor. I remember reconnecting with and balancing my rage the evening of the shooting and the following Father's Day Sunday when I was invited to preach at a historic Black church in Princeton, NJ that I would later be called to Pastor. We were all reminded again that the struggle continues. We continue to move back and forth along that threefold path. As our Black national anthem intones, "God of our weary years, God of our silent tears. Thou who has brought us thus far on the way. Thou who has by they might, led us into the light. Keep us forever in the path we pray."

Black rage changed me. Black rage cleansed me of any notions of easy acceptance of answers that did not answer and solutions that did not solve. Black rage emotionally inspired me in my "Red Stage" to 'debate the hate' and resist any effort to rationalize racism or the ravages of white supremacy. As I transitioned from red stage to the enlightened reasoning of the green stage, I resolved to more fully unpack the words echoed by both President Kennedy and Dr. King that warned that those that make peaceful revolution impossible will make violent revolution inevitable. The more enraged I became about the things that I identified with my pain, the more committed I became to that which promised change.

As I considered the seemingly impossible possibilities of both violent and non-violent revolution, I realized that even if Black people decided to kill white people for a week as Sister Souljah had imagined we still would not be free. Black rage freed me up to commit more deeply to the full range of freedom possibilities and to transition to the enlightenment of the Green Stage and the sustenance of the Black Stage where my study of the history and theology of violent rebellions prompted me to go deeper than the mass mobilization emotion that inspired me to simply take to the streets in protest. Black rage ultimately helped me to clearly know that I would never be the kind of "Uncle Tom Preacher" that applauded rebukes of prophets of rage, Stokely Carmichael's or Black Lives Matter protests. Inspired in my rage, enlightened by a call to a biblical justice/righteousness (dikaiosune) and sustained by a power that was greater than any that could be encapsulated in a clenched fist, I was led to explore a theology of liberation that integrated a commitment to what I was fighting against with a devotion to what I was fighting for.

As much as Black rage and its expressions are critiqued from political platforms and pious pulpits, the function of Black rage as a phenomenon has inspired and encouraged both mass uprising and unprecedented collective consciousness and discussion of the reality of oppression in this country and the world. The threat of the next riot creates the space for the Church to truly live into its call to do justice, love kindness and walk humbly with our God (Micah 6:8). The crowd needs the compassionate understanding of the Church. The Church needs the movement of the crowd.

Endnotes

1   *James H. Cone, Black Theology and Black Power, p. 151; cited in Hans Schwarz, Theology in a Global Context: The Last Two Hundred Years* (Grand Rapids, Michigan: Wm. B. Eerdmans Publishing Company, 2005), p. 473.

2   David Mills, "Sister Souljah's Call To Arms," Washington Post, May 13, 1992, https://www.washingtonpost.com/archive/lifestyle/1992/05/13/sister-souljahs-call-to-arms/643d5634-e622-43ad-ba7d-811f8f5bfe5d/

3   Gayle Pollard-Terry, "The 'First Black President," in Person," *Los Angeles Times*, June 25, 2004, https://www.latimes.com/archives/la-xpm-2004-jun-25-et-pollard25-story.html

4   Thomas B. Edsall, "Clinton Stuns Rainbow Coalition," *Washington Post*, June 14, 1992, https://www.washingtonpost.com/archive/politics/1992/06/14/clinton-stuns-rainbow-coalition/02d7564f-5472-4081-b6b2-2fe5b849fa60/

5   Peniel B. Joseph, "What Bill Clinton Got Exactly Wrong About Stokely Carmichael's Role in the Black Freedom Struggle," *Washington Post*, August 4, 2020, https://www.washingtonpost.com/nation/2020/08/04/bill-clintons-misunderstanding-what-stokely-carmichael-brings-black-americas-long-struggle-freedom/

6   Pollard-Terry,   https://www.latimes.com/archives/la-xpm-2004-jun-25-et-pollard25-story.html

7   "Three-Fold Path" (pamphlet provided by the author; pamphlet updated by the "Malcolm X Grassroots Movement," December 31, 2014.

8   Walter Rodney, *Groundings With My Brothers*, p. 22; published by Frontline Distribution International, first edition (2001); originally published in 1969 (New York, London).

9   Martin Luther King, Jr., "The Other America," speech delivered

at Grosse Pointe High School, March 14, 1968; accessed, October 15, 2020, https://www.gphistorical.org/mlk/mlkspeech/

10   Franz Fanon, *The Wretched of the Earth*, p. 94; published by Grove Press, New York; originally published by Présence Africaine, Paris, 1963.

11   New York Times News Service, "N.Y. Train Killings Called Bias Crime," *Chicago Tribune*, December 9, 1993, https://www.chicagotribune.com/news/ct-xpm-1993-12-09-9312090162-story.html

12   Richard Pyatt, Interview transcript with Dr. William H. Grier, co-author of *Black Rage* with Dr. Price M. Cobbs, Published by NYPR Archive Collections, January 21, 1969, https://www.wnyc.org/story/interview-with-william-h-grier-author-of-black-rage/

13   Judd F. Sneirson, "Black Rage and the Criminal Law: A Principled Approach to a Polarized Debate," *University of Pennsylvania Law Review*, Vol. 143, Issue 6, June 1995. https://www.questia.com/library/93357/black-rage

14   Ron Kuby & William Kunstler, "An Insanity Defense in L.I.R.R. Massacre," *New York Times*, April 28, 1994, *https://www.nytimes.com/1994/04/28/opinion/l-an-insanity-defense-in-lirr-massacre-920509.html.*

15   John McQuinston, "Murder Trial in LIRR Case Goes to the Jury for Deliberation," *New York Times*, February 17, 1995, https://www.nytimes.com/1995/02/17/nyregion/murder-trial-in-lirr-case-goes-to-the-jury-for-deliberation.html

16   People v. Ferguson (1998), 248 App.Div.2d 725, 670 N.Y.S.2d 327.

17   Samuel A. Cartwright, "Diseases and Peculiarities of the Negro Race," *Debows Review* (1851).

18   *Stedman, Thomas Lathrop, Practical Medical Dictionary, 3rd ed. (New York: W. Wood, 1914), p. 268,* https://babel.hathitrust.org/cgi/pt?id=ien.35558005332206&view=1up&seq=286&q1=drapetomania

19   Cartwright, XI.

20   Martin Luther King, Jr., "I Am Proud to Be Maladjusted," speech delivered at Western Michigan University, December

18, 1963, http://ronniestanglermd.com/martin-luther-king-i-am-proud-to-be-maladjusted/

21   Hanif Abdurraqib, "By the End of His Life Martin Luther King Recognized the Validity of Violence," *Timeline*, June 16, 2017, https://timeline.com/by-the-end-of-his-life-martin-luther-king-realized-the-validity-of-violence-4de177a8c87b

22   Jack Hunter, "Denmark Vesey Was a Terrorist, *Charleston City Newspaper*, February 10, 2010, https://www.charlestoncitypaper.com/story/denmark-vesey-was-a-terrorist?oid=1756179

Lukata A. Mjumbe, M.Div., Th.M.

The Reverend Lukata Mjumbe is a veteran grassroots community organizer, public policy advocate, interfaith leader and dynamic community pastor. He describes his calling as one in which he is, "called to bring together people of diverse traditions who are deeply committed to freedom and justice".

On March 10th 1836, Black members of the First Presbyterian Church of Princeton (now, Nassau Presbyterian Church) in Princeton, New Jersey were "dismissed to form The First Presbyterian Church of Colour of Princeton." The church became the spiritual home of those enslaved and formally enslaved. Located in what is the historic center of the Black Princeton community, the church became what is now the Witherspoon Street Presbyterian Church where the Reverend Lukata Mjumbe serves as Pastor.

It is from this church platform that Mjumbe teaches, preaches and ministers to an expanding community in a diversity of ways. He has struggled against urban internecine and police violence, structural poverty and the community erosion of gentrification. He is a founding member of the Black Alliance for Peace and an advocate for racial and environmental justice, the protection of immigrants, cooperative economics and the development of public policy strategies to abolish the system of mass incarceration. Mjumbe seeks to explore and challenge the intersection of multiple forms of oppression. As a spiritual and community leader he is called to bring together people of diverse traditions who are deeply committed to freedom and justice.

Reverend Mjumbe was one of the more than 100 men who signed a "statement of solidarity" with the more than 700 women who called for a Black woman Vice President. He is committed to holding elected officials accountable to both people and principles. Starting his organizing work in the "Black Belt" south with Black farmers, Mjumbe has been an advocate for Black freedom and justice movements and a variety of social justice issues from his teenage years.

Speaking at a local rally in Trenton, NJ protesting the police murder of an unarmed Black man in May of 2020 he declared, "There is a difference between "creating peace" and "keeping the peace." *Keeping* the peace is characterized by keeping people quiet and in obedience to systems of domination and repression and calling it justice, or law and order. Governments *keep* the peace with guns, riot shields and tanks. We *make* the peace through our demanding, cultivating and nurturing right relationships with God, with our neighbors, and within ourselves! We must fiercely love and labor for the justice of this kind of peace! In the unjust world in which we live--tragically and ironically, we have to fight for peace! This is how we will come to *k-n-o-w* justice and *k-n-o-w* peace!"

CHAPTER NINE

The Wrong Question:
On Forgiveness, Fury, Rage, and Reconciliation

Rev. Jameel Morrison

Abstract

Aglobal pandemic. Skyrocketing unemployment. Absentee leadership. A horrifying viral video. America stands at a familiar inflection point. Its faults are again visible. Its wounds are still open. Its patterns of oppression, of turning a blind eye and a deaf ear to the needs of Black people (and numerous others by extension), are apparent. Triggered by imagery, traumatized by memory, and taunted by authority, Black people are angry, morally outraged, and demanding change. The white Christian theologies offer outright denial with their simple and paternalistic solutions to systemic racism—the centuries-old, airborne, highly contagious virus that has disproportionately destroyed the lives of Black and Brown people and savaged their communities: "Forgive, even as God forgives" (Matt 18:24-35); "Be quick to listen, slow to speak, slow to anger" (Jas 1:19-20); and "Be angry, but do not sin, do not let the sun go down on your anger, and do not make room for the devil" (Eph 4:26-32). But what does forgiveness look like when injustices and transgressions persist? Is forgiveness possible under such circumstances? How "slow" is slow enough for the acknowledgement and expression of anger? Under what circumstances does God sanction or even sanctify our anger? When is rage not only appropriate, but necessary? What function does rage serve in Christian discourse? What does the pursuit of reconciliation look like when the involved parties fail to agree on reality?

And what of forgiveness, that undeniably essential spiritual and emotional Christian practice? In discussions of anger and racism, forgiveness is always an issue that is made focal. But when the work of forgiveness is co-opted by whiteness and conflated with repentance and reconciliation, all while being divorced from the transformative and redemptive work of those processes, it gives rise to Black fury. When this condition of false piety persists alongside continued injustices, Black fury becomes Black rage—a bright line that identifies and reclaims reality and demands reconciliation. To the extent that this rage is concerned with reconciliation—restorative work rooted in transparency, resolution, and re-union—I propose to argue that that rage is holy.

These are the critical questions that I raise and address in this article.

>>

Introduction

What is the place and purpose of anger in the African American observance of the Christian faith? When does anger color and define the experience of Black Christians and what does it look like? How might we make sense of the ends it accomplishes, and what are the implications of naming Black anger as *holy*?

Anger is a God-given emotion and God-granted capability that galvanizes, equips, and resources people who have been beaten down, silenced, and marginalized. Anger in concert with hope and resilience animates people who have been subjected to a condition of recurring injustice without recourse or remedy. *Holy* anger bolsters boundaries that have been breached, reclaims and re-centers dignity that power aims to diminish or deny, and affirms the sacrality of life as it sounds the trumpet of accountability and reckoning.

Plausible Deniability

George Floyd was murdered on the evening of May 25, 2020, when Minneapolis Police Officer Derek Chauvin kneeled on his neck for 8 minutes and 46 seconds with his hands in his pockets as onlookers protested. Floyd was already handcuffed face-down on the ground and non-combative, yet two additional officers restrained him as a fourth officer prevented onlookers from interfering. Floyd was said to have allegedly passed a counterfeit $20 bill at a local grocery store. The excessive force deployed while responding to the alleged crime drew sharp attention to the widespread problem of police brutality disproportionately directed at Black bodies in America.

The triggering and traumatic viral video of the execution ignited uprisings across the nation as hundreds of thousands filled streets in large cities and small towns with cries of "Black Lives Matter!" and "No justice, no peace!" Thousands more around the world marched through their respective cities and towns in solidarity with these protests, all while negotiating the ravages of a global pandemic.

The moment surfaced America's continued failure to reckon with its complicity in and culpability for the "cancer" of racism, the evil born of "a history of the powerful acting to protect their self-interest."[1] Chillingly, the same day Floyd was murdered in Minneapolis, a white woman threatened a Black man with police violence in New York's Central Park. CNN reported:

> Amy Cooper was walking her dog Monday morning while Christian Cooper (no relation) was bird-watching at a wooded area of Central Park called the Ramble. They both told CNN their dispute began because her dog was not on a leash, contrary to the Ramble's rules, according

to the park's website. Christian Cooper recorded video of part of their encounter and posted it on Facebook, where it has since been shared thousands of times and became a trending topic on Twitter. In the video, he is largely silent while she frantically tells police he is threatening her and her dog. "I'm taking a picture and calling the cops," Amy Cooper is heard saying in the video. "I'm going to tell them there's an African American man threatening my life." In comments to CNN as the video spread widely, Amy Cooper said she wanted to "publicly apologize to everyone." "I'm not a racist. I did not mean to harm that man in any way," she said, adding that she also didn't mean any harm to the African American community.[2]

In apprising a white woman of her failure to observe the rules of a public park by leashing her dog, a Black man earned a label, not of neighbor, fellow park patron, or advocate for the protection of the park, but of a "threat" to the woman and her dog. This claim was made even though the white woman wielded the apparatus of the state as a weapon, simultaneously securing her safety, salving her ego, and stanching her embarrassment. The video of their encounter documents the transformation of her voice from threatening to frantic and fearful as she switches from talking with Cooper to contacting a 9-1-1 dispatcher.

Despite the seamless if not subconsciously self-righteous pivot between the roles of accuser, judge, executioner, and innocent victim, Amy Cooper maintained "[she wasn't] a racist," though her invocation of racist ideas in her threat and subsequent 9-1-1 call belied her protestation. She said she "did not mean to harm that man…[or] the African American community" when her hostile disposition toward Cooper and her protracted vocal inflections while speaking with the 9-1-1 dispatcher intimated precisely that intent.

Amy Cooper stated in an apology issued to NBC News that "[she thought] of the police as a protection agency, and unfortunately, this [experience] has caused [her] to realize that there are so many people in this country [who] don't have that luxury."[3] Zeba Blay contests this claim, linking Cooper's behavior to the false accusations Carolyn Bryant [Donham] and Sarah Page made against 14-year-old Emmett Till and Black shoe shiner Dick Rowland, respectively. In 1955, Emmett Till was beaten, tortured, and killed because of a claim Bryant would later admit was not true. Page's accusation in 1921 incited a race massacre that saw an affluent Black neighborhood in Tulsa burned to the ground as hundreds of residents were killed and others were injured. Blay comments that Cooper's volley between action and apology reveals "a kind of savviness, a calculated racism showing she was already aware of that privilege...[and that] white people are far more aware of the structure of the thing than they care to admit."[4]

The unconfessed awareness that Blay identifies is echoed in James Cone's examination of the connection between the cross and the lynching tree. Cone writes:

Whites lynched blacks in nearly every state, including New York, Minnesota, and California ... a black man could be walking down the road, minding his business, and his life could suddenly change by meeting a white man or a group of white men or boys who on a whim decided to have some fun with a Negro; and this could happen in Mississippi or New York, Arkansas, or Illinois ... white communities made blacks their primary target, and torture their focus ... Lynching became a white media spectacle, in which prominent newspapers, like the Atlanta Constitution announced to the public, the place, date, and time of the expected hanging and burning of black victims. Often as many as ten to twenty thousand men, women, and children attended the event ... a ritual celebration of white supremacy, where women and children were given the first opportunity to torture black victims ... Postcards were made from the photographs taken of black victims with white lynchers and onlookers smiling as they struck a pose for the camera. They were sold for ten- to twenty-five cents ... [Spectacle lynching] could not have happened without widespread knowledge and the explicit sanction of local and state authorities and with tacit approval from the federal government, members of the white media, churches, and universities.[5]

Lynchings were public affairs. They were widespread, accepted and tolerated, promoted in prominent newspapers, and attended by staggering numbers of white people. Children were allowed to be present and encouraged to participate in lynchings. Souvenirs were taken, often directly from the victim's bodies, and postcards were made and sold to commemorate the events and circulate knowledge of the same among those who hadn't attended. The desensitization to violence against Black bodies was not only ritualized, but to the extent many white people today insist "they weren't aware"—of the persistent widespread violence against African Americans or the nature of their lived experience in America—it was ostensibly redacted from American History curriculums and/or subjected to revisionism[6] before being released into the general social consciousness. For too many then, the history of lynchings may as well be the scent of food that lingers in a kitchen (and in the nostrils and consciousness of the brutalized) that has already been cleaned.

After George Floyd's murder, and amid concurrent controversies with police involvement in the deaths of Ahmaud Arbery and Breonna Taylor, many white Americans, Christian and otherwise, suggested, like Amy Cooper, that they were "not aware" of how different life was for African Americans living in America. Amy Cooper's conduct during her encounter with Christian Cooper cost her her job[7] and, for a time, possession of her dog.[8] It seems doubtful that Amy Cooper would have apologized if her reputation, employment prospects, and custody of her dog weren't all at stake. I raise this point to underscore that the apology, although framed as a denial of malice against Christian Cooper or the African American community, was no indication of Amy Cooper's desire to repent, rectify, or rehabilitate her behavior. As "unacceptable" as she characterized the behavior to be, no assurances were made that she would assume responsibility for her transgression, educate herself, or alter her behavior because of her revelatory awakening. In fact, there is little indication that she grasped the depth and destructive nature of her instinctive actions (or the conditioning that gave rise to them), much less their connection to a tragic history of truth-twisting at the expense of Black lives.[9]

Not a Game

In the summer of 2002, Philadelphia 76ers shooting guard Allen Iverson made headlines after giving a press interview where he interrogated journalists who were questioning his practicing habits. The press conference happened following the 76ers' elimination in the first round of the NBA playoffs. In the prior year, Iverson had earned league MVP and led the 76ers to the Finals before losing to Shaquille O'Neal's and Kobe Bryant's Lakers.

At the time, rumors suggested that Iverson was to be traded, that he was unhappy with the 76ers organization, and that the organization desired to release him in order to secure other talent. Media rumors and speculation suggested that Iverson's failure to take practice seriously was a sort of final straw.

The quote that made the rounds, "We talking about practice" was played excessively in the media, made into a song by Philly native DJ Jazzy Jeff, and became a sort of synecdoche for Iverson's reputation—the gilding on what was often considered to be a countercultural, brash, and impetuous image. This image, which had not yet become mainstream in the NBA, was enshrined in his cornrows, tattoos, entourages, and baggy clothing.

In Iverson's words:

> If I can't practice, man, I can't practice. If I'm hurt, I'm hurt. I mean, simple as that. It ain't about that ... it's easy to sum it up when we just talk about practice ... Not the game that I go out there and die for and play every game like it's my last ... When you come in the arena and you see me play, you see me play, don't you? You see me give everything I got, right? ... it's funny to me too. It's strange to me too, ... We not even talking about the game, the actual game, when it matters ... Whatchu mean I'm the superstar? Why? Why am I the superstar? Aight. Oh right. So why we talking

about me getting traded, or leaving, or it's a problem with me? … If I'm the best in the world, if I'm the best if I'm a superstar, then why is this happening man? Why is this going on? Why do my daughter gotta deal with this? Why does she have to deal with this everyday she go to school? … I'm just—I'm upset. I'm upset for one reason man. Cause I'm in here. I lost. I lost my best friend. I lost him, and I lost this year. Everything is going downhill, for me, as far as just that, as far as my life. And that I'm dealing with this right here. I don't want to deal with this man.[10]

Iverson's meta-commentary on the moment—on teachers and staff at his then 7-year-old daughter's school talking to her about her Dad's employment prospects, on grief over a recently murdered close friend (whose killer was facing trial at the time of the press conference), on still smarting from the first-round elimination, and on the indignity of being a league-MVP-franchise-caliber player whose commitment to and focus on the game was questioned over practice attendance—was visceral.[11]

All-star athlete though he may have been, he was human first, and he was hurting. The journalists had a job to do, and however frivolous or callous their questions may have been, no matter how much he wished to avoid it, he had a job to do. As the character Omar from HBO's *The Wire* would remark, "It [was] all in the game." And for Iverson, it presented a palpable conflict. The expectation was that he would present a buttoned-up, austere-if-not-mournful, reserved, and respectable disposition. He was to commend his competitors, thank his coach and handlers, and promise to try harder next year. By that metric, cross-examining those who questioned his character and commitment was out of bounds. Iverson was expected to be composed and conciliatory, but he showed up in his humanity and demanded to be seen and heard.

As violence, anxiety, grief, and the threats of violence cast shadows on the Black experience in America, and as injustices are highlighted and reported on but remain unaddressed and unresolved, Blacks are expected "to do their jobs" even as apologies are abundant and accountability is absent. This attitude has been leveled at those who have stepped into streets around the country to lift their voices, fists, signs, hopes, and prayers in protest of justice too-long denied, as well as public figures who make comments, and professional athletes who kneel during pledges of allegiance to draw attention to problems with policing and inequality.

It is not the responsibility of Black people or Black Christians to engage in virtue signaling, wherein whites are assured that anger is not part of the agenda and forgiveness is the default order of the day. Black people are not required to put on happy faces when their bodies are cast down and destroyed. Black people are allowed to "hang their harps on the willows" (Psalm 137:1-2) when traumatic and stressful events beset them, and when their children are snatched from them coldly and cruelly; they have the right to acknowledge and express the disappointment, grief, and rage that appeals to God to remember their adversaries when punishment is meted out (Psalm 137:7-9).

The observance of Christianity does not require Black people to suppress or disguise their indignation, disgust, contempt, or disappointment when they are maligned or intentionally placed in harm's way. Oppressed people are under no obligation to soothe or console the silent majorities who assure them that justice delayed is forgivable, understandable, or the best that could be done—anything other than justice denied.

A great disconnect lies in the failure on the part of white people to recognize that "walking down the road, minding one's business" was a perilous act if one could encounter "a white man, or a group of white men or boys" with the capacity to decide "on a whim" that randomized terror against Black people, even harassment resulting in a fatality, could all be in good "fun." Under these conditions, actions that characterized Christian piety and actions that accomplished Black survival were conflated. Eye contact was not avoided as a matter of Christian duty. Crossing the street to allow whites to pass was not evidence of Black comprehension of the Christian catechism. These were adaptations internalized by Black people in service to survival.

As Cone wrote about his development of a liberation theology that could be both Black and Christian, "it was not easy because even in the black community the public meaning of Christianity was *white*."[12] Black survival demanded participation in assimilative behaviors that bore the appearance of a particular brand of Christianity, and whites' unwillingness to confront the mirror of America's past has "made it difficult for them to even recognize their cultural and spiritual arrogance," much to the detriment of any conversation oriented toward an idea of reconciliation, racial or otherwise.[13]

The distinction between Christianity and African American experience is significant, because although Amy Cooper's apology had no teeth, her offered apology functions as an appeal for forgiveness.

Seeking Forgiveness Without Repentance

The import of reconciliation becomes visible when something has been ruptured in a relationship. A transgression creates, promotes, sustains, or reinforces inequity, indignity, or a denial of intrinsic value. A meaningful reconciliatory process begins with awareness and acknowledgment of transgression.

Awareness refers to the capacity to know or perceive a situation or fact. It may start in the gut. It might just be a feeling. Or there may be visible, palpable, tangible evidence. There may be boxes of reports, terabytes of data, or hours worth of footage. The evidence may be obvious, but the eyes required to interpret it as such may not have been refined. Our capacity for awareness is often compromised by distractions and diverted by denial.

Acknowledgment accepts or admits the existence or truth of a situation or fact. In the reconciliatory process, awareness knows and perceives transgression. Acknowledgment identifies the transgression and labels it. The reckoning begins when one party in a relationship moves from awareness and acknowledgment of transgression toward action designed to neutralize the transgressive condition. Reconciliation culminates with affected parties articulating awareness of the transgression, engaging in mutual acknowledgment, and taking up collaborative/constructive action to remedy both the transgression and its effects.

In financial language, the term "forgive" is used to refer to the cancellation of a debt. A debt that has been canceled is no longer held against the debtor. In human relations, the term usually describes a condition wherein one party ceases to hold anger or resentment toward another for an offense, a flaw, or a mistake.

Forgiveness is a component of the reconciliatory process that is particularly concerned with restoration. If a relationship between concerned parties is overdrawn, forgiveness makes the continuance of a relationship possible, subject to whatever remedies are determined through the reconciliatory process. Forgiveness says, "This won't be held against you in perpetuity. We can still maintain a functional, working relationship."

The reconciliatory process is disrupted when one party seeks restoration without repentance. This would be the equivalent of a person running over someone in their car and then attempting to secure a promise that no police report or insurance claims will be filed before backing up their car off of the person and "assuming responsibility" for their problematic behavior.

Forgiveness is the property of the offended party. It does not belong to the offending party. It is not due to the offending party. The offending party is not guaranteed forgiveness. Asking for forgiveness when there is no repentance, or when no changes that are meaningful to the offended party are undertaken, is to ask for absolution without accountability and restoration without responsibility. It is to re-offend. In fact, the offense is compounded because the offended party is being further subjected to indignity while the original offense persists.[14]

When offenses persist without remedy or acknowledgment—when violence against Black bodies is downplayed or dismissed and leaders demur on discussions of change—they produce disappointment, despair, anger, and resentment. There is a grace to forgiveness that functions for the offended party even as its function for the offender is delayed. Forgiveness enables the offended party to create space between themselves and the offense emotionally, spiritually, and psychologically. I believe this space can be occupied by hope and stave off resentment even as the offended party seeks a reckoning toward reconciliation. The restorative quality of forgiveness that is experienced by the offending party is not compromised by whatever delay precedes repentance, because the efficacy of forgiveness that is extended to the offending party is made possible through repentance. The question, then, is not whether or not Black people will forgive the injustices, atrocities, traumas, and indignities visited upon them by whites caught up and carried away with what Sonya Renee Taylor terms the white supremacist delusion.[15] The question is: "Will whites repent?"

Righteous Indignation as Rebuke

Joshua L. Lazard writes that, while forgiveness is important, Christians should not be taking a shortcut around anger to get there. He posits that the inclination to do so reinforces escapist observances of Christianity, avoids confrontation with racism and white supremacy, and denies humanity the gift of a spiritual encounter with righteous indignation. An equally critical problem that emerges from this traditional practice of suppressed or muted anger is that the absence of its expression can lead to a wholesale rejection of the Christian worship experience. To the extent that patterns of prompt forgiveness can be conflated with white appeasement, those seeking change are apt to be persuaded that Christians deny the need for or place of rebellion and revolution in transforming society.[16]

Dante Stewart describes how confusion became rage as he observed white responses to President Trump and the shootings of unarmed Black people in the evangelical church he served. After encountering insensitivity to Black trauma, a re-fusal to acknowledge the breadth and depth of injustice that has affected and continues to affect Black people, and repeat-ed insinuations that he did not belong to the community that he was serving, he observed that rage animated what others tried to weaken:

> Rage shakes us out of our illusion that the world as it is, is what God wants. Rage forces us to deal with the gross system of inequality, exploitation, and disrespect. Rage is the public cry for [B]lack dignity. It becomes the public expression of a theological truth that [B]lack lives matter to God. Rage is the work of love that stands against an unloving world .... To protest violence against black people is a spiritual virtue, moral obligation, and political practice. In a world that wounds the souls of black folk, it represents the Spirit of God at work resisting the evil of white supremacy and murder with impunity. It's holy work.[17]

Anger asks: "If Amy didn't mean any harm, why did she say Christian Cooper was threatening her life when he wasn't? If African Americans have no demonstrated history of organized, pre-meditated violence against whites or other Americans in general, why are peaceful protests of police brutality met with expressed fears of Black retribution or genocidal behavior? If 'All Lives Matter,' as a general principle, then why is there reticence and waffling and equivocating about the value of Black Lives in particular? If there is a shared confession of faith, freedom, and salvation through Jesus Christ that crosses color lines, why have so many white pulpits and parishioners remained silent about the systemic evils that beset their Black sisters and brothers in Christ?"

Anger cries out: "Are you serious? Are we really debating whether Black lives are sacred, God-breathed, and fearfully and wonderfully made? (Ps. 139:13-14). Do streets really have to be flooded with people protesting the world over before there can be agreement that there is a critical problem with law enforcement in America? How is there a debate over police brutality when there are decades of video footage depicting police violence against Black bodies?"

Furthermore, asks Anger: "Why isn't the problem recognizable when video footage also depicts police officers attacking crowds of people peacefully protesting violence against Black bodies? How can traffic stops be more fraught than drive-by shootings if there is not a problem? Is the problem really invisible? Are American Christians committed to ignoring these transgressions wholesale?" To witness these conditions is to worry, to wonder, and to wail. Witnessing, whether first- or second-hand, gives rise to indignation—"Wait, you're *okay* with this?"

James Cone writes that Reinhold Niebuhr, who was "widely regarded [as] America's most influential theologian in the twentieth century, and possibly American history... failed to connect the cross and its most vivid reenactment in his time [i.e., lynchings]. To reflect on this failure is to address a defect in the conscience of white Christians and to suggest why African Americans have needed to trust and cultivate their own theological imagination."[18] It was Reinhold Niebuhr who posited that "forgiveness was the final form of love."[19]

Niebuhr's assertion regarding forgiveness resonates deeply with the Christian theology of the cross, wherein Christ's death is evidence of God's love (John 3:16, Romans 5:8). The ethic of forgiveness as love is evident in Christ's teaching to his disciples—generosity in extending forgiveness to members of the church (Matthew 18:22, Luke 17:3-4), forgiveness of others as a precondition to receiving forgiveness (Matthew 6:14-15, 18:35), the centrality of forgiveness in prayer (Matthew 6:12, Mark 11:25), and the healing that forgiveness renders (Matthew 9:6, Mark 2:10, Luke 5:24).

It is curious that forgiveness is seated at the same table as rebuke and repentance (Luke 17:3). A rebuke is necessary when a lack of awareness and acknowledgment results in continued assault. If an offense has been committed, a rebuke is designed to provoke and promote apology and adjustment (repentance), which then clears the way for absolution. I believe the emphasis on forgiveness in Scripture is paired with confession and repentance to function as a purifier and preservative for the believing community (1 John 1:9). The ebb and flow of confrontation, confession, contrition, and commitment cauterizes the community even as it strengthens the community and fortifies its bonds.

What are the protests, direct actions, vigils, and loud laments—what are the bodies in the streets breathing together against and in spite of brutality—if not rebukes? What are the unarmed bodies of peaceful protesters bearing signs if not cries and pleas to be heard, seen, understood, and respected?

What should we make of the deaf ears these rebukes fall on, and have fallen on for some 400 years? If African Americans are not and have not been in a position to offer rebukes, does that mean they are not believers? If white Christians won't hear and heed rebukes, or if they think themselves above good-faith rebukes from Black believers, should they still be considered/recognized as Christian? (Matthew 7:20, John 13:35).[20]

Black rage has rarely been seen as normative, acceptable, or justified. Though efforts to reject and discredit its existence abound, I believe there is a salvific element to its expression. James Baldwin called out this tension when he wrote the following words to his nephew:

> There is no reason for you to try to become like white people and there is no basis whatsoever for their impertinent assumption that they must accept you. The really terrible thing, old buddy is that you must accept them. And I mean that very seriously. You must accept them and accept them with love. For these innocent people have no other hope. They are, in effect, still trapped in a history which they do not understand; and until they understand it, they cannot be released from it...we cannot be free until they are free.[21]

The expression of anger, of righteous indignation, of moral outrage, of grief and lament because of evil that remains— these are expressions born of love. They reject things as they are in pursuit of things as they ought to be. The cries for justice—for Black lives to be seen, heard, and honored—are cries for whole communities that acknowledge, appreciate, and uphold the worth of all persons. They are cries for equality, not for revenge.[22] The expression of Black rage offers whites a mirror—an understanding of history and themselves that they have yet to grasp and sincerely reckon with. Black rage is the embodiment of an unyielding determination to raise that mirror in response to and in the face of disenfranchisement, danger, and death. Black rage is a modern-day manifestation of loving one's neighbor as oneself.

Endnotes

1   See Ibram X. Kendi, *How To Be an Antiracist* (New York: One World, 2019), p. 230.

2   "White Woman Who Called Police on a Black Man Bird-watching in Central Park Has Been Fired": https://www.cnn.com/2020/05/26/us/central-park-video-dog-video-african-american-trnd/index.html; retrieved August 31, 2020.

3   "White Woman Who Called Cops on Black Man in Central Park Issues Apology | NBC New York,": https://www.youtube.com/watch?v=jbA9rWo89gQ at 2:37 time stamp; last accessed August 31, 2020.

4   "Amy Cooper Knew Exactly What She Was Doing": https://www.huffpost.com/entry/amy-cooper-knew-exactly-what-she-was-doing_n_5ecd1d89c5b6c1f281e0fbc5; last accessed August 31, 2020.

5   James Cone, *The Cross and the Lynching Tree* (New York: Orbis Books, 2011), pp. 24-25.

6   "Mother Shares Textbook Describing African Slaves as 'Workers":https://www.nbcnews.com/news/nbcblk/mother-shares-textbook-describing-african-slaves-workers-n438836; last accessed August 31, 2020.

7   "White Woman Who Called Police on a Black Man Bird-watching in Central Park Has Been Fired": https://www.cnn.com/2020/05/26/us/central-park-video-dog-video-african-american-trnd/index.html; last accessed August 31, 2020.

8   "Dog Returned to White Woman Who Called Police on

Black Man Bird-watching in Central Park": https://www.cnn.com/2020/06/05/us/amy-cooper-dog-returned-trnd/index.html; last accessed August 31, 2020.

9 "Woman Linked to 1955 Emmett Till Murder Tells Historian Her Claims Were False": https://www.nytimes.com/2017/01/27/us/emmett-till-lynching-carolyn-bryant-donham.html; last accessed September 02, 2020.

10 "Allen Iverson's Legendary Practice Rant [FULL] | ESPN Archives": https://www.youtube.com/watch?v=K9ZQhyOZC-NE&t=1236s; last accessed August 31, 2020.

11 "Stephen A. Explains Why Allen Iverson Was So Upset during 'Practice' Rant | SportsCenter": https://www.youtube.com/watch?v=FAgAlmkzex4; last accessed August 31, 2020.

12 James Cone, *The Cross and the Lynching Tree* (New York: Orbis Books, 2011), p. 15.

13 James Cone, *The Cross and the Lynching Tree* (New York: Orbis Books, 2011), p. 25.

14 Waltrina N. Middleton, "I Don't Forgive the Man Who Murdered My Cousin DePayne at Mother Emanuel," The Christian Century, June 16, 2020: https://www.christiancentury.org/article/first-person/i-don-t-forgive-man-who-murdered-my-cousin-depayne-mother-emanuel; last accessed June 17, 2020.

15 Sonya Renee Taylor, "Why Talking to Your White Family about Black People Is the Wrong Approach (ASL)": https://www.youtube.com/watch?v=s-R-VR5AJ7U; (2:55 for context; expression occurs at 3:12).

16 "A Theology of Anger: Forgiveness for White Supremacy Derails Action and Alienates Young Black Activists": https://religiondispatches.org/a-theology-of-anger-forgiveness-for-white-supremacy-derails-action-and-alienates-young-black-activists/; last accessed June 18, 2020.

17 "Black Rage in an Anti-Black World Is a Spiritual Virtue": https://sojo.net/articles/black-rage-anti-black-world-spiritual-virtue; last accessed September 15, 2020.

18 James Cone, *The Cross and the Lynching Tree* (New York: Orbis Books, 2011), p. 46.

19 Reinhold Niebuhr, *Irony of American History* (New York:

Charles Scribner's Sons, 1952), p. 63.

20   "The Racist Message of Do-Nothing Religion, Courtesy of Texas Lt. Gov. Dan Patrick": https://religiondispatches.org/the-racist-message-of-do-nothing-religion-courtesy-of-texas-lt-gov-dan-patrick/; last accessed June 18, 2020.

21   James Baldwin, *The Fire Next Time* (New York: Dell Publishing, 1963), pp. 19, 22.

22   "Kimberly Latrice Jones BLM Video Speech Transcript": https://www.rev.com/blog/transcripts/kimberly-latrice-jones-blm-video-speech-transcript; last accessed August 31, 2020.

Jameel Morrison, M.Div.

The Rev. Jameel A. Morrison is an Itinerant Elder in the African Methodist Episcopal Church, who has served in pastoral ministry since 2010. He has a Master of Divinity from the Theological School at Drew University, and a Bachelor of Arts in Communication from Rutgers University. He is an avid home cook and professional photographer with a deep and abiding appreciation of hip-hop music and culture. He also harbors the belief that only he can appreciate the intersections of stand-up comedy, preaching, and battle rap. He has pastored four congregations in New Jersey and currently serves as the pastor of Grant AME Church in Chesilhurst, N.J. He lives with his wife and their three children in Southern New Jersey.

CHAPTER 10

Coping with Holy Rage and the Concept of a "Good" God

Susan K. Smith, M.Div.

Abstract

This essay will examine how rage is a part of the very relationship with God, birthed and nurtured in our spirits because of the lack of a monolithic concept and interpretation of God and of "goodness." The rage comes as a result of being disappointed with God concerning our expectations of how a "good" God would order and run the world.

Despite there being one Bible, there is not one way of reading or of interpreting what we read therein. The Rev. Dr. Jeremiah Wright teaches that our theology (the way we see God) determines our anthropology (how we see society), which in turn determines our sociology—i.e., our relationship with others. Dr. Wright says that how we see God is how we see other people.

Oppressed people tend to see God as a liberator, a champion of the poor and the downtrodden, while those who oppress others see God as one who seeks to dominate and control. These two interpretations of God necessarily clash, and the oppressed are left wondering about the goodness of God, the presence of God, and God's concern for them.

God's silence—be it perceived or actual—in the face of oppression and suffering only feeds the rage. This essay will argue that God is often silent in the midst of oppression, even though God is always present. On perceived silence, it may be that God has in fact "said" something, but it has not been what the oppressed have wanted or needed to hear. Hence, historically, people have railed at God for God's silence. In much of the book of Job, God remains silent. Viktor Frankl said that during the Holocaust, many Jews were angry at God because they could not hear God or see God acting against the evil that was eliminating them. The psalmist wrote "fret not thyself because of evildoers," but other psalmists scream out for God. "Where are you?" they ask. Looking for God and not finding God in the way we need to find Her, causes not only rage but a weariness in looking.

What, then, is a "good" God? What does God's goodness look like? Is there an aspect of goodness that we do not understand because our definition of "goodness" is limited by our humanity? In the midst of oppression, what does "good" look like?

The problem for many is that, logically, a "good" God would not allow such unmerited suffering, and the fact that the suffering and oppression has not only existed but festered—in spite of the presence of God—has fed the rage. Is our rage justified? Is a silent God still a "good" God?

>>>

In a discussion that took place several years ago at the Children's Defense Fund's Child Advocacy annual conference, young activists faced veteran civil rights workers in what could only be described as a heated dialogue. The young activists charged the veteran civil rights workers with having betrayed and abandoned the movement, leaving them to pick up the pieces. As the older people listened, some brought up how their faith in God had been a major part of their work, but the activists wanted none of it. "What has God done?" asked one of the young people, cryptically. "Not even with all your praying and calling on God did racism die." As the other young people nodded or mumbled in agreement, it was not difficult to ascertain that in their hearts was a fair amount of "holy rage."

If we are honest, most of us must admit that at some time during our faith walk we have wondered about the "goodness" of God. As an adjective, "good" means "something to be desired or approved of," and as a noun, "good" is "that which is morally right." From Biblical days, however, there must have been some tension between the human and the divine understanding of "good," as the psalmist notes that, in spite of his trying to live a morally upright life, those who seemed to reject or ignore the need for such seemed to experience the benefits of what life offered more so than himself. In coping with that reality, the psalmist in Psalm 10 asks:

> Why, O Lord, do you stand far off? Why do you hide yourself in times of trouble? In arrogance the wicked persecute the poor...the wicked boast of the desires of their heart, those greedy for gain curse and renounce the Lord. (Ps. 10:1-2a, 3)

The wicked, says the psalmist in Psalm 73, "have no pain; their bodies are sound and sleek. They are not in trouble as others are; they are not plagued like other people." (Ps. 73:4-5). Noting that the "evildoers" seem to prosper, the psalmist in Psalm 37 advises those who are struggling with what appears to be the "good life" of the wicked not to worry: "Do not fret because of the wicked; do not be envious of wrongdoers" (Ps. 37:1). Try as hard as they might, it seems that the writers of the psalms are in a struggle to understand God. They have at least two questions: (1) "Why are you so far off?" which might be interpreted to mean, "Why are you letting this happen to me?" or (2) "Why is it that the lives of 'the wicked' seem to be so much better than mine?"

In these questions, it is not beyond the realm of possibility that there is a fair amount of rage against God. A good God, one would suppose, would demand "morally right" behavior, and if it were not happening, this same good God might be expected to punish those who were out of line. Our humanness leads us to a dialectical way of thinking and processing our experiences. Something is good or bad, right or wrong, left or right, up or down. There seems to be little room for middle ground. We expect God to be an either/or deity, to act in the way that we think, but that is not the case.

We believe in the concept of monotheism, but even if there is one God, the problem we wrestle with and must deal with in our understanding of God is that there is no monolithic understanding or interpretation of God. The oppressed and the oppressor might call on the name of God, but they have radically different understandings about who God is and what God's words mean. It is significant that both enslaved Africans who were forcibly brought to this country and English pilgrims who deliberately landed in this country both considered the story of the Exodus as their own story. For the enslaved Africans, the story of the Israelites' passage through the wilderness resonated with them as proof that God was with them in the wilderness called America and that it was God's will that they would one day reach the Promised Land. The English considered their journey across the Atlantic to the New World as their exodus, with the ocean being their wilderness. The difference between the two understandings is that the enslaved Africans believed that their wilderness journey would one day end, while the English proclaimed that their wilderness journey had ended—with the full blessing of God—once they landed on the shores of the Americas.

From the beginning, then, there was a division and a difference in the understanding of what a "good" God was. Walter Bruggemann talks about God being a God of promise and a God of blessing. Abraham and Sarah lived in the shadow of the surety of receiving God's promise. Their waiting increased their faith as they waited for years for God's promises to come to fruition. By the time their grandchildren came along, the promise had been fulfilled, resulting in them benefitting from the blessing that came from the waiting. While Abraham's faith grew, the faith of their grandchildren—Esau and Jacob—became less prominent as they sought to increase and hold onto their blessings, which had come about only because of their grandfather's faith. Jacob and Esau were more concerned with money and power—getting it and keeping it—than their grandfather ever had been. Jacob and Esau were beneficiaries of God's goodness, but not because of anything they had done. They might be compared, for purposes of this discussion, to the Pilgrims who traversed the Atlantic and lived in the blessings afforded them in the New World. The enslaved Africans, on the other hand, seemed to be more the people of promise, like Abraham, steadfastly believing in the promise of God, which, in their case, consisted of deliverance from racial oppression.

People who live believing in the promises of God hold a different kind of faith. They dare not turn away from God or forsake God, but they do *question* God. Why, they ask, are they made to suffer, even as they wait? Since they are living in the promise of God—waiting for the fruition of the words of Isaiah, in a way, "They that wait upon the Lord shall renew their strength; they shall mount up on wings as eagles, they shall run and not be weary, they shall walk and not faint"—they wait with the expectation that their "good" God will come through in due time. They see the evil around them and at times they question God, but they never lose their hope that the exodus experience will one day end. Those who live in the blessing of God, however—i.e., those who hold power and property—seem to put God aside, or so it seems, continually increasing their wealth and power while ignoring those who are still in exodus.

The oppressed cannot afford to let go of the notion of a good God, a God who hears and who will one day bring justice. It is their lifeline, the thread, so to speak, that holds their faith together. James Cone correctly teaches us that white people introduced Christianity to black people, but, from the very beginning, their understanding of God—coming from the perspective of people who live in the state of blessing—was radically different than the understanding of God they desired black people to have. There could be no sharing of power; black people were taught that it was God's will that they be enslaved. God was on the side of the oppressor. What was absent in their teaching of God was an ignorance about the relationship, says Cone, between life and theology. Black people could not possibly believe in the God they were being taught. That God would have been **complicit** in their subjugation, and that was not acceptable or palatable to them. So, while the enslaved Africans used the same words as did white people about God, and studied from the same Bible, the Africans, as people of promise or who lived in promise, conceived of God in an entirely different way than did their white teachers. And the more they studied the stories in the Bible, the more they were convinced that their concept of God—and of God's goodness—was far more accurate than the white concept of God they were being taught. God was good because God saw them, God heard them, God cherished them, and God would deliver them, just as God had delivered the Israelites.

Enslaved blacks were, like Abraham, willing to wait for the promise of God for deliverance to be fulfilled. But as they waited, they sometimes wrestled with God. Why was the wilderness journey taking so long? They had probably read or heard the story about Abram as he lived in the promise, but they might not have heard the entire story. The text reads that Abram fell into a deep sleep, where "a terrifying darkness descended upon him," and God said: "Know this for certain, that your offspring shall be aliens in a land that is not theirs and shall be oppressed for four hundred years, but I will bring judgments on the nation that they serve, and afterward, they shall come out with great possessions." (Gen. 15:12-14; NSRV).

According to this story, it took 400 years of being oppressed before there was deliverance! The span of time between God's promise and the blessing God has promised is often long in the scriptures. Abraham and Sarah waited almost 20 years for their promised child, and that may have been acceptable to their ears, but the 400-year wait for deliverance, as expressed in Genesis, was probably not often talked about.

Because of the time span between promise and blessing, however, there were times when the enslaved Africans grew weary, and wondered, as did the psalmists, where God was. It is the waiting, the being in the promise phase of one's relationship with God, that sometimes causes rage. The psalmists ask where God is and why God is forsaking them? (Psalm 22). They ask God to incline his ear toward them; perhaps he has not heard their cries? (Ps. 31: 1-2). They wonder if God is angry at them (Ps. 38) and if that is perhaps the reason God has not heard them. They demand the presence of God:

> "Give ear to my prayer, O God; do not hide yourself from my supplication. Attend to me and answer me; I am troubled in my complaint. I am distraught by the noise of the enemy because of the clamor of the wicked...." (Ps. 55:1-3a)

The words of the Bible make it clear that God is on the side of the oppressed, the poor, the widows, and the orphans, and that perspective is one that brings a sense of confidence in God to and for the oppressed. God in fact makes it clear that the tendency of people in power to not attend to the suffering is unacceptable to him: "The Lord rises to argue his case; he stands to judge the people. The Lord enters into judgment with the elders and princes of his people: it is you who have devoured the vineyard; the spoil of the poor is in your houses. What do you mean by crushing my people, by grinding the face of the poor, says the Lord God of hosts. (Isa. 3:13-15). But the waiting is difficult. The oppressed—those living in the promise—need deliverance. They need for God to move, act, and change their plight by reckoning with those who live in the blessing, apparently forgetting who they are and what they are suffering. There is a natural tension between promise and blessing, and the oppressed want to move into the latter category. But their situation does not change; their foes continue to "trample" on them all day long. (Ps. 56:2).

Because the wicked seem to have no regard for the oppressed, because the wicked use the bodies and the labor of the oppressed for their own gain and then discard them, a seedbed for their rage develops, grows, and ferments. The oppressors see God as having given them the right to have dominion over everyone and everything (Psalm 8). God, they believe, is not displeased with them. Quite to the contrary, the oppressors believe that God is pleased because they are doing God's will! Even as their oppressors tout their obedience to what they believe is God's will, the oppressed weep and moan. They remember the promises of God, they hold onto their surety that God's promises will bear out, but they grow weary. They continually cry out loud to God; they beg God to hear them and answer their prayers, but God seemingly does not answer. The seedbed of rage bubbles within them. "Hear my voice!" they cry, because it does not appear that God has in fact heard them. Their suffering continues and sometimes gets worse. Who is this God, they wonder, who allows such suffering? Why doesn't God deal with their enemies?

The notion of what a "good" God is and how that God should act becomes a theological crisis for some. The issue and understanding of God's ultimate sovereignty becomes an issue. If God is all powerful, and God demands that people "love the Lord their God with all their heart and all their mind and all their soul," and people who are trying to do that are still being oppressed, then what is divine "goodness?" Why would God allow the suffering of people at the hands of those who seemingly have little regard for the "great commandment" or little else that God has commanded? Does God care? In the words of the psalmist, *Why do the heathen rage?*

If goodness implies a certain set of morals, and those who are wielding power have morals that are antithetical and foreign to the oppressed, then what, exactly, does God expect?

What should the oppressed do differently in order to move from "promise" to "blessing?"

There are no answers, at least none that ease the suffering of the oppressed. In this time of political turmoil, the people of the blessing—i.e., the descendants of the Pilgrims who believed their landing in this world was their blessing, the proof of having entered the Promised Land after crossing the wilderness called the Atlantic—are wreaking havoc on the oppressed, gaining more power as they go. The prayers of the righteous are not stopping the train barreling down the tracks of power; the train is going ever faster. Those who have worked and struggled and prayed and been faithful to God can see only the end of the train. But, like black people who used to have to pay their bus fare, get off the bus, and go to the back door to get to their seats, the bus is leaving without them, even as they stand at the door ready to get on. They have paid their dues but they still have not received the reward for living in the promise of God. That reality produces a deep and resentful rage.

Would a "good" God allow this suffering to continue? What is God's "goodness"? How shall it be defined? Is God good because the oppression meted out by people in power has never succeeded in wiping everyone off the face of the earth? Do we adjust our definition of God's goodness based on our circumstances? Is the belief in God's goodness inextricably connected to people living in the promise, *hoping and believing* that the suffering of people will result in their "withering as the green herb" as Psalm 37 says? The God of the oppressed and the God of the oppressor seem to be two different deities. If that is the case, then the questions just posed are a little easier to answer. If my God is a different God than that of the oppressor, then my understanding of God's goodness is based on God's dealing with me, not with the predicament of the world. But if my God and the God of the oppressor are one and the same, there is no room to understand the concept of goodness. The God of the oppressor is not the God of the oppressed. The God who permits racism and sexism and bigoty of all sorts is not the God who in the Bible admonishes us to take care of each other and to love God above all else.

In summary, it is only if one acknowledges that there is a God of the oppressed and a God of the oppressor, and that there are people who live in the blessing and people who live in the promise, as illustrated earlier in this essay, that **the oppressed** can say "God is good." For the oppressed and the oppressor, the definition of "good" is also different. The God of the oppressed is "good" because She hears their prayers and gives them strength to keep fighting for justice. The God of the oppressor is one who apparently sanctions behavior that causes others to unduly suffer but who keeps them in power. Because the oppressed live in the promise that suffering will end and blessings will come, they experience rage as they watch "the wicked" prosper—too often at their expense—but the power of the promise of God that God will deliver them is enough to keep them convinced that God is good, all the time.

After much struggling, I have come to believe in the concept of there being two Gods—not in actuality but in the practice of Christianity. The God of my black church experience, the God who has kept black people on the battlefield in spite of all of the obstacles placed before them, is not the God of my white friends who have no problem with what seems to be a God who looks the other way when it comes to racism, sexism, and all of the other "isms" that cause people deep hurt—and rage. The issue is not God. The issue is the interpretation of who God is, how God acts, and what God requires. The God of my world would shudder at the thought of a "Christian" taking part in a lynching on a Saturday night and showing up for church on a Sunday morning. The hermeneutical understanding of God will always be tied to one's experiences and one's life. As a member of the family of the oppressed, I have to hold onto the promise that God will heal this diseased world and make a way for there to be a beloved community. My belief in God's desire for humans to treat each other with respect and dignity helps me to say "God is good." To hold onto and to ascribe goodness to the God of the oppressor would be committing spiritual suicide, and that is not a road our ancestors took. Nor, I expect, will it be the road the oppressed will take moving forward.

Susan K. Smith, M.Div., D.Min.

Rev. Dr. Susan K. Smith is an ordained minister, writer, social activist, and musician. A former news reporter, talk show host, and contributor to the *Washington Post*, she is the founder of Crazy Faith Ministries, an organization that functions as a "church without walls" in Columbus, Ohio. This unique ministry approach concentrates on teaching people to "pray with their feet" in their work with the homeless and on social justice issues.

She presently is a communications consultant with the Samuel DeWitt Proctor Conference, Inc.; is a consultant and writer with African American Ministers in Action (AAMIA), a division of People for the American Way; and is serving at this time as a co-chair of the Minority Vote subcommittee of the Nonpartisan Ohio Voter Outreach Campaign. (NOVOC).

She has written for the *Washington Post* and the *Huffington Post*, as well as her blog, *Candid Observations*. She serves as one of the tri-chairs for the Ohio Poor People's Campaign: A National Call for Moral Revival; as national scribe for the African American Ministers' Leadership Council (AAMLC) and as communications consultant for the Samuel DeWitt Proctor Conference. She is a graduate of Occidental College and Yale Divinity School and earned a D.Min. from United Theological Seminary. Among her previous publications are: *Crazy Faith: Ordinary People, Extraordinary Lives* (Judson Press, 2009); *The Book of Jeremiah: The Life and Ministry of Jeremiah A. Wright, Jr.* (Pilgrim Press, 2013); *Rest for the Justice-Seeking Soul* (Whitaker House, 2019); and her most recent, *With Liberty and Justice for Some: The Bible, the Constitution, and Racism in America.* (Judson Press, 2020).

CHAPTER ELEVEN

God Speak:
Countering and Healing from Spiritual Warfare's Racist Rhetoric

Janae Moore, M.Div., Ph.D.

Abstract

Words, like our lives, matter. For as long as the spiritual warfare of racism has existed, the perpetrators of this evil have used words to ontologically devalue, denigrate, and demonize who we are as an African people around the globe. Most particularly in the ironically named United States, it has been the intentional and persistent use of racist rhetoric that has insidiously seeped in to our hearts, minds, souls, and spirits to cause the erosion of our knowing the *imago Dei* that we are. This essay will counter the destructiveness of racist rhetoric with the healing love of God talk—God talk that speaks Truth into the centuries-old woundedness of our beings as only the Truth of God can heal us and liberate us from the racist rhetoric that tries, however cannot, ultimately destroy us.

>>

Only God Is Supreme!

We have all probably heard the saying, "Sticks and stones can break my bones, but words can never hurt me." Likewise, we have all probably experienced, via hurtful words hurled at us as well as those we have hurled at others, just how untrue this idiom is. Words can and do hurt, especially when intentionally and viciously used to devalue, demean, and even demonize the sacredness of our very being. Language, when used as verbal abuse, goes much deeper and lingers far longer than even physical abuse. Just as we are told in The Book of Proverbs (18:21) that "[t]he tongue has the power of life and death," words, like our lives, matter. Hence, language, as a structured system of communication, can be and is used as a means to obtain either constructive or destructive ends. The words we speak can be used to lift up or to tear down, to motivate or to mutilate, to encourage or to dissuade, as well as to liberate or to oppress. With these almost endless contrasting possibilities before us, for those of us who work for freedom, it is imperative that in our quest to dismantle systems that seek to oppress us, we must be attentive to and intentional about the language we use to do so. This includes giving credence and expression to the holy rage we experience as a consequence of the litany of words and deeds that racists inflict upon us daily.

As an African born and reared in America, I ask, "So, what happens when language is menacingly misused and intentionally put forth as convoluted rhetoric to maintain a system that is blatantly destructive and deadly like that of systemic racism?" From its origins in this country, racism, as well as the language that supports it, has detrimentally been used to construct and maintain a human hierarchy that God did not create and never intended. It is a hierarchy that arbitrarily places utmost value on those who created it, Europeans (European Americans or Whites), while also, over time, arbitrarily assigning a pecking order of other ethnic groups (Asian Americans, Latinx, and Native Americans), with the least value placed on those this European-imposed system has relentlessly sought to *keep in their place* since they brutally enslaved us as a people: Africans (African Americans or Blacks).

How do we relinquish racist rhetoric and all that it symbolizes when it has been so shrewdly devised, defined, and concretized at every level of social life for over four hundred years, purposely to assure that its intended captives are never set free? How do we heal and shift from utilizing language that helps to hold in place the very thing we need to be liberated from? As we seriously engage these questions and many others germane to our freedom, most especially for those of us who identify as Christians, the wisdom of activist Audre Lorde, spoken at an academic conference in 1979, remains instructive for us today. She contends that "the master's tools will never dismantle the master's house. They may allow us to temporarily beat him at his own game, but they will never enable us to bring about genuine change" (Lorde, "Quotable Quote").

For racists, language, and more accurately, racist rhetoric, is a critical tool they use to maintain the house that racism built long ago. Even the terminology of master and slave is racist rhetoric. It is racist rhetoric intentionally used to justify the aforementioned human hierarchy the enslavers (not "masters") imposed. It is racist rhetoric intentionally used to keep the enslaved (not "slaves") perceived by all—especially the enslaved—as both theologically and ontologically inferior (i.e., minorities, meaning "less than"), while maintaining their dangerous illusion of superiority. Racist White enslavers were so fanatical, pathological, and evil in their commitment to fully exploiting the enslaved while elevating themselves that they went as far as making the enslaved *their property* while viewing and treating them like—or, even worse, less than—they did their animals; hence, chattel slavery. Both terms, *master* and *slave*, like the racist term *nigger*, theologically misrepresent who and how God created all human beings *to be*: in God's Trinitarian image and likeness with equal ontological design and value.

Just like the word *nigger*, *white supremacists* and *minority* are words that should literally elicit holy rage within nanoseconds of hearing them for those of us who are the wrongly viewed and treated. All three terms, I believe, as racist rhetoric, are theological and ontological abominations to God. They cannot help but be. They are outright blasphemous refutations of who God is as well as of who we are as God's creations. *Supremacists*, when used to identify the ontology of racist Whites, is an abomination because its users seek to recreate, and then replace, the human archetype that God created all to be. It is in this theological, anthropological, and ontological refutation that racists (and spiritually unconscious) Whites falsely believe they are more divinely favored and valued by God than all other ethnic groups. Even more so, the diabolical actions of racist Whites against God and humanity do not warrant such a lofty descriptor, but rather, its very opposite: Satanists (satan followers) in truth, and dominants (dominating immorally and evilly) at best. Those of us who use the terms *supremacists* and/or *supremacy* to describe racist Whites only reinforce their idolatrous belief that they are both superior and supreme, above and beyond God. The intentionally wicked lies of White dominants distort and blaspheme God as well as God's creation. They are lies that grieve and enrage God while bringing untellable detriment, destruction, and death to millions.

I believe that the term *minority* is also abominable because, for those of us for whom it is used to pejoratively reference, it only reinforces our being viewed and treated as though we are *less than*—less than the *fearfully and wonderfully* created beings God created us to be. Thus, when we as African Americans who are wrongly viewed and treated as less than, continue to use the term (i.e., "minority"), not only do we label and limit ourselves, but we also corroborate, even if unintentionally, our own ontological diminishment. All acts by racist (and spiritually unenlightened) Whites against us as Blacks can be attributed to their first and foremost viewing us as "other," as "minority. Maintaining this illusive superior position requires the presence of a juxtaposed inferior group who can consequently be seen as and justifiably be treated as less—less valued, less deserving, less respected, and less important—to the point that, even if murdered (including wrongfully by the police, as were George Floyd, Breonna Taylor, Michael Brown, Sandra Bland, Tamir Rice, Freddie Gray, Philando Castille, Eric Garner, and countless others), we have to wage a life and death battle to make the point that Black lives matter!

Just as the word *nigger*—a word that has, with evil, racist White intentions, been made almost synonymous with being Black—should be an affront to us, so too should the words *white supremacy* and *minority*. For those of us who know and love God, these words, along with all racist rhetoric, must become affronts to us as we proclaim and be the Truth of who we are in God. It is God and God only in whom "we [all] live, move and have our being" (Acts 17:28a). Consequently, we must become so offended by all racist rhetoric that we find other language to communicate the truth of what we're reckoning with, as Pulitzer Prize author Isabel Wilkerson demonstrates in her intentional shift in her usage of the term *racism*.

In her masterfully written book, *Caste: The Origins of Our Discontents*, an Oprah's Book Club selection, Wilkerson tells of speaking before an audience of Indian scholars based in America who, learning of her research, invited her to their inaugural conference on caste and race at the University of Massachusetts in Amherst:

> There, I told the audience that I had written a six-hundred-page book about the Jim Crow era in the American South, the time of naked white [domination], but that the word *racism* did not appear anywhere in the narrative. I told them that, after spending fifteen years studying the topic and hearing the testimony of the survivors of the era, I realized that the term was insufficient. *Caste* was the more accurate term, and I set out to [tell] them the reasons why. They were both stunned and heartened. The plates of Indian food kindly set before me at the reception thereafter sat cold due to the press of questions and the sharing that went into the night. (Wilkerson, 2020, p. 30)

Wilkerson's sharing with the American Indian scholars of her heuristic discovery about caste in America, a discovery that personally resonated with them, generated the kind of energy and open and free engagement that only Truth genuinely brings. Her recognition and naming of caste, not racism or race, as the real infrastructure of our divisions in America is mammoth. Wilkerson identifies *caste* as "the architecture of human hierarchy, the subconscious code of instructions for maintaining, in our case, a four-hundred-year-old social order. Looking at caste is like holding the country's X-ray up to the light" (Wilkerson, 2020, p. 17). Wilkerson further defines and describes her discovery about America's caste system:

> A caste system is an artificial construction, a fixed and embedded ranking of human value that sets the presumed inferiority of other groups on the basis of ancestry and often immutable traits, traits that would be neutral in the abstract but are ascribed life-and-death meaning in a hierarchy favoring the dominant caste whose forebears designed it. A caste system uses rigid, often arbitrary boundaries to keep the ranked groupings apart, distinct from one another and in their assigned places.... A caste system endures because it is often justified as divine will, originating from sacred text or the presumed laws of nature, reinforced throughout the culture and passed down through the generations.... Race does the heavy lifting for a caste system that demands a means of human division. If we have been trained to see humans in the language of race, then caste is the underlying grammar that we encode as children.... Caste, like grammar, becomes an invisible guide not only to how we speak, but to how we process information.... We may mention "race" referring to people as black or white or Latino or Asian or indigenous, when what lies beneath each label is centuries of history and assigning of assumptions and values to physical features in a structure of human hierarchy.... Race, in the United States, is the visible agent of the unseen force of caste. Caste is the bones, race the skin. (Wilkerson, 2020, pp. 17-19)

Mark Lawrence McPhail, in his preface to (the new edition of) *The Rhetoric of Racism Revisited: Reparations or Separations?*, states that:

> [T]he language that we use to talk about racism implicates us in its perpetuation, and ... we will ultimately need to articulate what Cornel West describes as a "new language of empathy and compassion" if we are to move beyond reducing racism to material and ideological problematics, and instead recognize it for what it is: a problem of moral and spiritual incoherence. When we are willing to honestly address our racial histories and identities on these terms, we shall begin to move beyond a simple revisiting and toward a substantive reparation of the rhetoric of racism. ((McPhail, 2002, p. x)

The rhetoric of racism is the intentional manipulation and use of language to sustain a system that is ungodly in its origins, as well as its implementation. Racist rhetoric is not only ungodly; it is—like its progenitor, rac*ism*—satanically sourced. The historical and unprecedented slaughter and elimination of people and their cultures by racist Europeans around the globe—via genocide, enslavement, colonization, land and resource confiscation, unjust wealth procurement, and a myriad of other dehumanized horrors—remain almost unfathomable. Yet, the inhumane, dastardly, and demonic deeds of racist Whites are sickeningly real for far too many of us. And, justifiably, their evils evoke great pain and holy rage within us. The pain and rage are exacerbated all the more, knowing that the whole system of racism is based on and built upon the most fallacious of fallacies.

In the preface to his 1964 classic examination of the origins and implications of race theory, Ashley Montagu begins by identifying race as a problem whose assumed position of importance during that time was both alarming and exaggerated. Alarming, he states, "because racial dogmas have been made the basis for an inhumanly brutal political philosophy which has resulted in the death or social disenfranchisement of millions of innocent human beings; exaggerated, because when the nature of contemporary 'race' theory is scientifically analyzed and understood it ceases to be of any significance for social or any other kind of action" (Montagu, 1964, p. 13). While Montagu states upfront that his undertaking is not a treatise on race, he, nonetheless, declares at the onset that:

> This book then is designed to expose the most dangerous myth of our age, the myth of "race" by demonstrating the falsities of which it is compounded.... The fact is that there are numerous differences between ethnic groups, and even regional segments of such groups, in many bodily traits.... Differences are not denied where they exist. What is denied is that they are biologically either great or significant enough to justify men in making them the pretext for social discrimination of any kind.... In the past the tendency has been strong to overstress the differences.... this drive to find differences in the 'races' of mankind grew out of the general social climate.... A natural stratification of the races mirrored the social stratification of the classes, and in the light of the doctrine of 'the survival of the fittest' justified the exploitation and oppression of both. Differences were therefore maximized and exaggerated.... But the facts make it abundantly clear that these differences constitute proof of the fundamental unity of all [hu]mankind." (Montagu, 1964, pp. 14-15)

In Montagu's reporting, we not only hear the fallacy upon which the system of race is built and, thus too, racism, along with the selfish, sinister purposes for which it was intended, we also hear the Truth about God's creation. The Truth that, as diverse as our differences are, the sciences reveal that there is unity and oneness amongst us, not despite our differences, but rather, because of them. This great Divine Paradox from the Supreme Being, that "out of many, one" was even recognized by this country as it has its Latin equivalent as the traditional motto of the United States appearing on its Great Seal: *E pluribus unum*.

While Montagu calls race a myth, Princeton's James S. McDonnell Distinguished University African American Studies professor, Eddie S. Glaude, Jr. goes even further and calls both the concepts of democracy and the value gap imposed by racism a *lie* in his recently published book, *Begin Again: James Baldwin's America and Its Urgent Lessons for Our Own*. In his preeminent social critique of James Baldwin, who was a social critique extraordinaire of America's struggles with these intersectional lies, Glaude comments:

> Since the publication of *Notes of A Native Son*, Baldwin had insisted that the country grapple with the contradiction at the heart of its self-understanding: the fact that in this so-called democracy, people believed that the color of one's skin determined the relative value of an individual's life and justified the way American society was organized. That belief and justification had dehumanized entire groups of people. White Americans were not excluded from its effects. 'In this debasement and definition of black people,' Baldwin argued, white people "debased and defined themselves.'
>
> Baldwin's understanding of the American condition cohered around a set of practices that, taken together, constitute something I refer to … as *the lie*. The idea of facing the lie was always at the heart of Jimmy's witness, because he thought that it, as opposed to our claim to the shining city on the hill, was what made America truly exceptional. The lie is more properly several sets of lies with a single purpose. If what I have called the 'value gap' is the idea that in America white lives have always mattered more than the lives of others, then the lie is a broad and powerful architecture of false assumptions by which the value gap is maintained. These are the narrative assumptions that support the everyday order of American life, which means we breathe them like air. We count them as truths. We absorb them into our character. (Glaude, 2020, pp. 6-7)

The above commentary by Glaude, along with Baldwin's, addresses how deeply entrenched and prevalent the American lie has (and lies have) been amongst us. *The lie* about American democracy and race is as common in this White-dominated culture as is apple pie and baseball. The primary lie, and its many sub-lies, have been poured in and covered up with the very concrete that helped lay America's stolen foundation. His-story narratives as told by Whites have demonized and named as savages the indigenous peoples of the land as their own roles in the genocide and land confiscation of the indigenous people were sanitized and romanticized. (Europeans were amoral murderers and stealers, not moral pioneers and settlers—yet another lie.) This same sanitizing and romanticizing of their roles was extended to justify the chattel enslavement Europeans imposed on Africans while simultaneously debasing, devaluing, and demoralizing them. This spirit of evil remains alive and all too well in our midst today, as does the prophetic knowing of Baldwin about the true America still struggling to be the democratic, Christian nation it likes to deceive others (and many of us) to believe that it is.

The disregard that racists have for God (although many have always attributed the success of their bloody conquests to their being ordered and ordained by God), along with their arrogant disdain for the sanctity of human life, is hauntingly perverse. Thereby, the idea of affixing a term such as *white supremacy* to describe them despite their evil exploits—a term so antithetical to who and how they actually are—is beyond ludicrous. It is sacrilegious, idolatrous, and blasphemous. Like their evil actions, racists use racist rhetoric as a means to their ultimate end, which, like satan, is to "steal, kill and destroy" (John 10:10a). They deem all a threat whom they, out of fear, believe seek to usurp their determination to rule, reign, and dominate, not just a few or some, but the entire world. Racist Whites have sought "by any means necessary" to dominate the world through European imperialism, of which racism is a part. (Apologies to our late, beloved brother, el-Hajj Malik el-Shabazz, also known as Malcolm X, for applying his well-known phrase to the strategy of his nemesis!)

Given the past and continued present day horrors of racists, there is absolutely nothing supreme or superior about their comportment as members of the human family. They not only reject the human family, they ultimately reject, without a modicum of reverence or respect, the Creator of the human family as well. In fact, if Jesus were still in flesh form, He would render a sharp reprimand to all racists today as He did the pseudo-pious religious leaders of His day for their hypocrisy and lack of love millenniums ago:

> Jesus said to [the nonbelieving Jewish leaders], "If God were your Father, you would love Me, for I proceeded forth and came from God; nor have I come of Myself, but He sent Me. Why do you not understand My speech? Because you are not able to listen to My word. You are of *your* father the devil, and the desires of your father you want to do. He was a murderer from the beginning, and does not stand in the truth, because there is no truth in him. When he speaks a lie, he speaks from his own *resources,* for he is a liar and the father of it. But because I tell the truth, you do not believe Me. Which of you convicts Me of sin? And if I tell the truth, why do you not believe Me? He who is of God hears God's words; therefore, you do not hear, because you are not of God." (John 8:42-47; NKJV).

Jesus' *truth*, not rhetoric, delineates our purpose for being on this earthly journey we call life: *to be* clear in choosing whom we are going to serve. "No one can serve two masters; for either he will hate the one and love the other, or else he will be loyal to the one and despise the other. You cannot serve God and mammon" [i.e., money, empire, nationalism, racism, imperialism, the world] (Matthew 6:24). Jesus also defines the parameters of our choosing. It is a choice to serve God, the Father of Truth; or, to choose to be of the devil, the father of lies. There are no other options offered, not by God and not even by satan (intentionally lowercased by the author to symbolize his true stature).

As Satan relentlessly wages spiritual warfare (Ephesians 6:12), ultimately against God and primarily through us as God's finite and fickle creatures, he is ever on the prowl to destroy souls. Like a prowling lion, he is ceaselessly enlisting the selfish, the greedy, the arrogant, the ignorant, the prideful, the judgmental, the coldhearted, and yes, the racist, and all others of us who choose to side with him. Even those of us who attempt lukewarm posturing are ones Satan patiently waits for. He waits, knowing that it will be but a short time before God spews us out of His mouth for our conflictual doublemindedness and our useless cowardice (Revelation 3:16). And since it is abundantly clear that racists have made a distinctive decision about the evil one they are serving, they are undeserving of language or labels appropriate for and only applicable to God, for only God is Supreme!

According to the *Online Etymology Dictionary*, "supremacist" is a noun that, "by 1948, originally with reference to racial beliefs and in most cases with white, [derives] from supremacy + -ist [and is defined as] a person who advocates the supremacy of some particular group or racial group over all others" (www.etymonline.com). The adjective "supreme," from which "supremacist" is derived, is defined as "highest in excellence or achievement; greatest in status or power; greatest or maximal in degree; extreme. [It reportedly originates in the] 1520s, from Middle French *supreme* (15c.) and directly from Latin *supremus* "highest," superlative of *superus* "situated above," from *super* "above" ... Supreme Being ... God" (www.etymonline.com).

By mere definitions alone, it is obvious that while racist Whites dominate almost around the globe, they do not do so because of supremacy. They do so, rather, because of wickedness and evil, ruthlessness and godlessness. Thus, if any term is going to be affixed to them, it should originate from the root source of who and how they *be*. Again, Jesus' critique of the so-called religious leaders of His day is informative here and worthy of repeating: "You are of *your* father the devil, and the desires of your father you want to do. He was a murderer from the beginning, and does not stand in the truth, because there is no truth in him. When he speaks a lie, he speaks from his own *resources,* for he is a liar and the father of it." The most horrendous thing about this whole racialized system that is responsible for innumerable sufferings, misery, rage, grief, and death, is that it is all based on that which does not exist—not in spirit, not in truth!

For the many millions denied the liberties touted by this country, we, and our loved ones, too often deal with the harsh realities of generational oppression, mass incarceration, failing educational systems, racial profiling, inadequate and substandard housing to no housing, health and wealth disparities and injustices, job discrimination, unemployment, and police brutality, just to name a few. Our forced realities defy the notion that we live in a democracy or that whites are supreme. In fact, both, for the marginalized and oppressed, are experienced as the exact opposite—just ask the family of George Floyd and the many other families of Black and Brown bodies mercilessly killed by the police and, increasingly, by so-called White vigilantes who have been emboldened by the racist rhetoric of Trump to protect the illusion of white space and, ultimately, white domination.

In a June 1, 2020 NPR article written exactly one week after and in response to the inhumane public-square lynching of George Floyd, a 46-year-old African American father of five, James Baldwin is again quoted. The quote's context is a 1961 interview he had with a radio host who asked him what was it like to be a "Negro" in America. Baldwin's captured response is used to frame the article's title as well: "To Be in A Rage, Almost All the Time":

> To be a Negro in this country and to be relatively conscious is to be in a state of rage almost, almost all of the time—and in one's work. And part of the rage is this: It isn't only what is happening to you. But it's what's happening all around you and all of the time in the face of the most extraordinary and criminal indifference, indifference of most white people in this country, and their ignorance. Now, since this is so, it's a great temptation to simplify the issues under the illusion that if you simplify them enough, people will recognize them. I think this illusion is very dangerous because, in fact, it isn't the way it works. A complex thing can't be made simple. You simply have to try to deal with it in all its complexity and hope to get that complexity across. (www.

npr.org, "To Be In A Rage Almost All the Time", June 1, 2020, 2:55 PM, ET)

As poignant and piercing as Baldwin's response expectedly was, the great tragedy and yes, rage, is that just one-year-shy-of-sixty-years-later, his assessment of what it's like to be a "Negro" in America is just as applicable and harrowing. While the ethnic descriptor has gone from *Negro* in Baldwin's time to Black and/or African American in ours, those of us who are extra melanin-kissed children of God still find ourselves in a rage almost all of the time, if not (for some of us) *all* of the time. And it is precisely because we know that we are children of God—children endowed with the unalienable right to be viewed and treated accordingly—that we have, not just rage, but *holy rage*! We have holy rage that our ontological quest to *simply just be* in this country has for 401 years been met with vitriolic resistance and assiduous attacks that have been and continue to be daunting, dangerous, and, far too often, as for our beloved brother Mr. Floyd and countless millions, deadly.

So how do we free ourselves from the myths and the lies long enough to get our inner bearings to know how *to be* despite the many forces arrayed against our very existence? How do we connect and remain connected to help each other to "fix our thoughts on what is true and honorable, and right, and pure and lovely and admirable" (Philippians 4:8; NLT)? My response: We go back to in the beginning, remember, and *be*.

For those of us who identify as Christians, our biblical texts and sacred scriptures tell us that "in the beginning God created the heavens and the earth" (Genesis 1:1). It was God who spoke, "Let there be light" to the dark, formless void that earth was as His Spirit hovered over the deep waters, and light was. It was God who divided the (day) light from the (night) darkness, and affixed the firmament in the sky, which He called Heaven, and created the Seas and dry land which He called Earth, and then proceeded to fill the seas with sea life and the land with animals and seed-bearing plants and all that we have come to know and respect as Mother Nature (Genesis 1:2-26). And then, it was after all of this—the heavens and the earth—that God created, that God decided to make His greatest earthly creation: humans in God's Trinitarian image and likeness. Thus, God said:

> Let U̲s make man in O̲ur image, according to O̲ur likeness; let them have dominion over the fish of the sea, over the birds of the air, and over the cattle, over all the earth and over every creeping thing that creeps on the earth. So, God created man in His *own* image; in the image of God He created him; male and female He created them. Then God blessed them, and God said to them, 'Be fruitful and multiply; fill the earth and subdue it; have   dominion over the fish of the sea, over the birds of the air, and over every living thing that moves on earth. (Genesis 1:26-28)

In this creation story, it is important to note that God predates Creation. As the Creator of all, to include us as human beings, God is the Supreme Being. God's first issued command to His newly created likenesses is to reproduce themselves and to both fill and subdue the earth. God gave them dominion over all the creatures in the sea, air, and on the land that He created. There is no hierarchy established in God's creation of humans. And the greatest commandment that has been given to us since our creation is that we first love God with all that we are and to, likewise, love our Self and each other as God loves us (Matthew 22:36-40). As love dominates, there is no caste or race, there is only the yearning of the heart and soul for union with God and the creation of the Beloved Community with our God-imaged sisters and brothers.

As I remember God as the beginning of all that is, I experience the clarity Jesus says we must have: clarity to choose. And in this lucid moment, unencumbered by the ravages and rages evoked by racism, I choose to serve God and honor the Truth that Only God Is Supreme. I take comfort in knowing that lies can never alter Truth and this includes the Truth that only God is Supreme and no human being can ever, not in spirit, not in truth, usurp God's place, power, or position of Supremacy. My confession is that I have been responding to the lies spewed and the evils inflicted by White dominants as though God's Truth as the Supreme Being of and over all isn't true. It is in this place of being affected by the lies of racists and the devastations caused by them that my rage—my holy rage—is most acute. I have the holy rage expressed by David in Psalm 139 as well as his desire for God's vengeance against the wicked perpetrators of the evil that racism is: "If only you, God, would slay the wicked! Away from me, you who are bloodthirsty! They speak of You with evil intent; Your adversaries misuse Your name. Do I not hate those who are in rebellion against You? I have nothing but hatred for them; I count them my enemies" (Psalm 139:19-22).

The primary thing about perfect hatred toward those of us who make ourselves enemies against God as racists do, is that the holy rage we experience must be channeled into positive and constructive outlets for love and for good. To hold holy rage without mindful releasement can easily result in putting us in a place as displeasing to God as racists are. While intense energies, these energies can and will work against us as much as they can work for us if not engaged properly. And the most proper engagement is to release the holy rage we feel in our village communities with like spirits. With kindred spirits, we can move synergistically in the energies of holy rage as we collectively dismantle systems of evil like caste and racism by building God's Kingdom and the Beloved Community in our midst. A guiding principle for holy rage releasing is "as within, so out with." We want to release holy rage energies as a creative force and not hold on to them until they become a destructive force within—a consequence that has already occurred far too frequently in our communities.

I acknowledge that there is an undeniable heaviness to this Life journey. The heaviness is particularly true as we find ourselves at the intersection of multiple pandemics bearing down upon us as a people. A people who, after four centuries, are still dealing with grave social, racial, political, economic, ecological, environmental, health, and a host of other disparities, injustices, and inequities intentionally structured against us. A people who, in the current pandemic of COVID-19, are again the ones most impacted and devastated by its presence, to include in infections and deaths as well as the paradox of being both the primary frontline workers and those most prone to losing our jobs, being evicted and, consequently, faced with even more diminished wealth and quality of life. We face the dregs of this unprecedented virus and the negative results of global warming as there is an increase of brutality and racial negativity against us, including from police in various states, all the way to the president of the nation.

Given the seeming unrelenting hardships we keep enduring as Africans in America, becoming clear and remaining consistent in the choice of whom we are here to serve is perhaps one of our greatest life needs and challenges. And while I know that, in my own choosing, I'll continue to reject the racist rhetoric of White supremacy, minority, nigger, and all other pejorative terms (and actions) intended to keep the spiritual warfare of racism intact along with the caste system that undergirds it. I also know we each have to come to our own heuristic discoveries and, like Wilkerson, determine, in our own way and in our own time, the terminology that best defines our seeing, believing and, ultimately and prayerfully, our own true knowing. We have no greater example to follow than that of Jesus, who, in the midst of dying a brutal death for our sins, knew that His Truth in the Father still prevailed. Death did not destroy Him, but instead gave us, as His believers and followers, abundant and eternal Life—Life that the world did not give, and the world cannot take away.

I can hear Jesus saying now:

"Don't be afraid of those who want to kill your body; for they cannot touch your soul. Fear only God, who can destroy both soul and body in hell" (Matthew 10:28, NLT). This speaks to the Power and Authority that God has as the Author and Finisher of our lives. Therefore, in the midst of all the worldliness and racist evil that surrounds us, I'm putting all I that I am in Him; for after all, only God is Supreme!

Nothing real can be threatened.
Nothing unreal exists.
Herein lies the peace of God.
(*A Course in Miracles*, 3rd Edition, 2007, p. x)

References

A Course in Miracles, 3rd edition. (2007). Novato: Foundation for Inner Peace.

Glaude, E. S. (2020). *Begin Again: James Baldwin's America and Its Urgent Lessons for Our Own.* New York: Crown.

Lorde, A. "Quotable Quote": www.goodreads.com/quotes/291810-for-the-master-s-tools-will-never-dismantle-the-master-s-house

McPhail, M. L. (2002). *The Rhetoric of Racism Revisited: Reparations or Separation?* New York: Rowman & LIttlefield.

Montagu, A. (1964). *Man's Most Dangerous Myth: The Fallacy of Race.* Cleveland: The World Publishing Company.

Online Etymology Dictionary: www.etymonline.com

"To Be in A Rage Almost All the Time": www.npr.org, June 1, 2020, 2:55 PM, ET: https://www.npr.org/2020/06/01/867153918/-to-be-in-a-rage-almost-all-the-time

Wilkerson, I. (2020). *Caste: The Origins of Our Discontents.* New York: Random House.

Janae Moore, M.Div., Ph.D.

Rev. Dr. Janae Moore is an Itinerant Elder in the African Methodist Episcopal (AME) Church and serves in the Capital District of the Washington Conference at Mt. Zion AME Church in Laurel, Maryland. She is a clinically trained chaplain and licensed clinical social worker who is currently on staff with the Samuel DeWitt Proctor Conference. She also provides consultancy to a family- and community-based nonprofit organization in Washington, D.C. She has been an adjunct professor in the School of Social Work at Morgan State University and has taught incarcerated women through the University of the District of Columbia. Dr. Moore is the founder and operator of Taranga House Spiritual Retreat & Practice Center and Lov'N Poetry Ministries. She is the author of *What Is that Thing: Poetry for Spiritual Introspection and Dialogue that Leads to Action.* She is the grateful mother of two sons, a daughter-in-law, two grandchildren, and a third one due in January of 2021.

CHAPTER TWELVE

Expressing Rage Without Becoming Rage:
Mentors Mastering Psycho-Spiritual Paradigm

Alfonso Wyatt, M.Div., Ph.D.

Abstract

This essay arises from the clinical, pastoral, and teaching experiences born of a calling dedicated to the transformation and survival of Black youth in general and inner city Black male youth in particular.

In his own unique style, the writer offers his psycho-spiritual methods of analyzing and addressing the important issues of anger, rage, grief, death, and spiritual warfare.

Addressing the issue of Black Rage, the author stresses the importance of "speaking life" and discusses an approach he characterizes as "love to hate" and puts forth lifestyle choices for producing what he calls "Love Warriors."

Through the exegesis of Pauline texts, quotes from Black elders, a personal vignette, original poetry, and spiritually-based words of instruction and wisdom, we are offered a formulated Black Christian intervention for imparting and nourishing wisdom for use by all Black youth, Black male youth, and those who are similarly called to educate and support and empower youth of the Black community.

>>

> My people, hear my teaching; listen to the words of my mouth. I will open my mouth with a parable; I will utter hidden things, things from of old—things we have heard and known, things our ancestors have told us. We will not hide them from their descendants; we will tell the next generation the praiseworthy deeds of the Lord, his power, and the wonders he has done. He decreed statutes for Jacob and established the law in Israel, which he commanded our ancestors to teach their children, so the next generation would know them, even the children yet to be born, and they in turn would tell their children. (Psalm 78:1-6)

I am a lifelong youth developer, public theologian, national role model, and mentor of mentors. I have been blessed to change the lives of countless young people, most outside of the faith community. I have worked with youth in juvenile detention facilities, gangs, foster care, LGBQT youth, as well as young people eligible for advanced college placement. I have mentored the children of incarcerated parents; spoken hope to children (now adults), known as 80s Babies, who came of age during the crack pandemic; as well as young people growing up in single-parent households. It is from these experiences that I will advance my perspective on how to talk to young people about expressing rage without becoming rage from a psycho-spiritual paradigm.

Parents, mentors, activists, and elders in and out of the church, it is important to model and teach how to deal with rage because our children are dying in the streets—not just at the hands of police but also from young hands shooting guns. It is the job of parents, preachers, teachers, "reachers," mentors, community parents, and elders to equip our present and future leaders, many of whom will lead this current Black

Lives Matter fight well into the 21st century. The language, and techniques may change from generation to generation, but the truth, as I understand it and have been given to share, will always stand the test of time.

Speak Life

I was asked by one of my clients to lead a delegation of a dozen diverse individuals, all with a dream to become high school special education teachers. I took these future educators to a church located across the street from a housing project in "the hood" to meet children and teens enrolled in the house of worship's self-funded summer camp program. After entering the sanctuary, I could tell that both groups were wary of each other. My experience told me to do an "icebreaker" to facilitate group interaction. I asked the teachers-to-be to tell the young people the foundational reason why they wanted to teach. I then asked the youth to give their advice on how to be a successful teacher. I picked several eager "advisers." Their responses centered on being fair (children in school have a hard life), be consistent, know their students' names, and be a good communicator. There was one response from a 13-years-old boy that blew all of us away. In a voice beyond his years, a resonant voice filled with authority as if destined to speak in this moment, the young man said, "Speak life to the students."

We are living in a time where it is more acceptable to use words to kill the hopes and dreams of others. Every day, the incessant barrage of disparaging put-downs and "clap-backs" airs as trending news on television, social media, and in personal conversations to the extent that speaking life to one another can seem passé. There are people (trolls) who amass a following by taking advantage of a person's weaknesses, blunders, or presenting embarrassing private details without context, or, in many instances, without regard to truth. This is the opposite of speaking life. Do you have someone who speaks life to you? If you do, let me say you are fortunate. A person who speaks life generally lives a life that allows lessons learned to be gleaned, processed, and shared. This person does not want to control your life but wants you to get the best out of the life you are living. As mentioned, the inspiration for this dispatch centers on a boy living in the projects across the street from the church he attends.

While I sense he is trying to do the right thing, there are dismal demographics working against him. With that said, I was so moved by his speak-life proclamation that I had to go back and speak life to him. Following is the paraphrased conversation:

> Son, I want you to know that you are not ordinary but extraordinary. What you told those teachers about speaking life to their students was deep. I came back because my spirit told me that I had to speak life to you. I don't know your life story, but I do know many young people your age are headed in the wrong direction. I want to ask you a question; do you think you are doing the best you can in school? If not, you must ask yourself why not—then search for answers. You don't have to tell me your answer. I must say it is one thing to end up on the street and you don't care. It is another thing to be on the street and you know, deep down inside, you don't belong there. Speak life to your problems. Speak life to your obstacles. Speak life to yourself.

We must speak life to sisters and brothers of all ages. We must share the joy that comes from finding release from destructive life traps. We must always encourage, never discourage. We must always empower, never overpower. We must work hard to keep our personal lights shining bright so we may find and then speak life to a people struggling to live.

words

has compassion ever been enough
gestures...tears...words...
this day fades
then alone you stand resolve shaken
questions abound

just the other day dancing eyes
soaring spirit and smile
to melt the coldest heart
all radiating from love's core
boundless friendship and warmth
grows strangely cold supplanted by
rage…
fear…
hurt…
your sorrow shall pass
oh brave warrior
my words
offered
in fervent prayer
seeks
justice…
peace…
strength…
to
love
again

You have heard that it was said, "Eye for eye, and tooth for tooth." But I tell you, do not resist an evil person. If anyone slaps you on the right cheek, turn to them the other cheek also. And if anyone wants to sue you and take your shirt, hand over your coat as well. (Matthew 5: 38-40)

Most men in and out of the church have a hard time with turning the other cheek, an admonishment presented by Jesus in his Sermon on the Mount. Men, by nature and/or nurture, are supposed to be tough, remote, no-nonsense, strong, and ready to defend their being, home (territory), honor, or ego at the drop of a hat. This mentality is drilled into young boys when told they are not supposed to cry even when hurt, when crying is called for; or stand their ground and fight no matter the cost. One emotion that some men suffer little or no shame expressing is anger. There are positive things that can come from anger. Unfortunately, many negative issues can result from an angry impulsive outburst that overrides time to process cause and effect. Anger, when out of control, can escalate into full-blown rage. As I struggled with the concept of turning the other cheek, I read in a commentary that Jesus made the turn the other cheek pronouncement through a legal lens and not from an act of violence. After all, Jesus took offense at the moneychangers in the temple, so much so, that He overturned their tables and drove men and animals out of the temple using a whip fashioned on-the-spot in what could be termed a fit of rage (John 2:13-16). This image of Jesus is not in line with the image of The Shepherd looking for lost sheep.

It is difficult to reconcile the continued atrocities committed against Black people and not harbor rage. It is frustrating being blamed for trying to navigate a rigged system where the rules can change to suit the oppressor of the moment. It is tiring trying to prove who you are not as opposed to who you are. It is difficult sending children to schools that are still separate and unequal. It is spirit-defeating to witness the over-incarceration of men, women, boys, and girls of color. It is a travesty our elders fought in World War II only to be denied GI benefits given freely to White soldiers so they could get back on their feet. Rage is a proper response to injustice, but rage must link to a strategy that leads to a desired outcome; if not, rage becomes its own costly reward.

> What you say can preserve life or destroy it; so you must accept the consequences of your words. (Proverbs 18:21)

Counseling young people about negotiating life is difficult, as folkways and mores change from generation to generation; talking about negotiating the streets is another thing altogether. In many neighborhoods, where Black churches of all sizes and denominations are located, it can be said that violence rules the streets, especially at night. I work with formerly incarcerated men and women called "Credible Messengers." These brave brothers and sisters patrol dangerous streets in an effort to deter violence or retaliation after shootings occur. Some credible messengers work in hospital emergency rooms where death and rage meet after a shooting. The hospital is where vows to seek street vengeance are made. It is in this highly charged, rage-filled, spirit-killing, gut-wrenching environment that the Credible Messengers plead with enraged youth with a mind and means to kill, to, essentially, turn the other cheek.

Romancing Death

When I was four years old, I, along with my older brother, had to move down south for a year due to a Christmas Eve fire in my family's South Bronx apartment. We were sent to our grandparent's home in Bessemer, Alabama. It was there that I had my first brush with death. I was playing in the backyard with my cousin. We were chucking (a southern term for throwing) rocks at each other. If you know anything about four-year-olds, you appreciate the fact that they seldom connect with their target. Out of nowhere, I got the bright idea to throw a rock at a furry yellow baby chick, pecking in the corner of the yard. As soon as the rock left my hand, I had a bad feeling. I felt worse when the stone struck the chick and it died. I can still remember the emptiness and guilt I felt because of my action. My God, I was a chick murderer. I enlisted the support of my cousin and we hastily tossed the lifeless yellow corpse under the house. In the most innocent way, death became real to me.

My young brothers and sisters, you live in a time marked by death and dying. You see it and live it every day. You are fed a steady diet of blended imaginary violence via video games, movies, and television shows. You see real death on the streets caused by rage, robbery, retribution, new diseases, and a he-said/she-said-now-someone-is-dead mess. There are people who would rather kill other people because that is easier than getting a job, getting off drugs, or being responsible. There are desperate people who are so insecure, angry, and misshapen that they think nothing of blowing away someone for their sneakers, jacket, cellphone, or because of some perceived act of disrespect (looks can kill!). Life is too precious to die at the hands of someone who woke up angry at the world. You can wear the wrong colors and die these days. Where you were born could be the reason where you will die. If someone who is looking for trouble challenges you by asking, *"what-chu"* looking at, you have my permission to say, "Absolutely nothing" and keep on stepping.

> Let no corrupting talk come out of your mouths, but only such as is good for building up, as fits the occasion, that it may give grace to those who hear. (Ephesians 4:29)

Our ancestors were victims of hate in this country while they fought to reveal the presence of hate. Along this historical timeline, a false narrative was invented, supported, shared, and transported all over this country—and indeed, around the world. Hate will not back up in the face of hate. In fact, when hate meets hate all it can do is create more hate. I remember when an act engendering a surge of hate overtook me and, as a result, I wanted to exact some "Black man justice" (you ever been there?). I did not know what I wanted to do in response but felt the egregious wrong I suffered called for direct confrontation. All I recall is what I heard in my spirit: *Vengeance is mine, I will repay.* I went on a rant, saying to myself, "Why do I always have to be the good person, the rational person?" The next evening, The Lord spoke to my spirit, saying, "Go pray over the desk of your adversary." I said, "I ain't doing that," in a fit of rage-inspired rebellion— even as I was moving toward the desk. I was surprised that I was able to pray a fairly long, generous prayer for the person. The next day I came into work. I discovered that the person did not change... but I did.

Love To Hate

The National Memorial for Peace and Justice in Montgomery, Alabama, a project of the Equal Justice Initiative, stands as a stark reminder of the deep, dark legacy of hate in America, manifested in the lynching of 4,064 black men, women, and children from The Reconstruction Era to 1950. This new museum, also known as The Lynching Museum, symbolically presents the names of people of color hanging from the rafters who were lynched by frenzied White mobs driven by hate. I was always fascinated by history; so much so, at 16 years of age, I decided to major in Civil War and Reconstruction at Howard University. I knew before going to college that hate, steeped in slavery's destructive aftermath, shaped this nation to this very day. We, the descendants of slaves, still feel hate manifested in pernicious social welfare policies, institutional biases, outright violence, hostile attitudes, and benign neglect. Hate at times can wear an acceptable mask to trap the unsuspecting or beguile the susceptible by making it seem natural for people to have a love to hate.

Let us take hate from the macro/historic level down to the individual space and look at how it targets people. I am talking about hate that respects no bounds or pains it may cause; hate that seeks retribution and despises any attempts at reconciliation. Hate should come with a warning sign, because it will eventually destroy any trace of decency in the person that harbors it. Hate is a corrosive; it will break out and poison the heart, mind, and soul of those foolish enough to believe he or she will never have to pay a price for hating others. Hate creates a welcoming environment for bitterness to thrive. The more hate one develops, the more bitter he or she becomes. Sadly, this hate cycle, as we can see and feel, can go on for generations.

If we look at hate on the historical level once again, one would think that people who have a love to hate are unstoppable. Historical hate in this country can be seen through the genocide of Native Americans, enslavement of Africans, and the harsh treatment of immigrants, as well as the over-incarceration of people of color. Hate kills with impunity. Hate can take on a spirit that engenders hate as a plausible reason to have a love to hate. The hate rolls on the guilty, the innocent, and eventually, the people standing on the sidelines watching the horror unfold but reticent or refusing to do anything about it, become unindicted co-conspirators or victims. Hate is insatiable. My training as an historian reveals that eras of intense hate ride on the pendulum of time. As we wait for it to swing back, know that the only antidote to combat people who love to hate is love—love yourself, love your family, love your community, love your freedom—love your God.

safe harbor

if we cannot take love
truly professed to another
then hopelessly we are lost
forlorn sister and brother
cast adrift on a turgid sea
sails billowed by hate
evil wind forever blow
a wider void create
can we find together
some shelter from the storm
rescue the words I love you
new bond form
this day into forever
offer this plea
who first speak the words
find save harbor
in
me

Love is patient, love is kind. It does not envy, it does not boast, it is not proud. It is not rude, it is not self-seeking, it is not easily angered, it keeps no account of wrongs. Love does not delight in evil but rejoices with the truth. It always protects, always trusts, always hopes, always perseveres. Love never fails. (1 Corinthians 13:4-8a)

I issue this call to Love Warriors against a backdrop of rising hatred, continued racism, and wrongful deaths. Love Warriors fight behind enemy lines on behalf of others, spreading a message of compassion, forgiveness, and hope. The "high ground" for Love Warriors is the heart, mind, and soul of people who are lost in a morass of hate, anger, and the all-too-human desire to seek retribution no matter the cost. Love

Warriors excel in the practice of functional dualism, bringing mind and heart together, transforming love from being merely a good idea to being a way of life.

The act of loving one's neighbor has become more difficult. This disturbing reality of suspicion, oppression, and perpetual hate is wrapped around skewed revisionist history, stilted politics, and biased rhetoric. The enemies of Love Warriors use their not-so-secret weapon of spreading lies evidenced by irreconcilable differences in order to diffuse and confuse their adversary's efforts. Love Warriors are aware of lying prophets (profits) and deceitful pontificators trying to convince the world that their darkness is really truth in disguise. It is my prayer that true Love Warriors will find renewed strength and validation to fight for change, dignity, and respect that leads to lasting justice, equity, and peace.

Love Warriors' Psycho-Spiritual Academy for Mentors

Love Warriors, called to mentor, allow me to use the teachings of Paul in a different and unique context given what we as a people—and, by extension, our youth—are dealing with in the streets of America. Before there was Paul, there was Saul, an oppressor of people he did not know, an accomplice to murder, and a notorious hater of people determined to follow The Way. Saul had the same behaviors as modern-day oppressors. It was not until Saul became Paul (psycho-spiritual transformation) that he was able to systematically and unapologetically reach, teach, and equip the very people he tried to destroy. With that said, here are some teachings that have stood the test of time from the school of Paul, updated for modern day Love Warriors mentoring future leaders.

Gym Class—Paul used sports as a way to relate and teach men and women of his time. What was true then is true today: "We wrestle not against flesh and blood…but spiritual wickedness in high places…." He told his mentee Timothy to fight the good fight of faith. He told the people of Philippi to press toward the mark of the high calling; in other words, never give up the struggle. Given the pressures of the day, the pressing spirit of our ancestors must be invoked, taught, and shared with our young people—and with each other.

Psychology Class—Paul says in Romans 12:2, "be not conformed to this world but be transformed by the renewing of your mind." Love Warriors, your mind is as important as your heart—both must be in alignment. If you are going to help a young person think through the nuances of cause and effect, consequential thinking and behavior, you must be clear, focused, strategic, and relevant. If you want to help in the transformation process of a young person's mind, you must become proficient at saying the right thing at the right time; too often, the right thing is said at the wrong time—or worse, the wrong thing is said at the right time.

Study Hall—Love Warriors, as stated, the mind is the first battleground one encounters, so think on these things: "whatever is true, whatever is noble, whatever is right, whatever is pure, whatever is lovely, whatever is admirable— if anything is excellent or praiseworthy think on these things." Given the documented explosive growth of all manner of social media, young people have plenty on their minds that most mentors never had to address "back in the day." It is important to find time to explore what is on the mind of our future leaders and plant seeds of love, hope, expectation, strategy, and perseverance. Mentors, always remember there is power in a seed because everything the seed is to become is already inside of it.

Seven Mentor "Be" Tools that every mentor should practice:

1. *Be Caring*—If a young person knows that you care about him/her as a person, he/she will allow you access into their inner domain. There are mentors who have a difficult time expressing compassion and become content

showing it rather than sharing it. That will not go far if it is the primary mode of intervention.[1]

2. *Be Consistent*—It is better not to mentor if you have trouble consistently sustaining the relationship due to not showing up or other "pressing" personal business. You cannot successfully mentor if you only come when you feel like it or disappear when you get too busy—or worse, don't feel like being bothered.[2]

3. *Be Real*—Please don't invent a more dynamic or hardcore past in a vain attempt to help you relate to your mentee. If you make up a life, you can't change a life. It is far easier to be yourself than to constantly have to remember a reinvented self. [3]

4. *Be Flexible*—This does not mean being weak. Know when to bend when bending is helpful. It is important to note the difference between bending rules and ignoring rules. The benefit of a flexible approach is that it gives options in the form of varied opportunities to reach, teach, and guide.[4]

5. *Be Patient*—Don't be quick to jump to hasty conclusions by giving advice before you know the full story or condemn after you've heard part of the story. First listen, then reflect, then react. If patience is a virtue, unfortunately, some mentors are "virtue-less." Men are taught to be active and insert themselves into problems and SOLVE them. Waiting may seem like a big waste of time.[5]

6. *Be Aware*—Take note of what is going on in the life of a young person, especially since your mentee, depending on his age, is on a physiological, social, spiritual, emotional, and hormonal roller coaster. It helps to remember when you were young and what you felt at the time. While times have changed, feelings are relatively consistent.[6]

7. *Be Confident*—You must believe that you have the ability, tenacity, and spirit to make a difference in the life of your mentee. Your unwavering belief that change is possible is the fuel a young person may need to travel beyond

the barrier of what is known and dissatisfying to what is unknown and potentially fulfilling.[7]

If you have gotten this far, you are now ready to receive your Spirit Warrior uniform for the battles ahead. I am talking about the Helmet of Salvation, The Breastplate of Righteousness, The Sword of the Spirit, and The Shield of Faith. An important lesson to teach young people is to not make the mistake of dressing up for the outward battle before properly attending to the inward battle. This is important because inner rage must be properly channeled in order for it to be an effective catalyst in changing people, policies, and institutions. Love Warriors, while your efforts may be mostly invisible, know that your work, birthed in love, taught with compassion, and transformed by the Holy Spirit, is evident inside of determined young servants called to be Love Warriors.

Ancestors/Elders Love Warriors' Words of Encouragement and Illumination

- "Prayer and the Bible became a part of my everyday thoughts and beliefs. I learned to put my trust in God and to seek Him as my strength." [8] —Rosa Parks
- "He who proclaims it a religious duty to read the Bible denies me the right of learning to read the name of the God who made me. He who is the religious advocate of marriage robs whole millions of its sacred influence, and leaves them to the ravages of wholesale pollution. The warm defender of the sacredness of the family relation is the same that scatters whole families, — sundering husbands and wives, parents and children, sisters and brothers, — leaving the hut vacant, and the hearth desolate." [9] —Frederick Douglass
- "I am in Birmingham because injustice is here… and just as the Apostle Paul left his little village of Tarsus and carried the gospel of Jesus Christ to practically every hamlet and city of the Greco-Roman world, I too am compelled to carry

the gospel of freedom beyond my particular hometown." [10] —Rev. Dr. Martin Luther King Jr.

- "I always tole God, 'I'm gwine [going] to hole [hold] stiddy [steady] on you, an' you've got to see me through.'" [11] —Harriet Tubman
- "The caged bird sings with a fearful twill, of things unknown, but longed for still, and his tune is heard on the distant hill, for the caged bird sings of freedom." [12] — Maya Angelou
- "IT IS THE RESPONSIBILITY of every adult—especially parents, educators, and religious leaders—to make sure that children hear what we have learned from the lessons of life and to hear over and over that we love them and that they are not alone."[13] —Marian Wright Edelman
- "There is no magic formula to success—just soul-searching, goal-setting, planning, and taking action. Stay true to your course—and you will have help along the way. Be grateful for those moments of support, because they can be few and far between."[14] —Rev. Dr. Floyd H. Flake

Iconoclast

Alfonso Wyatt (circa 1986 unpublished)
perception
they have no heritage
values
love or
sense of self
hopeless apparitions unfettered
to wreak havoc
upon
an unsuspecting world
mind war
hatred protected by ignorance
PERCEPTION
DEVILS CHILDREN
DESTROYERS OF CULTURE
THE VANQUISHED CRY
GENOCIDE
love warrior

> can you conquer
> perception
> images battle
> for control of reason
> losers all
> to this war
> perception vs. perception

In the last days, says the Lord, I will pour out my Spirit on all flesh, your young men will see visions, your old men will dream dreams...."(Acts 2:17)

Beloved, we are called to negotiate our thoughts, words, and deeds from our spiritual elevation as pastors, ministers, evangelists, intercessory prayer warriors, teachers, and mentors. Holy Ghost power has allowed me to help young people from all walks of life. I am proud to say I have mentored, loved, taught, consoled, encouraged, and, in sadder moments, buried children I did not birth. Life exists on multiple levels and there must be multiple strategies to bring on change. Many of my mentees are now in decision-making positions in the faith community, corporate America, government, and the nonprofit sector. It was love, unwavering support, compassion, and a Spirit many did not know that offered direction, correction, and protection.

A Day To Remember

I was asked to officiate at a funeral for a 14-year-old honor student who was shot on a city bus. This tragedy was reported by local news for almost a week. The innocent face of the slain teen shown on the television screen transfixed me. I wondered why the family picked me to conduct their child's funeral. I also wondered why "higher profile" religious leaders were not considered. I found out the answer before the funeral when I was told that I had baptized the slain girl when she was a baby. She had been brought to my parents' church where I happened to be preaching that particular Sunday. The funeral too was to be held at my church. I saw hundreds of young people enter the sanctuary. I stood at the pulpit as they walked by the coffin. (The funeral was paid for by rapper and mogul 50 Cent.) I could tell by the way the young mourners were dressed that this may have been their first time in church. Several speakers on the program thought their own scheduled remarks were the moment to set young people straight about church-dress protocol. As for me, I was happy to see them in church, albeit for a funeral.

When I got up to deliver the eulogy, I asked the mother of the deceased child if I could talk to the young people when I finished. She nodded her approval through her tears. I said to the young people, "I want to apologize for the adults who have perfected talking *about* you and forgot how to talk *to* you. I want to apologize for adults who have neglected to say 'I love you.' I apologize for adults who never told you that you have a divine destiny and that is not to be a sneaker pimp, corner warmer, drug dealer, baby machine—or die from street violence at an early age." I read in *The New York Times* the next day that young people who were interviewed after the service mentioned they had posted on Facebook that they have a destiny to be somebody in life.

There is something powerful and transformational about saying the right thing at the right time. You will not learn when it is the right time from reading books or schooling—you just know it when you feel it. Unfortunately, many people, even caring parents, mentors, and preachers say the right thing at the wrong time—or worse, say the wrong thing at the right time. The hurt, loss, and rage that was in the temple that day—and by extension, on the street—was met and arrested by love, concern, and respect. Shouldn't that be what a church offers in times of trouble, despair and rage?

who are you

I am comfort in the night
strength to go on and fight
can you see me
I am spirit in the wind

blowing away troubles my friend
can you see me
I am wisdom please understand
cling to my all-knowing hand
can you see me
I am patience here to stay
helping seekers find their way
can you see me
I am the calm in the storm
faith in love new bond form
can you see me
I am all but not one
born of the father
Sprit and son
can you see me

Endnotes

1   Alfonso Wyatt, *Mentoring from the Inside Out: Healing Boys Transforming Men* (Clermont, FL: True Perspective Press, 2012), pp. 92-95.

2   Ibid., p. 92.

3   Ibid., p. 92.

4   Ibid., p. 92.

5   Ibid., p. 93.

6   Ibid., p. 93.

7   Ibid., p. 95.

8   Scott Slayton, *ChristianHeadlines.com Contributor*, February 24, 2020.

9   Frederick Douglass, *Life of an American Slave* (Boston: Anti-Slavery Office, 1845), p.118.

10   James Melvin Washington, ed., *A Testimony of Hope: The Essential Writings and Speeches of Martin Luther King, Jr.* (San Francisco: HarperSan Francisco, 1991), p.290.

11   Harriet Tubman: The" Moss" of Her People, Christianity Today Inc., August 8, 2008.

12   Maya Angelou, *I Know Why the Caged Bird Sings* (New York,

Random House, 1968), p.74.

13   Marian Wright Edelman, *The Measure of Our Success: A Letter to My Children and Yours* (Boston: Beacon Press,1992), p. 15.

14   Floyd Flake, Donna Marie Williams, *The Way of The Bootstrapper,* (San Francisco: HarperSanFrancisco:1999), p. 133.

Alfonso Wyatt, M.Div., Ph.D.

Rev. Dr. Alfonso Wyatt is an A.M.E. Elder on the ministerial staff of The Greater Allen A.M.E. Cathedral of New York. He provides vital leadership to youth, young adults, and professionals in sacred and secular communities in New York and around the country. He retired as vice president of the Fund for the City of New York (FCNY) after serving for over two decades. The FCNY was established in 1968, with the mandate to improve the quality of life for all New Yorkers. For over three decades, in partnership with government agencies, nonprofit institutions, and foundations, the Fund has developed and helped to implement innovations in policy, programs, practices, and technology in order to advance the functioning of government and nonprofit organizations in New York City and Japan.

Dr. Wyatt is founder of Strategic Destiny: Designing Futures Through Faith and Facts, an organization that seeks to find common language and collaborative opportunities with socially engaged practitioners motivated by faith and secular practitioners motivated by evidence-based learning. He has mentored thousands, ranging from young people in foster care and juvenile detention facilities, as well as adults in prison, as well as individuals receiving their Ph.D.

He serves as an adviser and consultant to government, colleges, civic groups, community-based organizations, public schools, education intermediaries, seminaries, foundations, and to the broader faith community. He is the co-creator of The Rabbi Marshall Meyer Interfaith Retreat, the longest running interfaith effort in this country focused on addressing social issues confronting leaders of world faith traditions.

Among his books are: *Mentoring from the Inside Out: Healing Boys Transforming Men; Leadership By Numbers: For God's People Who Count; Madd Truth: Lasting Lessons for Students of Life;* and *Beware The Mind Hustler: Identifying Self-Destructive Thoughts and Distractions.*

A sought-after speaker in his role as youth-development expert, community/organizational capacity builder, leader of leaders, and public theologian, Rev. Dr. Alfonso Wyatt has transformed the lives of adults and youth in institutions, youth programs, faith-based settings, training programs, as well as the public and private sectors and colleges. He is the visionary and founding member of The Institute for Transformative Mentoring (ITM) for formerly incarcerated individuals at the New School for Social Research, where he serves as a Visiting Fellow, as well as the Credible Messenger Institute (CMI) based at Hunter School of Social Work/Silberman Center in Harlem. Both institutions address the needs of "credible messengers" working with court-adjudicated youth.

Rev. Dr. Alfonso Wyatt attended Howard University, Columbia Teachers College, The Ackerman Institute for Family Therapy, Columbia Institute for Nonprofit Management, and New York Theological Seminary, where he earned his D.Min. He is a founding Board member of The Harlem Children's Zone Promise Academy and The Interfaith Center of New York, as well as former Chair of The 21st Century Foundation.

CHAPTER THIRTEEN

How Lazarus Got His Revenge

Vernon R. Byrd Jr., M.Div., J.D.

Therefore many of the Jews who had come to visit Mary, and had seen what Jesus did, believed in him. But some of them went to the Pharisees and told them what Jesus had done. Then the chief priests and the Pharisees called a meeting of the Sanhedrin. "What are we accomplishing?" they asked. "Here is this man performing many signs. If we let him go on like this, everyone will believe in him, and then the Romans will come and take away both our temple and our nation." (John 11:45-48)

Meanwhile a large crowd of Jews found out that Jesus was there and came, not only because of him but also to see Lazarus, whom he had raised from the dead. So the chief priests made plans to kill Lazarus as well, for on account of him many of the Jews were going over to Jesus and believing in him. (John 12: 9-11)

Lazarus's resurrection brought great joy to his sisters, to his friends, and to Jesus. It was an astonishing, reality-bending moment. He had been dead and buried for four days, but when Jesus called him to get up, he got up. But in spite of all of the jubilation and excitement it created, his resurrection also caused great turmoil and anxiety within institutions of power. His resurrection was such a disrupting event that the Sanhedrin Council went into emergency session to deal with it.

According to the minutes of the meeting, someone articulated the danger this way: "If we let Jesus keep carrying on like this, everyone will believe in him and then the Romans will come and take away our Temple and our Nation." In other words: "If we don't do anything to stop Jesus from making the dead come alive, and the blind see, then everyone will follow him and not us and then we will lose our grip on the levers of Religious Authority and Secular Power." The leaders considered the life-changing, life-giving power of Jesus to be an existential threat to the status quo. His "carrying on" had to be stopped. The High Priest Caiaphas chaired the meeting and entertained a motion that Jesus be killed. The motion carried.

But they later realized that it wasn't enough to just kill Jesus; they also had to nullify a resurrected Lazarus. Even if they got rid of Jesus, Lazarus's resurrection would cause people to shift their allegiance to Jesus and away from them. Not only did they have to do something about the miracle worker, they had to clean up all residue of the miracle. The woman at the well (John 4) had been changed, but they didn't feel the need to kill her. They could always bring up her past to try to nullify the power of the living water. There was a man who was born blind but had his sight restored (John 9), but they didn't feel the need to kill him because they could always gaslight the community by saying it was a hoax and that he just *looked* like the man who was born blind. But concerning Lazarus... that was a different matter.

Lazarus had been dead four days and decomposing. But Jesus told the people to roll away the stone and he called Lazarus to come forth. And Lazarus got up and came forth at the sound of the voice of Jesus. And then Jesus told them to "loose him and set him free." They couldn't badmouth their way out of that one. They couldn't gaslight their way out of that one. So instead of celebrating his resurrection, the powers and the rulers and the principalities plotted to kill Lazarus too.

They never really liked him anyway. He and his sisters would praise the name of Jesus and not their names. They were glad when he died and mad as all of hell when he got up. But when he got up, the very breath of Lazarus threatened the Sanhedrin's power grip on the Temple and the Nation because people started moving away from them and moving towards Jesus. His very breath threatened their control over the religious and the secular spheres of life.

As Black folk, we need to remember that, collectively, we are Lazarus. The old preachers told us so. We were once dead and decomposing over 400 years ago. Our ancestors were brought to the not-so-united states in shackles by Bible-carrying, church-going slave merchants; to be owned by Bible-carrying, church-going plantation owners; to be stripped of legal personhood by Bible-carrying, church-going members of Congress. And these Bible-carrying, church-going oppressors made it clear that *they* were in charge of the Temple and the Nation.

Many of our African forebearers died during the Middle Passage. The rest were brought here to die a spiritual death, entombed in the shrine of slavery. The system of slavery required that we die. Our native languages had to die. Our native cultures had to die. Our identities had to die. Our definitions of beauty had to die. Our right to control our own bodies had to die. Our memories of great civilizations had to die. Our strong, intact families were condemned to die.

And we all should be dead right now! But we are not dead, because, while we were decomposing, the same God who created us called us back to life and commanded, "Lazarus come forth!" And we came forth as members of Congress and Senators and Presidents in the same land in which we had been pronounced dead. We came forth as artist and actors and rappers and teachers in the same place where they had buried us. And we came forth as business owners and civic leaders and preachers and writers and lawyers and doctors and journalists and police commissioners and scientists and hospital administrators and EMT personnel and nurses in the same land in which we had been coded dead.

And no matter what atrocities happen to us on an almost daily basis, they cannot overcome the larger truth that God has been good to us—because we were dead, but Jesus called us back to life. We are not overwhelmed by evil. We stand as witnesses of the resilience of the Good. And because we are alive and getting stronger, wickedness has gone into emergency session, afraid that they might lose control of the Temple and the Nation. "If Jesus keeps on calling the dead back to life we will lose control of the Evangelical Temple and the White Anglo-Saxon Nation" … "If Jesus keeps on calling the dead back to life we won't be able to get our people appointed to the Supreme Court" … "If Jesus keeps carrying on we will no longer be able to impose our racist world-view on everybody else" … "If Jesus keeps on carrying on we will lose control of the Temple and the power to declare that our people are saints and other people are sinners" … "If Jesus keeps carrying on we will lose control of the Nation and the power to declare who gets the contracts, and who is above the law and who is under the law"…. No wonder the High Priest of Racism went and took a picture in front of a Temple holding a Bible in the same way that slave traders and slave owners held their Bible—as something to be seen with, not something to live by. He did it because evil is in emergency session and afraid of losing the Temple and the Nation, because if Jesus keeps carrying on, more people will move away from hatred and towards love.

They really want to kill Jesus. They really want to kill the "whosoever will" ideology of Jesus. They really want to kill the "first shall be last and the last shall be first" truth of Jesus. But since they can't get to Jesus, they want to kill Lazarus. They want to kill the evidence that a compassionate God is the supreme authority. The hateful reckless culture of some police departments towards Black life is connected to activities of voter suppression around the country. All of it is designed to kill Lazarus and to retain control of the Temple and the Nation. It has taken until the year 2020 for the Senate of the United States of America to finally pass an anti-lynching bill!

And I've been waiting for Evangelicals to come out *en masse* to condemn the cold-blooded and reckless killing of unarmed citizens, unarmed fathers and daughters. I looked to see if Evangelical leaders who have given cover to the president and racism would say anything about the senseless and systematic killing of Blacks by white police officers and I didn't hear too much. They haven't said anything because they are the chief priests of the Temple, and they are complicit with the leaders of the nation in the assassination attempts on Lazarus. They are as guilty of aiding and abetting as much as police officers who stand around and watch another officer casually murder another human being.

And now, my brothers and sisters, the time has come to talk about how Lazarus gets his revenge. We are uncomfortable with the word "revenge." The truth is, we really don't talk about it enough. The Psalms talk about revenge. Jesus talked about revenge when he told the parable of the persistent widow and the corrupt judge. Her plea was for the judge to avenge her for the wrong that had been done to her. Since the church is not talking about divine sanctioned revenge, it leaves people to try to figure it out themselves. I'm *not* talking about an eye-for-an eye revenge that leaves everybody blind. I'm talking about what Paul said in Romans 12:19: "Do not take revenge, my dear friends, but leave room for God's wrath, for it is written: 'It is mine to avenge; I will repay,' says the Lord."

The best way to take revenge is not to burn down but rather to get out of God's way for the wrath of God to step in. The best way to get even is not to become the sin that is perpetrated on us but to leave room for God because he said to evildoers "it is better to have a millstone tied around your neck and be cast into the sea than to mess with one of my little ones." The appropriate revenge is not human-led revenge; it is giving room for God to right wrong and to make the crooked straight.

More specifically, Lazarus teaches us that you cannot get even until you get up. If you want to give room for the wrath and the judgment of God, you have to respond to the voice of Jesus and get up! If you want to make the enemy really mad, just get up when Jesus says get up. Get up and protest injustice. March. Cry aloud. Get up, Lazarus. Get voter registration up. Get the Black vote up. Get the Black high school graduation rate up. Get the applications to the police department up. Get the numbers of Blacks running for city, state, and national offices up. Get the numbers of jobs up. Get the income level for the working poor up. Get Black wealth up. Get up, Lazarus. Get up! The voice of Jesus is calling on us to get up, to not only demand justice, but get up and be the people at the table that make the critical policy decisions in the first place. The Pharisees want you to be discouraged with the repeated images of wickedness, but get up to do good. The Pharisees want you to be discouraged by the constant need to keep demanding what is right and moral for any human being. But get up and demand it.

The second way that Lazarus got revenge is that he walked in his resurrection and not in the Sanhedrin's hatred. He walked proactively in the power of Jesus and not reactively, in reaction to the weakness of his enemies. He had to walk out of the entrance of the tomb and keep walking until he got home.

Keep walking in the resurrection of Jesus.

Keep walking, mentoring, teaching, encouraging, marching, protesting, comforting, healing, loving, amusing, and blessing. Keep on walking until you get home. What you do may not seem like much to you, but it is more than what you realize. Because we are a part of a collective resurrection that started over 400 years ago, and the little piece that you do is connected to the piece that somebody else is doing. And every piece is connected to the ongoing mosaic that prior generations created. And one of these old days, when the mosaic is finally finished, I have a hunch that it will look like Jesus! Ours is a collective resurrection, so that if they kill one of us the rest of us have to keep walking for them until we all get home. Don't back up. Don't put back on the grave garments of despair.

Don't do the enemies' work for them by defeating ourselves. Keep achieving in spite of the odds. Keep exceeding expectations in spite of double standards. Keep doing your assignment. Don't let the agenda of hatred win and cause you to return to the grave clothes of defeat.

Finally, Lazarus got revenge because he just kept breathing.

His breathing was unlike anybody else's breathing because he breathed in resurrection air. Every breath he took was a testimony to the goodness Jesus. Every breath he took was evidence that Jesus was still carrying on. When Lazarus breathed, it upset the powers that be, because when he breathed it meant that a day is coming when the wicked will cease from troubling and the weary will be at rest. He didn't make a speech. He just kept breathing. And his breath alone testified to the sovereignty of God. Every time they saw him alive and well the chief priests got mad. If they saw him cutting his lawn, they got mad. If they saw him picking up his mail, they got mad. If they saw him buying his groceries, they got mad. He wasn't going back and forth with them. His breathing led to believing in Jesus.

When we breathe collectively as one, our breath is different from everybody else's. For we breathe the air of resurrection.

Our collective breath is evidence that "no weapon formed against us shall prosper and every tongue that shall rise against us in judgment shall be condemned." Our collective breath is evidence that JESUS is the supreme power—the King of Kings and the Lord of Lords. And one of these old days, Trumpism will have to go back to the pit of hell from whence it came.

Keep breathing, Lazarus!

They've tried to lynch us by tree, asphyxiate us by a knee—trying to take the Divine breath out of us. But we are still here. And our collective breathing means that there is still a God who sits high and looks low.

Keep breathing, Lazarus! Just keep breathing.

If some of us have to die because of these chief priests, the rest of us have to collectively keep breathing for them. Because if Lazarus is still breathing, it means that Jesus is still blessing.

If Lazarus is still breathing, it means Jesus is still working miracles. If Lazarus is still breathing, it means that many who used to hate will move over to the side of love. Keep breathing, Lazarus, and make room for the judgment of God.

And that's the story of how Lazarus got his revenge.

Vernon R. Byrd, Jr., M.Div., J.D.

Rev. Vernon R. Byrd Jr. is an attorney, and retired Assistant General Counsel and Vice President of Legal Education at Johnson & Johnson. Prior to this he served as a Senior Counsel for *The New York Times*. He is a member of the New Jersey, Pennsylvania, and New York Bar Associations.

He is an ordained Elder and presently serves as senior pastor of St. Matthew African Methodist Episcopal Church in Philadelphia, Pennsylvania. At the General Conference in July of 2012, the AME Church elected Rev. Byrd to serve as a member of the Judicial Council.

An anointed preacher and sought-after speaker, Rev. Byrd is also a composer, singer, and musician, who began conducting church choirs in his youth.

In his leisure time, he likes to golf and to hike. On September 11 of 2014 Rev. Byrd reached another life summit when he successfully climbed to the top of Mount Kilimanjaro in Tanzania. In May of 2017 Rev. Byrd also successfully climbed Machu Picchu in Peru.

He earned his undergraduate degree from Harvard University, his Juris Doctorate from the University of Pennsylvania School of Law, and his Master of Divinity from Princeton Theological Seminary.

CHAPTER FOURTEEN

The Other Side of Rage

Melinda Contreras-Byrd, M.Div., Psy.D.

A s we end our discussion of rage, I believe that it is important to address a critical goal of the collection:

i.   To distinguish important factors involved in the expression of the Holy Rage that we advocate.
ii.   To offer information that will assist those enraged, to choose informed and anointed methods for enacting a response.

In my mind, Holy Rage is distinguishable by several factors. These include at least its origin, its purpose, and its parameters. I would like to begin by exploring factors for consideration in developing the parameters of a Holy rage.

Determining a Legitimate Foundation for Holy Rage

While most angry behavior is tolerated in U.S. society, the acting out of any form of rage is typically viewed as unacceptable. Because rage is characterized as a response that is often extreme, visceral, and uncontrolled, it is feared and demonized. But the question that is being raised during this double pandemic is whether there are appropriate times when rage is legitimate and tolerable. Both directly and indirectly, Black people are being told that there is not.

Moreover, *the most televised and touted* White Christian or U.S. belief seems to suggest that rage is unacceptable *in all* settings and situations. "Race" realities in the U.S. — White mobs that have pillaged, burned, lynched, raped, falsely imprisoned, harassed — demonstrate the hypocrisy of this idea. One psychological underpinning is that there is fear of the potential destructive and personal violence that may accompany states of emotional rage in general and Black rage in particular.

These essays have sought to dissect the issues associated with Black Rage and create a foundation for Biblical interpretation, and parameters for decision-making regarding the legitimate avenues open to Black Christians in these increasingly perilous times.

For many if not most U.S. citizens, the topic of U.S. and worldwide systems of historically ongoing racism is a subject that has arisen powerfully enough to have been given a place on the discussion list (but not a top priority).

Past responses suggest that it is seen as an intellectual puzzle to be discussed, argued about, and intellectually mastered. There has been little indication that the powers-that-be have assigned this subject the status of crucial, or even urgent. This is a disheartening and egregious truth that Black Christians have been forced to become ever aware of as they sing, "We are one in the Spirit, we are one in the Lord...." We have had to face the "awe-full" truth that every facet of U.S. life goes on with the template of business as usual — even amidst a pandemic — and White self-proclaimed Christians salute and support a man who has made it crystal clear by his demonstrated values, talks, tweets, and the direction of his statements of support that he represents all that Jesus died and rose to stand against. As the pundits proclaim that we are at a precipice, as a nation, the critical issue for Black Christians, people of faith, and people of color is: "What will be the clarion call that releases and frees us to embrace a Holy Rage?"

Certainly, one foundational factor in the legitimacy of extreme acting-out behavior is the presence of imminent life-threatening danger.

While this country has tended to assess racist violence of all types within a template of "isolated incidents," Black communities have been able to see the connected and strategic qualities of these behaviors. We have been able to recognize them overtly and covertly. We have discovered them across generations, nationalities, down through history, and in multiple and diverse forms. We understand that our experience in this country has been a struggle for our lives on every level!

In the October 7, 2020 edition of the *New York Times* is an article by journalist Zolan Kanno-Youngs, titled "Delayed Homeland Security Report Warns of Lethal White Supremacy." Kanno-Youngs quotes a Homeland Security report that states that violent white supremacy was the "most persistent and lethal threat in the homeland."

He further references the words of Acting Secretary of Homeland Security, Chad Wolf: "I am particularly concerned about white supremacist violent extremists who have been exceptionally lethal in their abhorrent, targeted attacks in recent years."

There is little doubt that the variety of increasing racist-based situations that Black communities have been forced to endure fit the description of "imminent life-threatening danger." That being the case, the situation of Black America meets the first criterion for characterization as one that legitimizes a declaration of" just war."

Because we have been given ample information to firmly determine that the origin of Black Rage is a historic, all-pervasive, never-ending, and systemic imminent life-threat, we can therefore conclude that "our cause is just" and move on to a second area for investigation. A specific question here would be, "What steps are available to Black Christians and their allies when 'waging war' against those seen and unseen powers that continue to threaten the lives of Black people?"

Setting the Parameters of Holy Rage

Holy Rage, like rage itself, is a response to egregious wrongs being leveled against those enraged. One attempt at delineating moral guidelines for the taking of human life has developed in response to the establishment of moral guidelines for the declaration of war, and its ensuing violence. Early scholars who tackled this question included theologians, and the outcome, included the idea that the violence and aggression of war is only justified in situations of imminent threat, and as a last resort when there is no other alternative resolution.

Although the Bible is rife with Old Testament stories of God's messengers using and being told to use violent force against the designated enemies of God, any idea of violence has been eschewed by modern-day Christians as un-godly, with at least one exception. The Christian-based idea of "just war" stands as an example of how the use of violence can be acceptable and compatible with an idea of "the holy."

A consideration of this way of thinking can be found in the *Summa Theologiae* of Thomas Aquinas. From a theological/ moral point of view, he outlines four foundational conditions for engaging in the violence of war in a justified manner:

The group to wage war must overtly declare this intention. In my mind, this speaks to a sense of fairness in assuring that others of the group have discussed and are of one accord in this declaration, and that those to be attacked have been given due warning. With respect to this condition, there are myriad of writings by Black leaders that have outlined the ongoing and abject suffering that Black people have suffered under the U.S. systems of structural racism and racist violence. They have been given due warning of Black anger and unrest, by decades of Black activist leadership—the Civil Rights Movement, the Southern Non-violence Coordinating Committee, the Black Panther Party, the Nation of Islam, Black Lives Matter, and a host of other Black forms of uprising dating back to the Nat Turner Rebellion. The second half of this criterion is not technically enforceable, because people of the African Diaspora do not constitute the "sovereign authority" called for by Thomas Aquinas. Yet, I would argue that the ongoing, diverse, and united voices of Black people in the U.S. meet the basic *intentional* criterion.

1. The second criterion insists that *the war must have a just cause, one that is for the common good or against injustice.* There can be no greater common good than to grant innocent, law-abiding human beings and citizens of the republic the right to live without threat of death, assault, or injustice. That this struggle against racism is a struggle against injustice is axiomatic. The contributors to this collection have cited numerous cases of injustice borne by Black Americans and others of the African Diaspora.

2. The third criterion is that *this war/use of violence must have as its goal, a reason that is just.* At the root of the Black struggle is a fundamental struggle of God's children to be allowed to just "be.". It is a struggle for human equality. In the case of the Black struggle against all forms of racism, if we follow its trajectory over the years, the struggle against racism has also fueled and in certain instances supported the erasure of all kinds of bigotry—ableism, homophobia, elitism, sexism, anti-Semitism, xenophobia, etc. Its foundational goal is the establishment of a just and moral society.

3. Lastly, the final criterion is that *the war/violence must be one that will end in a" just peace."* The foundational goal of Holy Rage is not personal catharsis, revenge, or an evil delight in inflicting pain and suffering on one's enemies. The foundation for Holy Black Rage is firmly based upon the ubiquitous Biblical concept of justice, love, and the acting out of principles consistent with God's Kingdom. This meets the criterion of a "just peace."

While the above ideas related to "just war" theories have informed Christian thinking with respect to the legitimate use of deadly force, other considerations have been examined as well. These considerations include factors such as the just and humane treatment of enemies, the probability that the use of this extreme measure will result in the desired goals, etc.

We have seen that both Christian and non-Christian thinkers have resolved that, within certain situations, the use of violence is permissible, moral, and just. So, in the face of imminent threat, are Christians justified to use violence? The courts have made the use of violence justifiable in the passage of "stand your ground" laws. It was justifiable for an armed non-Black man to murder an unarmed Black teen because, based upon a racial stereotype, he was seen as a threat. Our courts have declared that deadly force and violence are justifiable in instances involving the protection of certain kinds of property.

But do we as Christians have the same value system as the courts? Is property as valuable or more valuable than a human life? What do scriptures teach us about the value of a human life within a Kingdom context? This is a point for discussion.

Holy rage is an anger response of elevated proportions. In almost all cases, a *Holy* Rage will exempt the acting out of physical violence against those persons posing an imminent threat. From a theological standpoint, human life is quintessentially holy and sacred unto God. The Bible teaches that all humans share one blood origin and all are given one universally meaningful and purposeful gift of life. All differences considered, we are all fundamentally creatures created by and for love, and this overriding point of origin renders murder and other forms of purposeful human death anathema—except in very unusual circumstances. Our theological foundations tell us that life is sacred, while also giving us examples where God instructs the people to wage war and chides them when not everyone is killed! Ours is a three-in-one God, who epitomizes great love but is also the exemplar of a sanctified leadership created to exact justice—death upon Babylon/the unrighteous:

> Raise a banner on a bare hilltop!
> Cry out loud to them!
> Give a wave of the hand,
> signaling for them to enter the gates of the nobles.
> I myself have commanded my consecrated ones;
> I have also summoned my warriors,
> those who rejoice in my triumph,
> to carry out my angry judgments
> Listen! There's a noise on the mountains
> like that of a great multitude!
> Listen! There's an uproar among the kingdoms,
> like that of nations massing together!
>
> The Lord of the Heavenly
> Armies is mustering an army for battle.
> They're coming from a faraway land,
> from the distant horizon—
> the Lord and the weapons of his anger—
> to destroy the entire land. (Isaiah 13:2-5)

Perhaps one answer to the question of the legitimate use of violent destruction is that the Bible does not rule it out, but a review of texts such as the above, juxtaposed with Jesus' response to Peter's drawing of his sword in the garden, and Moses' slaying of the Egyptian, might suggest that while a Holy Rage—*directed* by God, and for Godly *purposes*—is acceptable, other violent rage may not be.

Those who would be warriors of a Holy Black Rage are foremost spiritually focused persons who know who their real enemy is. They are aware that, despite what it looks like, this is not a racial or class war. The real enemy is evil in the form of racist injustice (among other forms).

Therefore, Holy Black rage must be aware of, well-versed, and centered in the art of "spiritual warfare."

The acting out of a Holy Black Rage must be born of informed spiritual interaction and direction from God, that is, as a heartfelt desire to live out Kingdom principles.

Holy Black Rage warriors are known by their humility, rather than a desire to demonstrate their position, power, or strength. These are warriors who are fully yielded to God with a strategic, group-approved, and set goal of bringing about peace and justice.

Unlike other forms of rage, Holy Black Rage struggles to incorporate the Kingdom principle of forgiveness of enemies, knowing that, beyond their own pain, the peace that accompanies justice cannot be fully experienced without the ability to forgive. And the truth of this struggle is this: that Holy Black Rage warriors are blessed to share in God's work, as conduits of personal, spiritual, and societal transformation.

CHAPTER FIFTEEN

[Epilogue]

Joy in the Valley of Baca: A Meditation

Rev. Vernon R. Byrd Jr., M.Div., J.D.

> Blessed are those whose strength is in you,
> whose hearts are set on pilgrimage.
> As they pass through the Valley of Baka,
> they make it a place of springs;
> the autumn rains also cover it with pools.
> They go from strength to strength,
> till each appears before God in Zion.
> (Psalm 84:5-7)

In Psalm 84, verse 6, there is reference to a place that many of us have never heard of. Most of us have heard about the Valley of the Shadow of Death from Psalm 23, the Valley of Dry Bones in the book of Ezekiel and even the Valley of Elah, where David defeated Goliath. But the Valley of Baca is unfamiliar territory. Terra incognita.

Its geographic location has drifted into obscurity. Its longitude and latitude are unknown. Where it was, who lived there, and what took place there are the stuff of speculation.

What little we know about it is stitched together from the fragments of this text itself. First, the name *Baca* in Hebrew means "weeping." It was a place of tears and sorrow. Second, the text suggests that Baca was a dry place, which means it was stagnant and not much grew there. Life could not thrive there. And third, the text suggests that the ancient valley was not the kind of place where anyone would want to go or stay.

Maybe the year 2020 has taken us to the Valley of Baca. More tears have been shed in 2020 than in any other year in recent memory. More hospital visits and more trips to the cemetery took place in 2020 than at any other time in recent history. In New York alone, the death rate spiked 700% between March and June. This means that the rate of weeping and grief and loneliness and anxiety spiked much more than 700%. Multiply that by countless cities and towns throughout the country. *We* are in the Valley of Baca.

Baca is not a place where anyone necessarily intends to go. But we must recognize when we are there. If we do not, we will treat Baca as a destination rather than just a stop along the way. If we treat Baca is a destination, then the absurd becomes normal and the unacceptable becomes acceptable. Here we are, under a cloud of oppression and in the midst of a pandemic. We have arrived in the desolate Valley of Baca.

How in the world then can anybody talk about *joy* in the Valley of Baca? The Psalmist must have lost his or her mind. Yet in that valley, ancient voices would sing:

> Blessed are those whose strength is in you,
> whose hearts are set on pilgrimage.
> As they pass through the Valley of Baca,
> they make it a place of springs;
> the autumn rains also cover it with pools.
> They go from strength to strength,
> till each appears before God in Zion.
> (Psalm 84:5-7)

What was it about these people that caused them to have joy in the worst of circumstances? What lessons can we take from their story and apply to *our* story?

The writer says that they were blessed because their strength was in the Lord. Their bodies were in Baca, but their trust was in the Lord. Their grief and pain were in Baca, but their trust was in the Lord. And because of that they were blessed.

We must understand that, in spite of everything, God is yet with us even in Baca. God still answers prayer in Baca. God still makes a way out of no way in Baca. God still opens doors in Baca. God still puts food on the table in Baca. Baca is a place that is too hard for us. But it is not too hard for God. We have to keep our trust in God in spite of all of our troubles.

Psalm 84 may have been one of the psalms people sang while they traveled to Jerusalem for the annual festivals. The psalm mentions that the people "have their hearts set on pilgrimage." They understood that they might have to spend a night or two there, but they were not settling in Baca. They were on their way to Zion!

Neither is Baca *our* final destination. This present darkness is not the end. We're on our way to a better place! We can have joy in the Valley of Baca because Baca is not where we are going to. It is what we are going through. And we can have joy about that.

Finally, joy is possible in Baca because the pilgrims in Psalm 84 did not allow the conditions in Baca to stop their praise. Instead, they changed a valley of weeping into a sanctuary of doxology. They turned a barren place into a place of new life. In Baca they sang, "Better is one day in your courts than a thousand elsewhere" (verse 10). In Baca they sang, "I'd rather be a doorkeeper in the house of my God than to dwell in the tents of wickedness."

Because of God's steadfast goodness to us, because God's record is that God never fails--somebody in Baca ought to hear our praise!

That's why the President of Baca is going to hear our praise when we vote his hateful self out of office.

The police department of Baca is going to hear our praise when we get rid of qualified immunity and bring criminals in uniform to justice.

The insurance companies of Baca are going to hear our praise when universal health care becomes a right for all instead of a benefit for a few.

The homeland security department of Baca and every politician that enabled the separation of families at the border in our name are going to hear our praise when they are held to account for the evil that has happened and is happening in this country.

In the Valley of Baca I will bless the Lord.

In the Valley of Baca I will sing praises unto the Most High King.

In the Valley of Baca I will declare the works of the Lord.

In the Valley of Baca I will extol him. I will magnify him. I will glorify him. I will tell of his goodness. I will have joy unspeakable even in the Valley of Baca. For this joy that I have Baca did not give and Baca cannot take it away.

> Sound the trumpet in Zion, and sound an alarm in my holy mountain; let all the inhabitants of the land tremble; for the day of the Lord cometh, for it is nigh at hand;

> A day of darkness and of gloominess, a day of clouds and thick darkness...a great people and a strong; there hath not been ever the like, neither shall be any more after it, even to the years of many generations...

> Fear not, O land; be glad and rejoice: for the Lord will do great things...and the floors shall overflow with wine and oil. And I will restore to you the years that the locusts have eaten.... You will have plenty to eat, until you are full, and you will praise the name of the Lord your God, who has worked wonders for you; never again will my people be shamed. (Joel 2: 25-26)

POSTLUDE

Listen.
Can you hear the voice of Mahalia Jackson singing?
How I got over
How I got over
You know my soul looks back and wonders
How I got over....*

---

*   *How I Got Over* is a noted "Negro hymn," written by Clara Ward in 1951. It was made famous outside of the Black church when Mahalia Jackson sang it at the 1963 March on Washington. It has been sung by many Black recording artists, including Patti Labelle, Yolanda Adams, Vicki Winans, among others.